Against

THE

Machine

T

Also by Paul Kingsnorth

FICTION

The Wake

Beast

Alexandria

NON-FICTION

One No, Many Yeses

Real England

*Confessions of a
Recovering Environmentalist*

Savage Gods

POETRY

Kidland and Other Poems

Songs from the Blue River

These Were the Stories of My People

Against

THE

Machine

On the Unmaking of Humanity

Paul Kingsnorth

THESIS

Thesis
An imprint of Penguin Random House LLC
1745 Broadway, New York, NY 10019
penguinrandomhouse.com

Most Thesis books are available at a discount when purchased in quantity for sales promotions or corporate use. Special editions, which include personalized covers, excerpts, and corporate imprints, can be created when purchased in large quantities. For more information, please call (212) 572-2232 or e-mail specialmarkets@penguinrandomhouse.com. Your local bookstore can also assist with discounted bulk purchases using the Penguin Random House corporate Business-to-Business program. For assistance in locating a participating retailer, e-mail B2B@penguinrandomhouse.com.

Grateful acknowledgment is made for permission to reprint the following:
Excerpt from "The Purse Seine" from *The Selected Poetry of Robinson Jeffers* by Robinson Jeffers, edited by Tim Hunt, published in 2002. Used with permission of Stanford University Press and Jeffers Literary Properties. Permission conveyed through the Copyright Clearance Center, Inc., and Jeffers Literary Properties.

Excerpt from "The Other" from *R. S. Thomas: Selected Poems 1946–1968* (published by Bloodaxe Books, 1986). Reproduced with permission of Bloodaxe Books (http://www.bloodaxebooks.com).

Book design by Alissa Rose Theodor

LIBRARY OF CONGRESS CONTROL NUMBER: 2025017959
ISBN 9780593850633 (hardcover)
ISBN 9780593850640 (ebook)

Printed in the United States of America
3rd Printing

The authorized representative in the EU for product safety and compliance is Penguin Random House Ireland, Morrison Chambers, 32 Nassau Street, Dublin D02 YH68, Ireland, https://eu-contact.penguin.ie.

It is easy for me to imagine that the next great division of the world will be between people who wish to live as creatures and people who wish to live as machines.

WENDELL BERRY

It may be that our role on this planet is not to worship God but to create him.

ARTHUR C. CLARKE

Contents

Caught in the Web of Its Song

AN INTRODUCTION

WHEN I WAS A CHILD, I wanted to live in a pine forest. Or, to be more accurate, a pine plantation. We have a lot of these in Britain, sown across the hills and mountains during the twentieth century for cheap paper and pulp. The tight ranks of conifer trees, planted so close together that most of their branches die for lack of light, and which acidify the soil for miles around, are hated by ecologists, landscape lovers and most of the local wildlife, which barely ventures into them. Perhaps that's what I liked about them. There seemed to be some kind of dark, mossy mystery in that maze of pillarlike trunks. Maybe I'd been reading too much Tolkien (this was a perennial problem), but I could imagine myself pitching camp in there, making a small tent of branches and leaves, wandering the soft forest floor, drinking from the streams, becoming something other than myself.

I've never been addicted to drugs or alcohol, but I have often been addicted to dreams. This is the lot of the writer. You become a writer because the world you encountered in the stories you read as a child is more exciting than the world you are actually living in. More exciting and, in a strange way, more real. Your world is school and suburbs and bus stops and breakfast cereals and maths homework and being forced to wash your dad's car at the weekend and wondering how to talk to girls and listening to the charts to work out what kind of music it's permissible to like. This is not Lothlorien, and neither is it Earthsea. The worlds created by Tolkien and Asimov and Verne and Howard are better than this, and there is no doubt at all that given a splinter of a chance you would prefer to live in them, just as you would prefer to live in a pine wood on the northern fells. Then, one day, you pick up a pen and realise that you can create your own.

Meanwhile, out in what is fondly called 'the real world' by people who often don't know very much about reality, you are living in a metastasising machine which is closing in around you, polluting your skies and your woods and your past and your imagination. If you have the kind of sensibility which prefers Lothlorien to Isengard, this means that you are a character in a tragedy rather than a heroic epic. Most of the things you like are fading away. The great forests and the stories made in and by them. The strange cultures spanning centuries of time. The little pubs and the curious uninhabited places. The thrumming temples and dark marshlands and crooked villages and folk tales and conviviality and spontaneous song and old houses which might have witches in them. The possibility of dragons. The empty beaches and wild hilltops, the chance of getting lost in the rain forever or discovering something that was never on any map. A world without maps, a world without engines.

This world, you can see, is on the way out, if it is not already long gone. The one that is manifesting to replace it is a left-brain paradise, all straight lines and concrete car parks where the corn exchange used to be. The future is STEM and chatbots and cashless parking meters and economic growth and asteroid mining forever and ever. There is no arguing with it. You can feel the great craters that it makes in the world, you can feel what is being tarmacked and neatened and rationalised into oblivion, and the depth of what is leaving, but you cannot explain or justify it in the terms which are now the terms we live by. You just know that something is wrong. Everybody tells you that you feel this because you are infected with something called 'nostalgia', or that you picked up a dose of 'Luddism' or 'Romanticism' at a party or in a doctor's waiting room. Basically, there is something wrong with you. You don't understand Progress, which is always and everywhere a Good Thing.

But you can feel something going on that is not a good thing, and it doesn't matter how many lies, damned lies or statistics are produced to prove otherwise. You can feel this something enveloping you. The Welsh poet R. S. Thomas described it chillingly in his poem 'Other,' in a verse I have never forgotten since I first read it:

> . . . The machine appeared
> In the distance, singing to itself
> Of money. Its song was the web
> They were caught in, men and women
> Together. The villages were as flies
> To be sucked empty.
> God secreted
> A tear. Enough, enough,
> He commanded, but the machine
> Looked at him and went on singing.

This, I understood when I read these lines, is what I wanted to hide from in that pine forest, and a Machine was as good an image as I had ever found for it. Another poet, the American Robinson Jeffers, a writer admired by Thomas, seemed to see the same thing one night, when he sat on a mountain looking at the lights of an American city and had a vision of a giant purse seine fishing net, slowly hauling in its prey:

> . . . I cannot tell you how
> beautiful the city appeared, and a little terrible.
> I thought, We have geared the machines and locked all together
> into inter-dependence; we have built the great cities; now
> There is no escape. We have gathered vast populations incapable
> of free survival, insulated
> From the strong earth, each person in himself helpless, on all
> dependent. The circle is closed, and the net
> Is being hauled in. They hardly feel the cords drawing, yet
> they shine already.

I read a lot as a child. After my fantasy-reading period, it was the poets who opened up the world for me, and a lot of them, I began to notice, in the centuries between Wordsworth and Merwin, were gesturing in some way towards the same thing: this Machine. Later I found that novelists had been writing about it as well, from Mary Shelley to Aldous Huxley, via George Orwell, E. M. Forster and Ursula Le Guin. The filmmakers, meanwhile, had been on the case from *Metropolis* to *The Matrix*. As for the non-fiction writers, they had been pouring forth great tomes on this force for over a century; this book will dig into some of them.

In other words, this was not a new story. This triumph of the mechanical over the natural, the planned over the organic, the centralised over the local, the system over the individual and the community: this was the tale of our time. As this Machine rose around them, all of these writers tried to pin it down in words. Many succeeded, and yet we are still here trying to work out what is going on and what to do about it and what it quite means. All we know is that some force has been unleashed in our world which we are struggling to contend with. A huge change is birthing itself; a change in our human relationship with nature, with each other, with our past, with our tools. With everything.

SOMETIMES I FEEL LIKE I'VE BEEN writing about this thing all my life, running from it and pursuing it all at once. Wanting to hide from it in a pine forest at the same time as I want to trap it in a jar, or a book, and examine it for what it is. Those suspicions or intuitions I had as a child—that something was off about the world I lived in, about its values and its direction—morphed as I grew older into a way of life, or perhaps an obsession. At university in the early nineties, my love of nature and my anger at the thing that seemed to be eating it turned me into an activist. Back then, I wanted to tackle this Machine head on, and *Earth First!* was my drug of choice. Later, my years of chaining myself to bulldozers, living in treehouses and turning up to any protest site I could find gave way to something else: writing as a form of activism.

Journalism, magazine editing, writing for NGOs, the bad poetry and the unpublished novels: it all counted. It was all, in the end, the same pursuit: an investigation into the Machine, and a friction against its onward march. After a few years helping to run *The Ecologist* magazine in London, I left to write a book of investigative journalism, wandering the world from protest site to tribal village to township to summit venue, writing about resistance to the new game in town, something called 'globalisation'. The name was different, but the values were the same—the values of money and numbers and profit and growth—and as usual I was against them. I was against them for years, through many more books of non-fiction, fiction and poetry, published now, but still circling around that same story: the tale of this Machine. Yet I still didn't have a name for it, and I still wasn't quite sure what it *was*.

A few decades later, I find myself still circling the monster, like Ahab pursuing the whale. I think I'm closer to the thing now, though: I can see it just ahead of me. I'm older now, married with children. My wife and I fled our urban lives in England more than a decade ago, bought a small house on a bit of land in Ireland, threw away our TV, and started growing food and homeschooling our children, all of it in an attempt, again, to fend off the excesses of the Machine. I kept writing, too, to understand it. This book is an attempt—a final attempt, I hope—to circumscribe this thing with words. To do my best to explain, to myself and to whoever is reading, the nature of this force that the poets have seen for so long. The nature of the Machine: where it comes from, how we built it, and what it is doing, finally, to our world and to our souls.

Things have changed since I moved to Ireland; the West has changed, and the wider world with it. Much of the culture I grew up with seems to be disintegrating, along with the natural world it was always rooted in, though we were able to forget about that part for a while. A cultural revolution has been brewing; a 'culture war', as we have all learned to call it. We know the battle lines of this by now, and maybe we have all chosen our sides. But I began this book with an intuition: that the roots of this culture war were much deeper than they looked. That it was related in some way to that Machine that had stalked me all my life. By the time I had finished the book, I was sure that this was true.

I was sure of something else too: that the political and cultural upheavals which continue to roil the West have historical, technological and ultimately spiritual roots. The 'decline of the West' which is so hotly debated right now is, in my view, not a matter of the wrong people being in charge, or the wrong economic policies being pursued. It is not due to the rise of China or Russia, or racism, or 'misinformation', or nasty populists, or the institutionalisation of 'woke' ideology. As such, it will not be solved by tougher border controls, or radical rightist governments, or revolutions, or 'decolonisation', or controls on freedom of speech in the name of 'protecting our democracy'. Any number of these things might or might not be real or true or desirable, but they are symptoms, not causes, of our malaise. The malaise is deeper, older, more interesting and far more consequential than any of this, and it affects the very basis of our humanity. What happens next will determine what it means to be human in the twenty-first century and beyond.

This book seeks to tell the tale of this Machine: what it is, where it came from, and where it is taking us next. Drawing from history, from religion, from current events and from the work of many other writers and thinkers, it aims to pin down the shape and genesis of this thing. My inquiry is divided into four parts. Part one explores the roots of the current Western cultural malaise. Part two explains where the Machine came from, and how it contributed to that problem. Part three examines how its values manifest around us today, and what they are destroying. Part four offers a guide to practical and spiritual survival and resistance.

I never ended up in that pine forest, but that was probably a good thing. Part of me has always wanted to be a hermit, but the job opportunities are just not there these days. Besides, I would probably just have gone mad. Here in the Irish West, I'm far enough away from the centre of the maelstrom to have, I hope, a useful perspective on it. If this book can be of some help in navigating the strange perils of the world that is rising—in pinning down this Machine in words, and offering up some alternatives to it—then it will have done its job; and, maybe, at last, so will I.

PART ONE

The Western Deviation

The whole modern world has divided itself into
Conservatives and Progressives. The business of
Progressives is to go on making mistakes. The
business of Conservatives is to prevent
mistakes from being corrected.

G. K. CHESTERTON

The Dream of the Rood

L ET ME TELL YOU A STORY.

This story begins in a garden, at the very beginning of all things. All life can be found in this garden: every living being, every bird and animal, every tree and plant. Humans live here too, and so does the creator of all of it, the source of everything, and he is so close that he can be seen and heard and spoken to. Everything walks in the garden together. Everything is in communion. It is a picture of integration.

At the centre of this garden grows a tree, the fruit of which imparts hidden knowledge. The humans—the last creatures to be formed by the creator—will be ready to eat this fruit one day, and when they do they will gain its knowledge and be able to use that knowledge wisely for the benefit of themselves and of all other things that live in the garden. But they are not ready yet. The humans are still young, and unlike the rest of creation they are only partially formed. If they ate from the tree now, the consequences would be terrible.

Do not eat that fruit, the creator tells them. *Eat anything else you like, but not that.*

We know the next part of the story because it is still happening to us all the time. *Why should you not eat the fruit?* says the voice of the tempting serpent, the voice from the undergrowth of our minds. *Why should you not have the power that you are worthy of? Why should this creator keep it all for himself? Why should you listen to him? He just wants to keep you down. Eat the fruit. It's your right. You're worth it!*

So we eat the fruit, and we see that we are naked, and we become ashamed. Our mind is filled with questions; the gears inside it begin to whir and turn and suddenly now here is *us* and *them*, here is *humanity* and *nature*, here is *people* and *God*. A portcullis of words descends between us and the other creatures in the garden, and we can never go home again. We fall into dis-integration and we fall out of the garden forever. Armed angels are set at the gates; even if we find our way back to the garden again, we cannot re-enter. The state of questless ease that was our birthright is gone. We chose knowledge over communion; we chose power over humility.

The Earth is our home now.

This Earth is a broken version of the garden, of our original integration with creator and creation. On Earth we must toil to break the soil, to plant seeds, to fight off predators. We will sicken and die. Everything is eating everything else. There is war and dominion and misery. There is beauty and love and friendship too, but all of it ends in death. These are the consequences of our pursuit of knowledge and power, but we keep pursuing them because we know no other means to escape from our exile. We keep building towers and cities and forgetting where we came from. Outside the garden, we are homeless and can never be still. We forget the creator and worship ourselves. All of this happens inside us every day.

There comes a time when the creator takes pity. After so many centuries of this, after so many years of humans missing the mark, of wandering from the path, of civilisations rising and falling and warring and dying, of eating the fruit again and again, the creator stages an intervention. He comes to Earth in human form to show us the way back home. Most people don't listen, naturally, and we all know how the story ends. God himself walks on Earth and what does humanity do? We torture and kill him.

But the joke is on us, because it turns out that this was the point all along. The way of this creator is not the way of power but of humility, not of conquest but of sacrifice. When he comes to Earth he comes not as warlord, king or high priest, but as a barefoot artisan in an obscure desert province. He walks with the downtrodden and the rejected, he scorns wealth and power, and through his death he conquers death itself, releasing us from our bondage. He gives us a way out, a way back home. But we have to work at it. The path back to the garden can only be found by giving up the vainglory, the search for power and the unearned knowledge which got us exiled in the first place. The path is the path of renunciation, of love and of sacrifice. To get back to the garden, we have to go through the cross.

Now imagine that a whole culture is built around this story. Imagine that this culture survives for over a thousand years, building layer upon layer of meaning, tradition, innovation and creation, however imperfectly, on these foundations.

Then imagine that this culture dies, leaving only ruins.

If you live in the West, you do not have to imagine any of this. You are living among those ruins, and you have been all your life. Many of them are still beautiful—intact cathedrals, Bach concertos—but they are ruins nonetheless. They are the remains of something called 'Christendom', a 1,500-year civilisation into which this particular sacred story seeped, informing every aspect of life, bending and changing and transforming everything in its image. No aspect of daily life was unaffected by this story: the organisation of the working week; the cycle of annual feast days and rest days; the payment of taxes; the moral duties of individuals; the very notion of individuals, with 'God-given' rights and duties; the attitude to neighbours and strangers; the obligations of charity; the structure of families; and most of all, the wide picture of the universe—its structure and meaning, and our human place within it.

Current arguments about the state of 'the West' usually begin with disputes about what it actually is, and the answer you receive to that question will depend on who you talk to. For liberals, the West is the 'Enlightenment' and everything that followed—parliamentary democracy, human rights, individualism, freedom of speech. For conservatives, it might signal a set of cultural values such as traditional attitudes to family life, religion and national identity, and probably broad support for capitalist economics. For the kinds of post-modern leftists who have dominated the culture for some time now, the West—assuming they will concede that it even exists—is largely a front for colonisation, empire, racism and various other historical horrors.

All of these things could be true at the same time, but each is also a fairly recent development. The West is a lot older than liberalism, conservatism, Marxism or empire. The West, in fact, is at the same time a simpler, more ancient and immensely more complex concoction than any of these could offer. It is the result of the binding together of people and peoples across a continent, over centuries of time, by a sacred order constructed around this particular religious story.

In his book *Religion and the Rise of Western Culture*, written shortly after World War Two, the medieval historian Christopher Dawson explained it like this:

> There has never been any unitary organisation of Western culture apart from that of the Christian Church, which provided an effective principle of social unity . . . Behind the ever-changing pattern of Western culture there was a living faith which gave Europe a certain sense of spiritual community, in spite of all the conflicts and divisions and social schisms that marked its history.[1]

Your personal attitude to that 'living faith' is beside the point here. So, come to that, is the entirely legitimate question of whether 'Christendom' was even Christian much of the time. People will be arguing about all of that forever. The point to focus on is this: that when a culture built around such a sacred order dies then there will be upheaval at every level of society, from the level of politics right down to the level of the soul. The very notion of an individual life will shift dramatically. The family structure, the meaning of work, moral attitudes, the very existence of morals at all, notions of good and evil, sexual mores, perspectives on everything from money to rest to work to nature to kin to responsibility to duty: everything will be up for grabs.

The West, in short, was Christendom. But Christendom died. What does that make us, its descendants, living amongst its beautiful ruins? It makes ours a culture with no sacred order. And this is a dangerous place to be.

The philosopher Alasdair MacIntyre argued in his classic work *After Virtue* that the very notion of virtue itself would eventually become inconceivable once the source it sprung from was removed. If human life is regarded as having no *telos,* or higher meaning, he said, it will ultimately be impossible to agree on what 'virtue' means, or why it should mean anything. MacIntyre's favoured teacher was Aristotle, not Jesus, but his critique of the Enlightenment and his prediction of its ultimate failure were based on a clearsighted understanding of the mythic vision of medieval Christendom, and of the partial, empty and over-rational humanism with which Enlightenment philosophers attempted to replace it.

MacIntyre, writing four decades ago, believed that this failure was already clearly evident but that society did not see it, because the monuments to the old sacred order were still standing, like Roman statues after the Empire's fall. To illustrate his thesis, MacIntyre used the example of the *taboo.* This word was first recorded by Europeans in the journals of Captain Cook, in which he recorded his visits to Polynesia. 'The English seamen had been astonished at what they took to be the lax sexual habits of the Polynesians', MacIntyre explains, 'and were even more astonished to discover the sharp contrast with the rigorous prohibition placed on such conduct as men and women eating together. When they enquired why men and women were prohibited from eating together, they were told that the practice was taboo. But when they enquired further what taboo meant, they could get little further information'.[2]

Further research suggested that the Polynesian islanders themselves were not really sure why these prohibitions existed, either; indeed, when taboos were abolished entirely in parts of Polynesia a few decades later, there were few immediately obvious consequences. So were such prohibitions meaningless all along? No: but when the context in which they once had meaning evaporates—once times change—the taboos, even if they are still standing, have less and less meaning. They eventually become relics. Once a society reaches this stage, one shove is all it takes to start a domino effect that will knock them all down.

MacIntyre believed—forty years ago, remember—that this stage had already been reached in the West. 'Modern moral utterance', as he put it, is best understood as a series of badly understood and fragmented survivals from a forgotten past. These 'fragmented survivals' are a remnant of that Western sacred order. Now, as MacIntyre predicted, the final taboos are falling like ninepins, and from all across the cultural spectrum the effects are being felt.

If you're broadly socially conservative, for example—which in practice means that you hold views which were entirely mainstream until about fifteen years ago—the questions are currently coming at you in a rolling barrage. Why should a man not marry a man? Why should a man not become a woman? Why should a child not have three fathers, or be born from a uterus transplanted into a man's body? Why should the state not assist people to commit suicide? Since the source of our old understanding of marriage, family, sexuality and perhaps even biological dimorphism was the now-problematic Christian story, these are the kinds of questions to which there is now only one logical answer.

Things are not much better, though, for those on the left who are concerned about the destructive inequalities created by the modern economy. 'Woe to you who are rich', said Jesus, in one of many blasts against wealth and power that we can read in the Gospels. 'Greed is a sin against God', wrote Thomas Aquinas, one of the giants of Western Christian theology. Not any more. Now our economy runs on greed, and it laughs in the face of any foolish and unrealistic romantic who rejects it. The shaky binding straps with which medieval Christendom kept the traders, the merchants and the urban bourgeoisie tied down have long since broken, leaving us with no better argument against rampant greed and inequality than against total sexual licence or the remaking of the human body itself.

This is what Friedrich Nietzsche knew, and what today's liberal humanists will too often deny: if you knock out the pillars of a sacred order, the universe itself will change shape. At the primal level, such a change is experienced by people as a deep and lasting trauma, whether they know it or not. No culture can just shrug off, or rationalise away, the metaphysics which underpin it and expect to remain a culture in anything but name—if that.

When such an order is broken, what replaces it? It depends on how the break happens. When the taboos were abolished in Polynesia, reported MacIntyre, an unexpected 'moral vacuum' was created, which came to be filled by 'the banalities of the New England Protestant missionaries'.[3] In this case, a certain colour of Christianity had stepped into the breach created by the death of an earlier sacred story. The end of the taboos had not brought about some abstract 'freedom'; rather, it had stripped the culture of its heart. That heart had, in reality, stopped beating

9

some time before, but now that the formal architecture was gone too, there was an empty space waiting to be filled—and nature abhors a vacuum.

It seems to me that we are now at this point in the West. Since at least the 1960s our empty taboos have been crumbling away, and in just the last few years the last remaining monuments have been—often literally—torn down. Christendom expired over centuries for a complex set of reasons, but it was not killed off by an external enemy. No hostile army swept into Europe and forcibly converted us to a rival faith. Instead, we dismantled our story from within. What replaced it was not a new sacred order, but a denial that such a thing existed at all.

In *After Virtue*, MacIntyre explains what happened next. The Enlightenment project of the eighteenth century was an attempt to build a 'morality' (a word that had not existed in this sense before that time) loosed from theology. It was the project of constructing a wholly new human being After God, in which a new, personal moral sense—no longer eternal in nature, or accountable to any higher force—would form the basis of the culture and the individual.

Did it work? In a word: no. Post-Enlightenment 'morality' was no substitute for a higher purpose. If the correct path for society or the individual is based on nothing more than that individual's personal judgement, then who or what is to be the final arbiter? Ultimately, without that higher purpose to bind it—without, in other words, a sacred order—society will fall into emotivism, relativism and ultimately disintegration. This was MacIntyre's prediction. It's starting to look like he was spot on.

In many ways, I am a roundhead at heart. Maybe we all are, we Western folk. The Enlightenment may have failed to create a new moral order that would last, but it taught modern Western people something useful: how to interrogate power and identify illegitimate authority. But while I learned this early, it was much later that I learned something else, dimly and slowly, through my study of history, mythology and, well, people: that every culture, whether it knows it or not, is built around a sacred order. This does not, of course, need to be a Christian order. It could be Islamic, Hindu or Daoist. It could be based around the veneration of ancestors or the worship of Odin. But there is a throne at the heart of every culture, and whoever sits on it will be the force you take your instruction from.

The modern experiment has been the act of dethroning both literal human sovereigns and the representatives of the sacred order, and replacing them with purely human, and purely abstract, notions—'the people' or 'liberty' or 'democracy' or 'progress'. I'm all for liberty, and it would be nice to give democracy a try one day too; but the dethroning of the sovereign—Christ—who sat at the heart of the Western sacred order has not led to universal equality and justice. It has led, via a bloody shortcut through Robespierre, Stalin and Hitler, to the complete triumph of the power of money, which has splintered our culture and our souls into a million angry shards.

This has been the terrible irony of the age of reason, and of the liberal and leftist theories and revolutions which resulted from it. From 1789 to 1968, every one of them ultimately failed, but in destroying the old world and its sacred order they cleared a space for money culture to move in and commodify the ruins. The vacuum created by the collapse of our old taboos was filled by the poison gas of consumer capitalism. It has now infiltrated every aspect of our lives in the way that the Christian story once did, so much so that we barely even notice as it colonises everything from the way we eat to the values we teach our children. Cut loose in a post-modern present, with no centre, no truth and no direction, we have not become independent-minded, responsible, democratic citizens in a human republic. We have become slaves to the power of money, and worshippers of the self.

The old taboos are not coming back, and Christendom will not be returning to Europe any time soon. Neither do we need to desire it. The point is not to make an idol of the past, but to recognise that when a culture kills its sovereign, the throne will not remain empty for long. Dethrone Christ if you like—dethrone any representative of any sacred order on Earth. But when you do, you will understand that the sovereign, however imperfect his rule, may have been the only thing standing between you and the barbarians massing outside—and inside—your gates.

A culture, I think now, is above all a spiritual creation. When the *cult* departs from the heart of the *cult*ure, the thing starts to fall apart. The centre cannot hold. This, I think, is where we are. If this is true, then the 'culture war' is the equivalent of two bald men fighting over a comb. We are not in an existential fight for the future of 'Western civilisation'. Western civilisation is already dead—and both sides of the current 'war' are reacting, in their own particular ways, to the vacuum that has replaced it—a vacuum which something must come to fill. The French philosopher and Sufi mystic René Guénon, writing in 1927 in his short book *The Crisis of the Modern World,* suggested that what he called 'the Western deviation' away from the sacred order had unleashed materialist demons which 'now threaten to invade the whole world'. Guénon could see that the power of materialist science, allied with the values of commerce, would cause the West to 'disappear completely' if it did not change course:

> Those who unchain the brute forces of matter will perish, crushed
> by those same forces, of which they will no longer be masters; once
> having imprudently set them in motion, they cannot hope to hold
> their fatal course indefinitely in check. It is of little consequence
> whether it be the forces of nature or the forces of the human mob, or
> both together; in any case it is the laws of matter that are called into

play and that inexorably destroy him who has aspired to dominate them . . . [4]

When a sacred order collapses, despair can ensue, even amongst those who would not want its return or who are not even aware of what is missing. But the cycle of rise and fall is an inevitable part of the human historical pattern, and a necessary one. 'The passage from one cycle to another', wrote Guénon, 'can take place only in darkness'.[5]

What if we are in that passage now? What if we are living in Guénon's 'darkness between worlds'? It would explain the strange, tense, shattering and frustrating tenor of the times. It would start, too, to get to the heart of what we are lacking, for we modern creatures are people with everything and nothing all at once. We—at least if we are among the lucky ones—have every gadget and recipe and website and storefront and exotic holiday in the world available to us, but we are lacking two things that we seem to need, but grasp at nonetheless: meaning, and roots.

II

The Great Unsettling

THERE IS NO SUCH THING AS a perfect society, and anyone who tries to build one will either go mad or become a tyrant. Humans are fallen, or just natural, and both of those words are synonyms for 'imperfect'. What is 'perfection' anyway? It is a concept designed by a part of the modern human mind—the part that likes clean lines, easy answers, plots that end by neatly tying up all the threads. The quest for perfection is a quest for homogeneity and control, and it leads to the gulag and the guillotine, the death camp and the holy war. Even if we could agree on what perfection amounted to, we would none of us be equipped to build it.

But. Though no human culture has been anything but flawed, all lasting human cultures in history have been rooted. That is to say, they have been tied down by, and to, things more solid, timeless and lasting than the day-to-day processes of their functioning or the personal desires of the individuals who inhabit them. Some of those solid things are human creations: cultural traditions, a sense of lineage and ancestry, ceremonies designed for worship or initiation. Others are non-human: the natural world in which those cultures dwell, or the divine force that they—always, without fail—worship and communicate with in some form.

We need these roots. We need a sense of belonging to something that is bigger than us, across both space and time, and we underestimate that need at our peril. A rootless society is like a society with no sacred order: it is adrift, and open to capture by dangerous forces. In her brilliant and singular book *The Need for Roots*, written in 1943, the French writer and reluctant mystic Simone Weil put the case starkly:

> To be rooted is perhaps the most important and least recognised need of the human soul. It is one of the hardest to define. A human being has roots by virtue of his real, active and natural participation in the life of a community which preserves in living shape certain particular treasures of the past and certain particular expectations of the future . . . Every human being needs to have multiple roots. It is necessary for him to draw wellnigh the whole of his moral, intellectual and spiritual life by way of the environment of which he forms a natural part.[1]

Weil was writing from exile in England, as her homeland was still under Nazi occupation. She saw National Socialism's perversion and capture of the notion of rootedness, and the evil that was being done with it. But unlike many intellectuals of the left, the Nazis' racial tyranny did not lead her to reject the notion of rootedness in favour of some universalist flavour of 'global justice'. She saw that for the perfectionism it was: the same flavour of perfectionism that, to the east, was leading the USSR to roll out the same kind of tyranny as the Nazis were building, right down to the barbed wire that surrounded the camps designated for those who did not fit into the model.

Weil saw beyond all of this: When she looked at Hitler and Stalin, she saw two tyrants leading nations that had already been uprooted—

by the Industrial Revolution, by Bolshevism, by the Great War, by the Depression, by the wider process of modernity. Both tyrants promised a return to security, power and meaning for their people through the imposition of a totalitarian ideology which they claimed would speak for the masses. Both delivered hell instead.

Weil's book was commissioned by the Free French in London, led by Charles de Gaulle. It was intended to be a manifesto for the renewal of France, and Europe, after the scourge of Nazism. Her prescription was radical. Europeans, she said, had been uprooted by industry, by the state and what she saw as a form of pseudo-Christianity which had lined itself up with 'the interests of those who exploit the people'. Both state nationalism and state socialism were con tricks: exploiters of the people posing as their liberators. The 'totalitarian idol' of grand world-saving ideologies such as communism and fascism was the scourge of the twentieth century. The whole game had to be junked, the terms redefined. 'The only punishment capable of punishing Hitler, and deterring little boys thirsting for greatness in coming centuries from following his example', she proclaimed, 'is such a total transformation of the meaning attached to greatness that he should thereby be excluded from it'.[2]

A transformation of the meaning attached to greatness. Perhaps this has always been the task, and perhaps it has always been urgent. But it certainly is now. Our society has attached a meaning to *greatness* that is not as far away from Hitler's as it would like to believe, despite our cant about democracy and freedom. Our idols today are economic conquest, unending 'growth' built on turning all life into 'resources' for human consumption, scientism disguised as objective inquiry, manic forward motion, and the same old quest for perfectibility.

What could such a 'transformation' look like? The conflagration that consumed the West in the twentieth century, as two vast materialist ideologies confronted each other and tyrants offering salvation rampaged across the continent, feels in retrospect like some sort of endgame.

If the West was, as the previous chapter argued, a spiritual creation, then this attempt to create heaven on Earth in the absence of God was a lesson in what a culture without a spiritual core can come to. The history of religion offers no shortage of tyrannies and persecutions, but its secular replacement has, if anything, fared worse. What does 'greatness' mean, then? Where should it aim its gaze?

Simone Weil found the answer in the eternal things, and the way she spoke about them could never be boxed in. She wrote in praise of God, tradition, roots, peoples and culture; but also of justice, freedom of speech and thought, honour and equality. She was a sort-of Catholic, but fought for the Republicans in the Spanish Civil War. She could be equally scathing about fascism, communism, established religion, liberal elites, capitalism and mass education. She incinerated the 'uprooted intellectuals obsessed with progress' who dominated the cultural elite of her time (and who have entirely conquered ours), assailed the left for its contempt of the peasantry and asserted that 'of all the human soul's needs, none is more vital . . . than love of the past'. But just when you imagined you were dealing with a conservative Defender of the West, you would read something like this:

> For centuries now, men of the white race have everywhere destroyed the past, stupidly, blindly, both at home and abroad. If in certain respects there has been, nevertheless, progress during this period, it is not because of this frenzy but in spite of it, under the impulse of what little of the past remained alive.[3]

Weil wasn't wrong. We in the West invented this thing called 'modernity', and then we took it out into the world, whether the world wanted it or not. Once, we called this process 'the white man's burden' and exported it with dreadnoughts. Now we call it 'development' and export it via the World Bank. But—and here is the point so often missed, especially by critics on the left—before we could eat the world, we first had to eat ourselves. Or rather: our states, our elites, our ideologues and power-mongers had to dispossess their own people before they could venture out to dispossess others. We were the prototype, the guinea pigs in a giant global experiment. Now we find ourselves rootless, rudderless, unmoored in a great sea of chaos; angry, confused, shouting at the world and each other. We have made of our world a *nihil*. We are both perpetrators and victims of a Great Unsettling.

Of course, 'Western' people are not the only ones responsible for the rolling destruction of culture and nature that is overwhelming the world, whatever progressive deconstructionists may claim. The culture of uprooting is global now. You can see it everywhere you care to look, accelerating in speed and destructive power. Witness the Indian government trying to undermine the power and agency of the nation's peasant farmers, and triggering a rural rebellion by doing so. Witness the Chinese state, which is increasingly looking like the most efficient machine ever invented for uprooting, resettling and controlling mass populations. Witness the Indonesians colonising the tribal cultures of West Papua, or African governments corralling the last of the bushpeople. This is what states do, whatever colour or culture their ministers are. It's the ancient human game of power and control, turbocharged with fossil fuels and digital surveillance technology.

However we dissect it, though, I believe that the heart of the crisis that is enveloping so much of the world today—cultural, ecological and spiritual—is this ongoing process of mass uprooting. It is also, as this book will explore further, the root of the West's current turmoil. We could simply call this process *modernity*, which is not a time period so much as a story we tell ourselves. But I prefer to call it the Machine, because a machine—as the poets showed me—is what it *feels* like. This process, which has been going on for centuries, of uprooting us from nature, culture and God, leads us into a mass society, controlled by and for technology, in which we have been on course to become, since at the least the Industrial Revolution, mere cogs in a giant mechanism that we have no control over.

Wherever we come from, wherever we are, we are almost all uprooted now. The power of the 'global economy' demolishes borders and boundaries, traditions and cultures, languages and ways of seeing wherever it goes. Record numbers of people are on the move as a result, and as the population increases and climate change bites, those numbers will rise everywhere, churning cultures and nations into entirely new shapes or no shapes at all. Even if you are living where your forefathers have lived for generations, you can bet that the smartphone you gave your child will unmoor them more effectively than any bulldozer could. The majority of humanity is now living in megacities, cut off from non-human nature, plugged into the Machine, controlled by it, reduced to it.

This process accelerates under its own steam because, as Simone Weil explained, 'whoever is uprooted himself uproots others', thus feeding the cycle. The more of us are pulled or pushed away from our cultures, traditions and places—if we had them in the first place—the more we take that restlessness out with us into the world. If you have ever wondered why it is *de rigueur* amongst Western cultural elites to demonise roots and glorify movement, to downplay cohesion and talk up diversity, to deny links with the past and strike out instead for a future that never quite arrives—well, I'd say that this is at least part of the explanation.

We are, I think, in this flailing, dissolving 'West' of ours, desperately in need of real culture. We want to go home again, but even when we know where home is to be found, we see that we can't return. And so a void is created, and into the void rush monsters: fake versions of the roots we are looking for. Identity politics, newly rigid racial labels, extreme forms of nationalism, endlessly multiplying genders, and 'identities' constructed online with no reference to reality. The mono-ethnic identitarianism of the far right or the 'diversity' identitarianism of the far left: take your pick according to your predilections and fears. We reach for toxic imitations of our lost roots, but they can never replace the real thing and the result is an orgy of anger, bitterness and wanton destruction. Meanwhile, the Machine pushes on, relentless.

If you are looking for a 'solution' to this—presuming, of course, you think it is a problem—then you will not find one in politics, nor in ideologies. The twentieth century shows us this clearly, and today's culture war, which sometimes seems like a 1960s nostalgia trip, shows it too. Once these rootless, curated 'identities' are the choices we are faced with, we are already a long way down the road that leads away from real culture. In all the time I have spent with people who live in genuinely rooted cultures—rooted in time, place and spirit—whether that be here in the remnants of rural Ireland, in indigenous communities in Mexico, Papua or India, on some of the last small farms in England, or talking to Maori or Native American or Aboriginal Australian people, I have been struck by one fact: people don't tend to talk much about their 'identity' unless it is under threat. The louder you have to talk about it, the more you have lost. Once an entire country is talking about nothing else, that's a pretty good sign that the Machine has sprayed the roots of its people with Roundup and ploughed the remains into the field.

'Our age is so poisoned by lies', wrote Weil, 'that it converts everything it touches into a lie'.[4] Everything deeper, older and truer than the workings and values of the Machine has been, or is in the process of being, scoured away from us. We turned away from a spiritual, rooted understanding of the world in order to look at ourselves reflected in the little black mirrors in our hands. Some people are quite happy with this, and have no time for romantic Luddites like me when we lament it. Even we romantic Luddites are doing much of our lamenting on the internet. But some day soon we will all have to look up and begin to turn back again. I have a feeling that this process has already begun.

When a plant is uprooted, it withers and then dies. When the same happens to a person, or a people, or a planetful of both, the result is the same. Our crisis comes, I think, from our being unable to admit what on some level we know to be true: that we in the West are living inside an obsolete story. Our culture is not in danger of dying; it is already dead, and we are in denial. This, now, is the reality we have to wrestle with— and transcend.

III

The Faustian Fire

SPRING IN IRELAND MEANS THE NIGHTS are still frosty, the fire is on in the evenings, and the birds are still hungry. Summer is slow in coming to this island, and sometimes it never really comes at all. Early this spring, as the first shoots appeared, I ploughed and raked a section of my field, and then sowed it with native wildflowers. A week later, the birds all got up earlier than me and ate the lot. There was barely a seed left; only a lot of telltale little patches of blue and white bird shit where my seedbed had been.

Working on the land is like that: an endless battle to protect your little space from every other creature that also wants its bounty. We can all identify with this in some way or another. Still, digging and sowing and leaning in to the last of the winter winds has a purifying side to it. Working on the land, I can clear my head of thoughts and questions. Sometimes, anyway. But there are times when the questions won't leave; they swirl around, they compost in my mind, they develop and grow tendrils and shoots. Sometimes they are answered, at least partially. Sometimes, they just give birth to more questions.

It's hard to work on the land without thinking about roots, because you're often working with them: trying to create them, or sometimes trying to dig them up. As spring began to ripen, in between planting seed and cursing the birds and wanting to work with the birds to avoid the cursing, I found myself thinking about those roots a lot. I knew that Simone Weil was right: I have been writing for years about the uprooting of things that seem to matter, both around me and within me. That uprooting is the story of our time; the story and the genesis of the Machine. In the end, all the digging and the thinking prompted me to sit down with a book I had been putting off for years: a book which, like its author, had an intimidating air but which I was sure would have answers to my questions.

Published in 1918, the book—or rather, the first of its two volumes—catapulted its author, a previously obscure private scholar, to fame. In that decisive year, the book's title might have been reason enough: *The Decline of the West*, by Oswald Spengler. Germany was emerging shattered from the First World War and beginning its spiral into two decades of catastrophe which would climax with the Second. Decline was very much in the air. But it wasn't just in Germany that the book took off. Across the West, after the horrors of the Great War, there was a sense that something was terribly wrong. A society that could create a hell like Passchendaele (where my own great-grandfather was a sniper), and pull much of the world into it, seemed to be suffering from some terrible sickness.

Spengler took the long view. *The Decline of the West* is a comparative history of civilisations, in which its author claims to have discovered a pattern of birth, growth and decline which can be applied to all major human cultures, from that of Ancient Egypt to that of the modern West. What sounds like a mathematical formula is then rendered in prose which is sometimes closer to poetry (Spengler preferred to call himself a poet rather than a historian), employing overarching metaphors, sweeping historical claims, layers of polemic and an often-overlooked spiritual undergirding. All of this resulted in both the instant scorn of professional historians, and an entirely original piece of work.

Spengler's poetic, intuitive and Teutonically wordy model divided the world up into discrete cultures, each of which had a distinct form. He then explained, through comparative examples, what he believed the standard cultural cycle was. First, a 'culture' is born, in a specific part of the Earth. The place itself is the primary influence on the feel and form of the culture, which cannot function properly outside its birthplace. A young culture is 'organic'; that is to say, it grows from the bottom up. The peasant, said Spengler—the 'eternal man'—is the base upon which a culture is built. A culture is at root a product of the countryside and the small town.

As the culture grows, it coalesces around a distinct 'Idea'. Each culture exists to fulfill this Idea, though it may not know it. The culture rises and grows, reaches its full potential and then flowers. The Idea floats off into the world like pollen on the wind. This is the golden age. Having fulfilled itself, then, the culture 'suddenly hardens, its blood congeals, its force breaks down and it becomes *civilisation*'. At this point, it may create great monuments, build empires, erect glorious buildings, produce great art—yet its life force is already seizing up. Its peasantry is gone, sucked into the urban slums; the small towns have become sprawling cities; its spiritual life has ossified; and its arts have become self-referential. Civilisation has triumphed, and civilisation ultimately only has one final arbiter of value: money.

Eventually, after a century or two of vainglory, such a civilisation evolves into a globalised 'cosmopolis'. Great 'world-cities', made up of people uprooted from landscapes far and near, are its heart, but despite their energy these cities—'the monstrous symbol and vessel of the completely emancipated intellect', where 'money and intellect celebrate their greatest and their last triumphs'[1]—are unable to create or maintain real culture. What was once animal has become machine.

At this point, the decline begins in earnest. The uprooting of every-thing and everyone, the quest for glory, the construction of empires and monuments, the accumulation of wealth and the subsequent dependency upon it: all of it creates an exploited, unhappy mass population in the 'barrack-cities' which are easy prey for corporations, media manipula-tors and demagogues. Here the arch-traditionalist Spengler comes into strange alignment with the communist Karl Marx, with his theory of alienation, and the uncategorisable Simone Weil with her reflections on the consequences of rootlessness. All are in agreement that the creation of vast populations in industrial megacities is the precursor to turmoil. What kind—and whether the turmoil is to be welcomed or feared—is another question.

Spengler's prediction on this front was clear: the age of cosmopolis was the beginning of the end of all civilisations, from China's Warring States to Ancient Rome. The resulting decline in each case paved the way for 'Caesarism': the rise of demagogues promising to bring order to increasingly formless chaos. After several hundred years of such cen-tralised tyranny, the civilisation finally succumbed to the weight of his-tory and was replaced by another. This, he said, would be the fate of the West; and soon.

So what did Spengler make of this thing we call 'Western culture': What did he mean by it, and what did he predict? The thing that seems to set Spengler apart from other comparative historians, aside from the poetry and the purple passages (always a plus for me), is the way he cat-egorised cultures. This is the part of the book that academic historians really hate, which may be why it is the most interesting bit. Spengler bunched up great chunks of historical time in unique ways. Rejecting the then-common division of past eras into 'ancient', 'medieval' and 'modern'—a schema which he said was too parochial and flattered the West by placing it at the centre of the world—he invented his own pat-tern instead.

First came 'Apollinian culture'—Spengler's term for the Classical world. Apollinian culture, like all others, had its own distinctive forms—arts, architecture, literature and the like, all accreting around key symbols. The symbol of the Apollinian world was the column. Growing out of the ruins of the Apollinian world came a culture invented especially for the occasion by Spengler: the 'Magian', which took in Judaism, Byzantium and early Islam. Magian culture, too, had its own forms and poetry: primarily, as the name suggests, it was a time of mysteries, of questions without answers, of trust in the higher will. Its symbol was the cavern.

Then came the culture in whose dying days we are now all living: the splendidly named 'Faustian' age. As the name suggests, the Faustian Idea—the soul, the essence which has driven the rise and fall of 'the West'—is expansion, curiosity and an endless forward drive. An endless need for conquest, invention and exploration define the Faustian soul, which believes to its core that the whole world should follow its example, and that its values are universal.

Faustian culture, said Spengler, was born around the year 1000. Its summer was the High Middle Ages, its symbol the great Gothic cathedral, its golden age represented by the music of Bach. By the time of the sixteenth-century Reformation the decay was setting in, and by 1800 Faustian culture had begun to atrophy into civilisation: Classicism and Romanticism were signs of an increasingly rigid civilisation already looking fondly back to its cultural or natural origins.

With industrial revolution, Enlightenment and empire, the Faustian fire was carried to all corners of the globe, and its core Idea—the onward push of economic growth, material expansion, 'development', 'progress' and all the other modern mythologies—was seeded across the world by the 'expansion power of the Western soul'. Organic lifeways were replaced by abstract systems, and modern science ('no other Culture possesses anything like it') became the *'servant of the technical*

Will-to-Power'. Religion declined, to be replaced first by liberalism ('freedom from the restrictions of the soil-bound life') and then socialism, which in Spengler's broad usage meant the urge to politically reshape the whole world according to egalitarian lights. The Western left, in Spengler's telling, as the Marxist revolution in Russia had so recently demonstrated, were Faustian too in their totalising universalism and their ruthless destruction of opposition.

But even as the West was conquering the world, its own soul was seizing up. By the twentieth century, the direction was clear, and for Spengler the Great War only confirmed it. Only disintegration, followed by Caesarism, and a 'return to thorough formlessness', awaited us now. The twenty-first century, predicted Spengler, would be the period in which this would begin. The only realistic response was to adopt some version of Stoicism, and hope for the coming of a cultured and suitably strong Caesar to steady the ship as she sank.

It's probably not necessary to labour the point that one of Spengler's readers did indeed become leader of Germany fifteen years later, and tried to fill the role he believed the author had allotted for him. Spengler was not impressed: the parvenu Hitler was not the Caesar he was looking for, and he had no time for Hitler's racial theories about 'Aryans'. But all Spengler's talk about 'blood' and the 'vigour' of nations, not to mention his fear of 'coloured races' usurping 'Prussians', and the need for a strongman to respond, had fed the tiger which would come to eat his country. He had discovered that we don't get to choose the shape of our Caesars, or their designs. Perhaps all we can do is try to make sure we do not prepare the ground for them to spring from.

I expect that those academic historians could still kick a hundred holes in the details of *The Decline of the West*, but it is hard to argue that the broad trajectory which its author offered was wrong. Now, as we watch a new period in our decline unfurl, I find it useful to keep his model in mind. I find it useful to remember that we are the men and women of the Faustian age: the age of the Machine. The values of this Machine are the values of Spengler's Faustian culture, and the upheaval that they create underpins all of our current cultural conflicts. We were formed by these values, even if we think we reject them; and like any people formed by any culture, we find it hard to see beyond the horizon to what might come next.

What is a culture? It is a story that a people tells itself. Whether or not that story emerges from the Earth and then creates a people to tell it—as Spengler believed and as I am tempted to believe too—we build and rebuild our cultures every day, in the stories we tell our children and ourselves. Stories about who we are, where we came from and where we're going. Stories about the deeper meaning of human life, about what matters, about what we stand for and what we will not. Stories, ultimately, about Truth. When the story stops being told, the people will disappear, and vice versa. And when the story is turned in on itself, when its tellers lose faith in it, when it is mocked or abused from within, or when it simply burns itself out—then the people begins to dissolve: to come apart, to slough away from the centre, to stumble and eventually to fall.

Spengler's answer to the crumbling of the West was to await the coming of his new Caesar. Others have their own responses: revolution, reaction, retreat, endless fights over policies and politicians. There are as many reactions as there are human personality types. But beyond all of it, there is another way that we could respond, one that is both more realistic and more likely to achieve ultimate success. Mythologist Joseph Campbell writes about it in his book about mythic traditions, *The Hero with a Thousand Faces*. Quoting the British equivalent of Spengler, the historian Arnold Toynbee, Campbell concludes that:

> Schism in the soul, schism in the body social, will not be resolved by
> any scheme of return to the good old days (archaism), or by pro-

28

grams guaranteed to render an ideal projected future (futurism), or even by the most realistic, hardheaded work to weld together again the disintegrating elements. Only birth can conquer death—the birth, not of the old thing again, but of something new.[2]

Only birth can conquer death. At the end of a culture, the real work is not lamentation or desperate defence—both instinctive but futile reactions—but the creation of something new. 'Peace then is a snare', Campbell continues; 'war is a snare; change is a snare; permanence a snare. When our day is come for the victory of death, death closes in; there is nothing we can do, except be crucified—and resurrected; dismembered totally and then reborn'.

What might come next? Weil suggests that a rootless culture will ultimately die. Alasdair MacIntyre predicted, forty years ago, the collapse of a Western world that had forgotten why it believed in any of its own shibboleths. Christopher Dawson, amongst others, taught us that those shibboleths had emerged, however imperfectly, from the Christian story: the story that built 'the West'. If our Faustian culture dethroned Christ from his place at the sacred centre of our culture, and if that Faustian urge has now burned itself out, what remains?

What remains is a void—or, to put it another way, an empty throne. But a throne never remains empty for long: something has to fill it. It has been a long time since the West was in any way Christian. It feels like a long time, too, since we have had any real roots, or any real sense of cultural purpose. And yet there is a sense of movement: a sense that we are being taken somewhere by some force which is restlessly pushing forward and whose values seem Faustian still. This thing has common words attached to it. Sometimes we call it 'the economy'. Sometimes we talk of 'growth' or 'progress'. I prefer to talk of the Machine: the force we met through the words of the poets in the introduction, and which we will begin to explore and define in part two.

For now, the useful work seems to be that outlined by Joseph Campbell: 'to conquer death by birth'. Simone Weil concluded her study of the rootless West by suggesting that the best response for we who find ourselves living in it is 'the growing of roots'—the name she gave to the final section of her work. Pull up some of the exhausted old plants if you need to—carefully, now—but if you don't have some new seed to grow in the bare soil, if you don't tend it and weed it with love, if you don't fertilise it and water it and help it grow: well, then your ground will not produce anything good for you. It will choke up with a chaos of thistles and weeds.

This, in practical terms is, the slow, necessary, sometimes boring work to which I suspect people in our place and time are being called: to build new things, out on the margins. Not to exhaust our souls engaging in a daily war for or against a 'West' that is already gone, but to prepare the seedbed for what might, one day long after us, become the basis of a new culture. To go looking for truth. To light particular little fires— fires fuelled by the eternal things, the great and unchanging truths— and tend their sparks as best we can. To prepare the ground with love for a resurrection of the small, the real and the true.

But first, we are going to have to be crucified.

PART TWO

Divining the Machine

The more machines there are to replace men,
the more men there will be in society
who are nothing but machines.

LOUIS DE BONALD

IV

Blanched Sun, Blinded Man

RECENTLY, I HAD TO BUY a lawnmower. For years now, I have strug-gled to contain the wild summer growth on my couple of acres of land with a scythe and various other hand tools, but there comes a time—and an advancing age—when a man has to admit defeat. I have a lot of grass, it grows too fast at this time of year, and my children are not strapping, interested or free enough to form a mowing team all summer. The hardware shop beckoned. There was no way out.

I live in farming country, so a trip to buy a mower is also a tour through the latest machinery being touted to landowners as labour-saving, forward-looking and impossible to do without if you want to compete with China. Tractors the size of barns, fancy new silage balers, sheer grabs, spreaders, slurry tanks, front loaders, chainsaws, industrial brushcutters: it's all here, if you can afford the loans. The current star of the show, though, is the robot mower. It's not a lot of use to a farmer, but to householders with lawns it's the must-have gimmick of the age. One of them was sitting on a pedestal in the middle of the shop I visited, festooned with ads and promises that this fantastic device, which will automatically mow your lawn without the need for you to even go outside, would save time, effort and energy.

The notion that new machinery equates to 'progress' is probably as old as civilisation, or at least as old as modernity. In my lifetime, all the labour- and time-saving technologies which have been pushed at us, from the microwave oven to the internet, have given us things we didn't previously have, and taken plenty more away, but one thing none of them has done is to save either time or labour. I'm old enough to remember, for example, when we were promised that the advent of email would save us hours of time: no more faxing, or opening and replying to letters! Now we spend, by some estimates, thirty days a year on email alone,[1] and it is increasingly impossible to be out of touch with anyone, anywhere.

This is the devil's bargain of the technological society, and we have been falling for it forever: embrace the new, lose the old, and find yourself more deeply entwined in a technological web from which you cannot extricate yourself even if you want to. Also available in all reliable outlets are such joys as smart fridges, robot vacuum cleaners, instant boiling water taps (no more tiresome boiling the kettle!), 'smart body analysers', smart watches, and of course the terrifying Alexa, who will helpfully monitor all of your private conversations and pass them straight on to Jeff Bezos.

It's often suggested that when we moved from Christendom via the Enlightenment into our current age, whatever we might call it, we desacralised or 'disenchanted' our culture: that we became pure materialists. For its proponents, this process was a move towards 'reason' and away from 'superstition'. For opponents, it represented a slide into decadence and moral dissolution. The best-known proponent of this notion first introduced it in 1917, around the same time that Oswald Spengler was publishing his theory of the West's decline and fall, and for some it has been one reason for that collapse. 'The fate of our times', wrote pioneering sociologist Max Weber, 'is characterized by rationalization and intellectualization and, above all, by the disenchantment of the world'.[2]

This 'disenchantment thesis', as we might call it, has been influential for over a century now. But is it really true? Historian Eugene McCarraher has taken issue with it. In his book *The Enchantments of Mammon*, he argues that modernity did not in fact dispense with the West's sacred order, leaving only a desiccated materialism in its place. 'Since the 17th century', he writes in an essay accompanying his book, 'much modern history has provided good reasons to show that "disenchantment" is more of a fable, a mythology that conceals the persistence of enchantment in "secular" disguise'. And what is being disguised? Love of money. 'Capitalism, it turns out', he continues, 'might be modernity's most beguiling form of enchantment, remaking the moral and ontological universe in its pecuniary image and likeness'.[3]

If McCarraher is right, we have not junked a sacred order for a profane one. We have instead enthroned a new god, and disguised its worship as the disenchanted pursuit of purely material gain. We have dressed up as a mere 'economy' our new idol and sovereign: what I am calling the Machine. But what exactly is this Machine, where did it come from and how might we pin it down? Can we? Is it real—or is it only a metaphor carried too far?

The man to ask is the American historian and cultural critic Lewis Mumford. His massive study *The Myth of the Machine*, published in two volumes between 1967 and 1970, is an exhaustive attempt to chronicle the rise and triumph of the system of power and technology which now entwines us all; a system he calls 'the megamachine'. He makes his position clear early in the first pages of volume one:

The last century, we all realize, has witnessed a radical transformation in the entire human environment, largely as a result of the impact of the mathematical and physical sciences upon technology . . . Never since the Pyramid Age have such vast physical changes been consummated in so short a time. All these changes have, in turn,

produced alterations in the human personality, while still more radical transformations, if this process continue unabated and uncorrected, loom ahead.[4]

My old hardback copy of Mumford's book smells musty and ancient
now, like a good second-hand bookshop. He wrote this paragraph when
colour TV was in its infancy and humanity had not yet landed on the
moon. The process did, needless to say, continue uncorrected. Mumford
died in 1990, before the internet, before smartphones, before the rising
age of AI and Smart Everything, but he saw precisely what was coming.
'With this new "megatechnics"', he wrote,

> the dominant minority will create a uniform, all-enveloping, super-
> planetary structure, designed for automatic operation. Instead of
> functioning actively as an autonomous personality, man will become
> a passive, purposeless, machine-conditioned animal whose proper
> functions, as technicians now interpret man's role, will either be fed
> into the machine or strictly limited and controlled for the benefit of
> depersonalized, collective organizations.[5]

Those 'depersonalized, collective organizations' are the giant world-
spanning corporations which now control most of our lives. They produce the food we eat, the clothes we wear, the technology we use, the
'entertainment' we consume and the 'news' we base our opinions upon,
all the while employing millions of us as labourers and harvesting us as
products ourselves, through the detailed personal information we freely
volunteer them daily all over the web.

These corporations operate via a global technological network of
staggering power and complexity—undersea cables, orbiting satellites,
monitoring devices in our homes and in our pockets, and, soon, web-
connected streets, buildings and appliances, all monitoring us in real

time and selling us what we didn't know we needed. They are facilitated by equally depersonalised collective states, which exist not to promote the interests of their citizens as expressed via 'democracy' (despite what those corporate-controlled media and entertainment systems would have us believe), but to service the corporations and provide for their interests: a process known as 'economic growth'.

This 'growth' is the overriding purpose of the 'global economy' which the Machine has built: everything else is of secondary concern. The growth has no specific aim and no end in sight, and can always be justified by pointing to problems—poverty, environmental degradation—which were in many cases caused by the growth, but which can now only be solved by more of it. It is facilitated by the production and consumption of 'goods and services', the desire (or 'need') for which has been manufactured by vast marketing and advertising concerns whose best minds are trained in the essence of psychological manipulation.

The rise and triumph of the internet—the neurological network of the Machine—has meant that there are now few places on Earth to which we can escape from the incessant noise of this state-corporate 'growth' and the incessant urge to contribute to it by clicking, scrolling, buying and competing. It has prescribed all of our values and proscribed the alternatives, and it shows no sign of stopping. It cannot stop, in fact, for to do so would mean collapse. Growth has become an end in itself, long-divorced from any means. And as the wilderness writer Edward Abbey once pointed out: 'growth for the sake of growth is the ideology of the cancer cell'.[6]

This, then, is the Machine. It is not simply the sum total of various individual technologies we have cleverly managed to rustle up—cars, laptops, robot mowers and the rest. In fact, such 'technics', as Mumford calls them, are the product of the Machine, not its essence. The Machine is, rather, a tendency within us, made concrete by power and circumstance, which coalesces in a huge agglomeration of power, control and ambition.

The Machine manifests today as an intersection of money power, state power and increasingly coercive and manipulative technologies, which constitute an ongoing war against roots and against limits. Its momentum is always forward, and it will not stop until it has conquered and transformed the world. To do that, it must raze or transmute many older and less measurable things: rooted human communities, wild nature, human nature, human freedom, beauty, faith and the many deeper values which we all adhere to in some way or another but find difficult to describe or even to defend. Its *modus operandi* is the abolition of all borders, boundaries, categories, essences and truths: the uprooting of all previous ways of living in the name of pure individualism and perfect subjectivity. Its endgame is the replacement of nature with technology, in order to facilitate total human control over a totally human world.

And yet, the Machine, and our tendency towards creating it, is not a new development. Indeed, it can be traced back much further than we might imagine, to the dawn of civilisation itself. 'A close parallel existed', says Mumford, 'between the first civilizations of the Near East and our own, though most of our contemporaries still regard modern technics, not only as the highest point in man's intellectual development, but as an entirely new phenomenon'. It was in fact not new at all, and we modern Western people did not invent it. Instead, it 'had its origin not in the so-called Industrial Revolution of the eighteenth century, but at the very outset in the organization of an archetypal machine made of human parts'.[7]

A machine made of human parts. This is what Mumford called the 'megamachine': an entire society ordered from the top down, justified by a *mythos* employed by its leaders and driven by a desire for 'order, power, predictability and above all, control'. The archetypal example of the megamachine, in Mumford's account, came not from modern Europe or America, but from Pharaonic Egypt, whose legions of enslaved pyramid-builders were conditioned to think and behave like cogs in a vast, inhuman mechanism. 'The workers who carried out these designs', he writes, 'had minds of a new order: mechanically conditioned, executing each task in strict obedience to instructions, infinitely patient, limiting their response to the word of command. Machine work can be done only by machines. These workers during their period of service were, as it were, stripped down to their reflexes, in order to ensure a mechanically perfect performance'.

If that sounds like a description of an English factory circa 1848—or a Chinese factory today—then that's because it is. The pyramids may be four thousand years old, but the legacy of the megamachine assembled to build them is horribly familiar to us now: 'a waste of destroyed villages and cities, and poisoned soils: the prototype of similar "civilised" atrocities today.' As for those pyramids, 'what are they but the precise static equivalents of our own space rockets? Both devices for securing, at an extravagant cost, a passage to Heaven for the favoured few'.[8]

Combine the analysis of Mumford here with those of Oswald Spengler and Alasdair MacIntyre, and a picture emerges of a rhythm in human history, in which centralised civilisations arise, accrue power to themselves through conquest, and then construct systems which coalesce into megamachines, with their parts made up either of human, mechanical or digital components—or, as today, all three. These megamachines grow and grow, pursuing ever more vainglorious goals—global economies, genetically modified organisms, interplanetary travel, the abolition of death—until they have swallowed cultures, devastated ecosystems and broken boundaries they didn't even know existed. Then they fall. But like Sauron, they will always rise again.

But, says Mumford, no society would go to all this effort for purely material ends. The Machine is not simply a vast, soulless mechanism for accruing material wealth. It is, in some deadly fashion, a sacral object in itself. It is its own enchantment. 'Communities never exert themselves to the utmost, still less curtail the individual life', claims Mumford, 'except for what they regard as a great religious end. . . . Where such efforts and sacrifices seem to be made for purely economic advantages, it will turn out that this secular purpose has itself become a god, a sacred libidinous object, whether identified as Mammon or not'.

This is what Mumford calls 'the myth of the Machine'. Sometimes, in our age, we call it growth. Sometimes we call it progress. Sometimes we don't need words, for no words can ever circumscribe a deity. But a deity it is—and throughout human history, from Egypt to Babylon, Sumeria to Rome, whenever the Machine falls, we work to build it up again, because at some level we need to hear the story that it tells us about ourselves. 'The one lasting contribution of the megamachine', concludes Mumford, 'was the myth of the machine itself: the notion that this machine was, by its very nature, absolutely irresistible—and yet, provided one did not oppose it, ultimately beneficent. That magical spell still enthralls both the controllers and the mass victims of the megamachine today.'

That it does. Across the spectrum, from conservatives to liberals, Marxists to fascists, believers to atheists, very little serious criticism of the entwined myths of progress, growth and materialism will ever be heard in the public sphere. Ultimately, most of us accede to our sovereign, happily or otherwise. We are told daily, after all, that there is no realistic alternative to pursuing what, in Mumford's telling, is the 'fundamental animus' of the Machine: 'the effort to conquer space and time, to speed transportation and communication, to expand human energy through the use of cosmic forces, to vastly increase industrial productivity, to over-stimulate consumption, and to establish a system of absolute centralized control over both nature and man'.

The novelists and filmmakers I mentioned in this book's introduction, issuing their now-quaint warnings about the eclipse of humanity by its own technology, had two curiously related characteristics: they were right, and their being right made no difference at all. We nodded sagely at 'The Machine Stops', as we did at *The Matrix* ninety years later, and then we went home and nothing changed. The great genius of the Machine, and one reason for its flourishing, is that it can absorb its own critics, co-opt their criticism, and then, very often, commercialise it. So pervasive are the Machine's values that often those who promote what they imagine is an alternative find themselves doing its work.

Consider, as an example, the two great totalitarian ideologies of the twentieth century. Communism and fascism—in reality variations on the same theme—sold themselves as alternatives to the 'decadence' of liberal capitalism. Both promised to create universalist utopian societies, but both were in fact Machine ideologies—arguably the purest manifestation of the politics of the Machine yet seen. Both were purist, materialistic, totalitarian, militaristic, technological and at least in theory 'scientific', manifesting the most twisted forms of rationalism imaginable. Consider Lysenkoism's claims, in the USSR, that genetic science was a 'bourgeois' notion; consider the measuring of skull shapes to determine racial makeup; watch a film of the Nuremberg Rally or a Soviet military parade in Red Square. Here is the Machine, naked and unashamed.

But today's milder forms of resistance are quickly co-opted too. The once-radical green movement, in which I cut my teeth, has been transformed into a Machine accelerant. A movement which began by calling for more simplicity and slowness, closeness to nature and simple living, has mutated into a crusade to coat wild landscapes with glass and metal, abolish farming, further industrialise the global food supply, track and trace our consumption patterns and promote a vision of 'sustainability' that would make any Fortune 500 company smile. Feminism, which began as a movement calling for the equal treatment of women, has become a device for filling the workforce with females while eroding the inconveniently un-Machine-like family unit. As for that 'social justice' movement that keeps conservatives awake at night: its 'radicalism' just happens to be Machine-shaped.

Here is where we find ourselves: in a world in which all of our desires, needs, projects and even attempts at resistance end up furthering the progress of the Machine. The values of that Machine are now so ubiquitous that we treat them as if they were as natural as rain or wind. Progress; 'openness'; an objection to limits and borders; therapeutic individualism; universalism; the rejection of roots, place and history; pure materialism; the triumph of 'reason' over 'superstition'; scientism; commercialism and the primacy of market values: all of these go to make up the unseen and unquestioned value system within which we live, and to which we feel there is simply no alternative. The Machine, in Mumford's words, feels 'absolutely irresistible . . . and ultimately beneficent'. Opposition to it is presented as naive idealism at best, and a dangerous denial of its benefits to the needy at worst.

About halfway through the first volume of *The Myth of the Machine*, pondering the various horrors this sovereign has unleashed, Mumford wonders why any of us put up with it. 'Why this "civilized" technical complex should have been regarded as an unqualified triumph', he writes, 'and why the human race has endured it so long, will always be one of the puzzles of history'. But this puzzle itself implies a faint light: a chink in the roof of the cavern that might point to some means of escape. If the Machine is a story, then the first step to its dismantling is neither monkey-wrenching nor revolution—it is to stop believing the story. The second step is to stop telling it to others; and the third is to begin the search for a better one.

To liberate ourselves, steadily, one human soul at a time, we simply have to walk away from the Machine in our hearts and minds, as the Israelites of the Exodus walked away from its original master, Pharaoh. Or, as Mumford has it in the conclusion to the second volume of his masterwork: 'For those of us who have thrown off the myth of the machine, the next move is ours: for the gates of the technocratic prison will open automatically, despite their rusty ancient hinges, as soon as we choose to walk out'.[9]

V

A Monster That
Grows in Deserts

THE FENS OF EASTERN ENGLAND WERE once considered untameable—
as were the people who inhabited them. A place of saltmarsh and
wide skies, this was a liminal territory where the land met the sea. A
pattern of islands, harsh peat bogs, sinking sands, marshes and causeways, they were so cut off that they gained a reputation for both mystery
and danger. Anglo-Saxon hermits and monks squatted on the peat islands, and eventually a great abbey was built on the marsh isle of Ely—
literally 'eel island'—which became the site of the final resistance of the
English to their Norman colonisers in 1070. Here, Hereward the Wake
fought off the Conqueror King for months, using such tactics as pouring
oil on the marshes and setting them alight, and burning the causeways
over which the Norman knights rode.

The people of these weird, wyrd lands were regarded with suspicion
by the flatlanders in more civilised parts. 'A thriftless race whose only
strong passion was a love of freedom,' is one of the more memorable
medieval descriptions of the fen-dwellers. The fen people, even more so
than the rest of the kingdom, were defending a unique way of life against
the invaders from the Frankish lands.

But though the Normans pacified the English in the end, they never really changed the essence of the fens. Over the centuries there was semi-regular talk from large landowners and the progress-minded elites of the day about 'improving' the messy, strange, inefficient fenlands, but since most of them were owned by small tenant farmers, or held in common by communities, there was neither the incentive nor the method to do very much about it.

All of this changed in the early modern period. From the sixteenth century onwards, the rise of the mercantile class signalled the breakdown of the old feudal order and the rise of the capitalism which would replace it. The state, increasingly controlled by the new merchant classes, began lending its strength to the 'improvement' of such 'unproductive' places. From the early 1600s, various plans, commissions and Acts of Parliament set out strategies for the enclosure and drainage of the fenlands, but it wasn't until the 1630s, with the employment of the Dutch drainage expert Cornelius Vermuyden, that the work began in earnest. Setting out an ambitious plan to drain the fens using wind power and the creation of a wide network of dykes, Vermuyden worked in concert with local aristocrats, imported French labourers and teams of 'gentleman adventurers' who received land grants in return for their labour, to turn the fens, finally, into productive and profitable land.

The people of the fenlands had lived for centuries by forms of local subsistence: fishing, waterbird harvesting, eel catching. They harvested the reeds, rushes and sedge for building materials and animal foods. They moved between the islanded settlements on causeways, or through the fens on stilts. The drainage scheme was designed to destroy all of this. Plans hatched in London and carried out by an engineer and labourers from across the seas would end their way of life. Some of them decided to fight back.

As in the eleventh century, so in the seventeenth: as William the Conqueror had discovered, attempting to defeat a people who knew their ground intimately was a strategic nightmare. Vermuyden and his teams faced groups of local guerrilla saboteurs known as the Fen Tigers who would materialise out of the fens at night and destroy dykes, causeways, dams and bridges. The Tigers would, like their ancestors, set fire to marshes to destroy pumps and equipment. They harried the engineers for years, slowing their work, re-flooding drained lands, destroying months or years of effort. It wasn't until the nineteenth century, with the coming of steam power, that the fens were finally claimed for the Machine.

This is a story from seventeenth-century England. It is also a story from nineteenth-century Africa and from eighteenth-century South America and from twentieth-century Indonesia and China and continental Europe. It is a story that is currently playing out in real time in northern India. It is the story of enclosure—the systematic concentration of land and resources in few hands—and it has been one of the basic building blocks of the Machine's rise and dominance since the pyramids were built.

The enclosure process in early modern England was intimately linked with the rise and subsequent global dominance of modern capitalism. As in the fens, much of the landscape of medieval England was subject to complex networks of rights and obligations. A peasant working land owned by a manor house, for example, might have the right to use common land for grazing their stock, or 'pannage rights' which allowed their pigs to forage in woodland. They would usually be entitled to collect fuel in the woods, and would receive help from either church or manor if they were unable to subsist at all. Farming in most lowland areas operated on the open-field system, in which families would farm individual strips of large areas of common land.

Between the early 1600s, when plans for the death of the fens were first laid, and the First World War, this old way of farming and living was changed utterly. A succession of Acts of Parliament, written and voted for by the landed gentry who stood to profit from the process, legitimised what was, in customary terms, a massive wave of land theft. Nearly seven million acres of land were taken out of common ownership and put into the hands of private landowners. The landscapes of fields, fences and hedges that we associate with the English countryside today are a product of this process.

The mass enclosure of the commons was, from the point of view of many ordinary rural families, a cultural tragedy which reduced entire communities to penury. The result at the grassroots level was noted by the eighteenth-century Rector of Cookham, Berkshire, who said of his local area that 'an amazing number of people have been reduced from a comfortable state of partial independence to the precarious condition of mere hirelings, who when out of work immediately come on the parish'.

Taking away peoples' 'comfortable . . . partial independence' and substituting it with 'the precarious condition of mere hirelings' has been the working basis of Machine capitalism worldwide since the 1700s. Once England's ruling class had perfected this process, through a system of experiments carried out on their own people, they were ready to take the system live. It was carried out into the world through trade and empire and it still goes on today, from eastern Europe to the Amazon.

But I always remember that my country, England, was the testing ground. Our great poet of enclosure—a man who mapped its tragedy on ordinary rural lives—was the 'peasant poet' John Clare. A man of the rural poor, his attachment to his local ground was so intense that the fencing-in of the small places that made up his very identity literally drove him mad, and he spent the last twenty-four years of his life in an asylum. But in his prime, he wrote the great ballad 'The Lament of Swordy Well', a poem written from the perspective of the land itself as it is fenced in and turned to profit:

There was a time my bit of ground
Made freemen of the slave
The ass no pinard dare to pound
When I his supper gave
The gipseys camp was not afraid
I made his dwelling free
Till vile enclousure came and made
A parish slave of me

A folk song of the time makes the same point in plainer language:

They hang the man and flog the woman
Who steals the goose from off the common
Yet leave the greater villain loose
That steals the common from the goose

The enclosure process set the scene for an ongoing immiseration of rural people across England, and turbocharged the ensuing Industrial Revolution, both by concentrating resources in few hands and by creating a landless underclass who had no choice but to traipse to the growing industrial zones and offer their labour to the new industries. For the first time, England would develop that key signifier of the industrial age, a 'proletariat'. The factory system which sustained it was built on the mass destruction of human-scale industries which had sustained urban and village communities just as the land had sustained the peasantry.

The impact of this on the country as a whole cannot be underestimated. In the 1790s, the writer Horace Walpole wrote to his friend Sir Horace Mann, who had left Britain to become envoy for Florence in 1737, that if he were to return home he would not recognise the country he had left behind. 'You left it as a private island living upon its means', he wrote. 'You will find it the capital of the world'.[1] Enclosure and industry had changed everything. Those who once lived on their means were now living at the mercy of those who were building a new world empire on their backs.

But as the Fen Tigers had resisted the drainers, there were those who strained against the rise of industry. The history of folk resistance in England, from the century beginning around 1750, is one of huge numbers of skilled artisans, craftspeople, farmers and labourers taking up arms against the theft of their independence and way of life. They knew that the machines had come to destroy them; the only action they could take in response, they believed, was to destroy the machines first.

The resulting uprisings were not sporadic, local protests. They were armed, organised and systematic. 'The rioters appear suddenly in armed parties, under regular commanders', reported one provincial English newspaper. 'The chief commander, be he whomsoever he may, is styled *General Ludd*'.[2] In his chronicle of ordinary lives, *The English: A Social History 1066–1945*, historian Christopher Hibbert records that Ludd's name

> was soon familiar throughout the country. It appeared as a signature at the bottom of inflammatory handbills and at the end of dire warnings to employers whose machinery had been marked for destruction. It appeared in ballads and in broadsheets. While nurses of middle-class children frightened their charges with it, conjuring up visions of a terrifying ogre, the children of the poor were taught to venerate it and remember it in their prayers.[3]

England's social revolution had generated a new folk hero: the mythical 'Ned Ludd'. The historian Kevin Binfield concludes that Ludd superseded the older, arcadian figure of Robin Hood as a freedom fighter more appropriate for the times. 'Robin had famously robbed the rich to give to the poor', he writes, 'but Ned Ludd epitomized the right of the poor to earn their own livelihood and to defend the customs of their trade against dishonourable capitalist depredators. While Robin, a displaced gentleman, signified paternal protection, Ned Ludd evidenced the sturdy self-reliance of a community prepared to resist for itself the notion that market forces rather than moral values should shape the fate of labour'. The mythical Ludd, in other words, 'was not only a symbol of plebeian resistance; he was an ideological figure as well, one who reflected the deep sense of history that underpinned the customary values of working communities in the manufacturing districts'.[4]

That 'deep sense of history' and attachment to 'the customs of their trade' are what connect the Luddites to the Fen Tigers, and to other rebels against the rising new order of money-power and factory-power that were reshaping the land. They also distinguish those earlier examples from the later universalist and theory-driven political movements so prevalent on the post-Marx left. Despite the claims of some later Marxist historians, the Luddite uprisings were not simply about 'class'. Wages mattered, and so did injustice, but what was driving these movements was a desire to protect a long-standing, self-willed way of life: an entirely different way of seeing and being to that of the profit-driven, utilitarian Machine. Enclosure is, more than anything else, a process of ground clearance. Its aim is not only to privatise land or resources, but to destroy older, more localised, customary communities and cultures. It is the basis of the Great Unsettling. Without uprooting older communities and ways of life, from English artisan weavers in 1800 to Papuan tribal people in the 2020s, the Machine cannot operate.

There's an argument you will often hear amongst the defenders of Machine progress: that global capitalism is something which has simply 'evolved' naturally from pre-existing conditions, as a jungle fowl is said to have evolved from a pterosaur. Global Machine economics, they will tell you at *The Economist* or around Thomas Friedman's dinner table, is simply a large-scale version of a local market economy. It's all about efficient resource distribution and labour specialisation, and it was inevitable that it would happen this way, as the 'laws' of economics demonstrate.

The notion that the Machine is inevitable and natural, and that there is no 'realistic' alternative to its reign, is a self-fulfilling prophecy. It is also a fiction, one which G. K. Chesterton skewered well when he wrote that its advocates 'talk as if ten miners had run a race, and one of them became the Duke of Northumberland'.[5] The reality is that Machine capitalism did not 'evolve' from small-scale artisan or peasant societies: they had to be deliberately destroyed in order that it might replace them.

In his short book *The Outline of Sanity*, written almost a century ago, Chesterton devotes an entire essay to this point. Capitalism evolved in England, he explained, not because it was a natural next step from a pre-modern society, but because land ownership was already so highly concentrated that the climate was favourable to it. Enclosure was easy when the landed gentry ran the show and made the laws. 'England became a capitalist country', he writes, 'because it had long been an oligarchical country'.

Chesterton's argument with both capitalism and socialism is that both were 'oligarchical' systems, in which small numbers of people owned everything and dictated to the rest of us how we should live. His own alternative model, distributism, called instead for 'equally distributed small property'. The only effective barrier against gigantist tyrannies of all kinds, Chesterton believed, was a society in which land, resources and power were reasonably evenly distributed—as they were in the best pre-modern cultures. In a memorable paragraph, he made his case like this:

Nine times out of ten, an industrial civilisation of the modern capitalist type does not arise, wherever else it may arise, in places where there has hitherto been a distributive civilisation like that of a peasantry. Capitalism is a monster that grows in deserts. Industrial servitude has almost everywhere arisen in those empty spaces where the older civilisation was thin or absent.[6]

Chesterton's observation explains why Britain and later America became the primary nerve centres of the Machine in the nineteenth and twentieth centuries, and remain crucial nodes today. In the US, once the brutal displacement of the Native Americans had taken place, nothing stood in the way of the Machine. The whole continent was a *terra nullius*, waiting to be turned to profit. In Britain, enclosure and concentrated land ownership had cleared the ground for the Machine's rise in a way that had not happened in other European countries. We made a desert of our countries more effectively than anyone else. Now we are home to the monster, and it is eating us at its leisure.

In this sense, we can see the guerrilla tactics of the Fen Tigers, the street warfare of the Luddites and the ongoing resistance of communities across the world today to contemporary enclosures as part of one historical arc: an often-doomed attempt to resist the new values of the Machine and keep alive the old values of place-based community. So successful has the Machine been at winning this battle in England that the very notion of older values of any merit is easily dismissed today as 'romanticism', 'nostalgia' or, of course, 'Luddism'.

But while the Luddites lost their war, their case was always correct. That war was not fought against technology *per se*—what Lewis Mumford called 'technics'. Most Luddites operated weaving looms themselves, and were quite comfortable with machinery. What mattered was who controlled it. They were fighting what they called 'the factory system'—the destruction of lived freedom, and the regimentation of both body and soul. Like the Fen Tigers and the many unnamed people who have stood up against the onward march of dehumanising 'progress', General Ludd and his legions were fighting the monster from the desert, and their struggle was existential. If they could see us today, transfixed by our glowing screens, deskilled and dependent on oligarchs for permission to earn, eat and speak, with the factory system gone global and the Earth heating up from its exhaust, they might be permitted a grim smile.

VI

A Thousand Mozarts

THE PETITION TO KEEP JEFF BEZOS in space forever had over 200,000 signatories by the time it was wound up. Bezos, the founder of Amazon, is among the richest men in the world, which also makes him one of the richest men in human history. His personal fortune at the time of writing stands at an estimated $200 billion, and he has channelled much of this into his own 'human space flight startup', Blue Origin. Bezos, like his fellow Silicon Valley Overlord Elon Musk, believes that inefficient governments have been too slow to expand human civilisation into space, and that nimble little companies like his can do it better. His own personal space flight was intended to be just one small step—as it were—towards much more ambitious goals, and it was this that had raised the ire of the petition's founder. 'Billionaires should not exist . . . on earth, or in space', declared the petition, 'but should they decide the latter, they should stay there'.

What were those goals? Bezos explained them to an interviewer in 2018:

> We have ever-improving lives in large part because we use ever-expanding amounts of energy . . . But in just a few hundred years,

we will have to cover the entire surface of the Earth in solar cells if we want to continue to grow our energy usage. And keep in mind, this covers all the things that you like: hospitals, air travel, all these things, modern childbirth, where children don't die.

We use a lot of energy to do these things. We've been getting more efficient at using energy with every passing decade, and still we use more. Our metabolic rate as an animal is 100 watts. That's how much the human body needs . . . But our civilizational metabolic rate as members of the developed world is 11,000 watts. Do we want that to continue, or do we want to freeze that in time? If we freeze it, by the way, there are millions of people who don't get to enjoy the 11,000 watts that the people in this room enjoy.

So, we will have to leave this planet, and we're going to leave it, and it's going to make this planet better.[1]

Put like this, there is a certain clear-eyed appeal to Bezos's logic. This is the Machine speaking, and if you accept the parameters of the conversation there is a kind of naive purity to the argument. But there is also a broken, autistic, clinical edge. 'There are a lot of other problems with planetary surfaces', he asserts, as if they were Lego bricks in the wrong order. 'But the main one is that they're not big enough. We have the resources to build room for a trillion humans in this solar system, and when we have a trillion humans, we'll have a thousand Einsteins and a thousand Mozarts. It will be a way more interesting place to live. The alternative, if we stay on this planet, is not necessarily extinction. We can defend this planet, but the alternative is stasis. We will have to stop growing, which I think is a very bad future. It's not the future that I want for my grandchildren or my grandchildren's grandchildren'.

It's always worth spending time with the unquestioned assumptions in passages like this. Here, for example, we see that our lives are 'ever improving'; that there is a universal 'we' in the 'developed world' that can be 'improved' with more 'growing'; that the entire world wants to 'enjoy' the American liberal-capitalist lifestyle; that 'we' can trust people like Jeff to 'make this planet better'; that a trillion people is more 'interesting' than seven billion; that a thousand Mozarts is a good target to aim for. Jeff doesn't say what we would do with all these extra Mozarts. Do we need that much classical music? Maybe the Mozarts could take turns: composing symphonies one day and doing charity work the next. I expect Amazon's Digital Assistant will be able to work it out when the time comes.

Anyone who has paid attention to the Silicon Valley Mindset over the last decade or two will recognise this kind of progress-obsessed, tech-fuelled optimism. We know these people by now. They are the global ruling class—or, at least, part of it—and their way of seeing and understanding the world is changing that world daily. Every time you search for something on Google, an algorithm is subtly shifting your attention towards something it wants you to see, and setting out the form within which you will comprehend it. The Satnavs and Google maps and drone deliveries and Alexas and AI personal assistants are re-engineering our relationships with each other, and to the wider landscape. Companies like Amazon and Google do not just have phenomenal economic heft, granted to them every time we use their services: they also design the parameters of the culture in which we live.

At some level we know this. As the space petition demonstrates, the degree of power and wealth held by people like Bezos naturally stirs up resistance and reaction. This was most starkly illustrated when a bunch of activists set up a guillotine outside his multimillion-dollar mansion, in a protest against the terrible pay and conditions that Amazon offers to its workers while its owner spends billions on castles in the sky. As a symbolic warning to plutocrats, a guillotine is hard to beat, but its symbolism goes beyond the obvious. If a version of the French Revolution were to erupt today, Bezos would certainly be likely to find himself in a tumbrel, perhaps with Mark Zuckerberg and Sergey Brin for company. But he is also, paradoxically, both a beneficiary and a manifestation of the chasm that opened beneath eighteenth-century France. The French Revolution took aim at people like Bezos—but, with some irony, it also paved the way for their triumph.

The eighteenth century brought two revolutions to the West, and thus later to the world. In the last chapter, I wrote about the Industrial Revolution and its discontents. But across the English Channel, at more or less the same time, another revolution was playing out. In France, the oldest of the West's old regimes, a complex interplay of corruption, poverty, political agitation, new philosophies of human origins, radical notions of 'liberty' and 'equality', an indecisive King and a series of unfortunate events led to an explosion of such force that Europe was permanently transformed.

Both of these transformations—and, indeed, the American revolution which inspired the French intellectuals who drove Liberté forward—acted as grand ground-clearing exercises. If the Machine is a monster that grows in deserts, then these two revolutions were instrumental in creating the desert that is modernity. Industrialism's physical clearances—the enclosures of land and the destruction of artisanship and the peasantry—were mirrored by the French tsunami, in which monarchy, aristocracy, church and customs of all kinds were to be swept away and replaced by a new world, designed along rational lines to promote Virtue through the rigorous application of that most vital of Enlightenment values: Reason.

It is almost impossible now to imagine the thrilling upheaval that the early days of the French Revolution must have represented to the intellectuals and radical aristocrats who were its progenitors. Like all revolutions of its kind, notably those which followed in Russia and China, the French Revolution was a product not of 'the people' but of a disaffected elite, inspired in this case by the ideas of philosophers like Voltaire and Rousseau who scorned ancient hierarchies and structures and promoted instead notions of individual liberty, radical patriotism, virtuous living, intellectual inquiry and market economics.

The historian Simon Schama, in his book on the Revolution, *Citizens*, emphasises several times that the forces which led to the end of the monarchy in France were led by a 'liberal nobility' rather than a starving peasantry. The working committees that drafted the revolutionary constitution, he explains, thus building the New France, 'were monopolised by a small intellectual elite, many of whom had known each other before the Revolution and a striking number of whom had been officers of the old monarchy in either the army, judiciary, government or church'.[2]

As with the Industrial Revolution in neighbouring England, the centre of society was violently wrenched into a new shape by an elite that claimed to be working on behalf of its people. The actual people, meanwhile, according to Schama, when they supported the Revolution, often did so not because they wanted to institute a new dawn of Reason and Virtue but because the old regime, led by King Louis XVI, had in their view been *too modern*.

Two years before the Revolution broke out, for example, Louis's regime had embraced the newfangled Enlightenment notion of 'free trade', sweeping away the old protections that had ensured affordable bread for the poor and good prices for farmers. This eighteenth-century equivalent of NAFTA inflamed an eighteenth-century populism amongst the people. But what those people wanted from the uprising against the king was not what the intellectual vanguard had in mind. 'While the *cahiers* of the liberal nobility offered an alluring picture of a briskly modernising France that would consummate the great alterations of the 1770s and 1780s by shaking off restrictions like a butterfly emerging from a chrysalis', writes Schama, 'those of the Third Estate [the general population] wanted, very often, a return to the cocoon. By implication they suggested a mythical France, governed by an all-seeing, just and benign monarch, cared for by a humble and responsible clergy'.[3]

The liberalism and individualism which fired the minds of the Revolutionaries were more repulsive to many French people than the corruptions of the Ancien Régime. The 'people' in whose name the execution of the monarch would be carried out didn't want more modernity, but less. Many of the ordinary folk who took to the streets in protest, explains Schama, 'had never been much enamoured of economic liberalism or individualism. Much of their anger had been a reaction against the unpredictable and impersonal operation of the market . . . They were not only indifferent, then, but actually hostile to much of the modernising and reformist enterprise embarked on, first by the monarchy and then by successive revolutionary inheritor regimes'.[4]

In France, as it turned out, the actual people (in contrast with the abstract notion of 'The People') wanted justice from their rulers rather than their beheading. Their aim, if they could be said to have one, was to make customary ways work better for them, not to overthrow them all from the bottom up. The elite Revolutionaries, though, had other ideas: those 'customary ways' were obstacles to be swept away, and once that was achieved, a new world would triumph. It's an old story now, and it usually leads to the same destination: the mass liquidation of those who don't fit the model.

But before the Revolution descended into Robespierre's Terror, there was a brief period in which that new world seemed to be possible. 'Bliss was it in that dawn to be alive,' wrote Wordsworth, who was in Paris as the old regime fell. The Romanticism that fuelled Wordsworth's poetic project fuelled many of the revolutionaries too. Inspired by the 'natural philosophy' of Jean-Jacques Rousseau, they hoped to re-create the 'state of Nature' in which humanity was said to have been born before being placed 'in chains' by unjust social conditions. In this state of Nature, the individual, untrammelled by cultural expectations, would live instinctively by 'uncorrupted morals'. Rousseau's philosophy, in some respects, would certainly have met with the approval of the Fen Tigers:

The first man who, having fenced in a piece of land, said 'This is mine', and found people naïve enough to believe him, that man was the true founder of civil society. From how many crimes, wars, and murders, from how many horrors and misfortunes might not any one have saved mankind, by pulling up the stakes, or filling up the ditch, and crying to his fellows: Beware of listening to this impostor; you are undone if you once forget that the fruits of the earth belong to us all, and the earth itself to nobody.[5]

Restoring this 'state of Nature' through 'true principles, rationally determined' was one of the aims of the French Revolution, and Reason— which would naturally flourish once the chains of society were removed— was to be its guide. The new systems designed to replace the baroque structures of the Ancien Régime would, in Schama's telling, 'strip away those "Gothic" accretions of history—arbitrary divisions of custom, habit and jurisdiction that were the products of ancient conquests. They would be replaced with rational, equalising institutions that would put men into relations with one another as citizens, bound by the same laws and subject to the same sovereignty: their own'.

Reason, rationalism, individualism, market values, the rejection of the past, the framing of custom and history as obstacles, the idealisation of progress and perpetual renewal: Jeff Bezos would recognise all of this, and perhaps nod in vigorous assent. In the turmoil of the early 1790s, the new French elite were laying the foundations of the world we inhabit today.

But the bliss of the new dawn was short-lived, and not just because of the appearance of the guillotine in public squares across the country, where Enemies of the People would be led by the thousand to 'shake the hot hand': my personal favourite euphemism for mass beheading. The bigger problem was that the new notions of the philosopher-Revolutionaries didn't actually work. Removing the old customs and strictures led not to a flowering of virtue but to mass outbreaks of revenge. Ideas which seemed intriguing in the intellectual salons of Paris—ideas like dividing the whole country up into eighty-one perfectly equal squares, each administered as a unit of local government—turned out to be ridiculously unworkable when actually tried.

Most of all, Reason was no replacement for the religion—Roman Catholicism—which the Revolution had ruthlessly downgraded and in many cases actively tried to eliminate through the mass murder of priests and the destruction of churches. For all the corruption and collaboration of the Ancien Régime church, the faith of the French people was not easily replaced by the ideas of philosophers and intellectuals. Many of the most extreme Revolutionaries, like their Marxist heirs in the twentieth century (Lenin and Trotsky consciously modelled their revolution on that of the Jacobins), saw religion as an irrational control mechanism which stood in the way of the people's liberation. The people themselves, though, would often defend their churches and priests against the secular replacements sent to them by the new regimes in Paris, and would later fight back, often in huge numbers, against attacks on religion itself.

As so often in radical history, the actual people were not behaving as the philosophy of the Revolutionaries suggested they ought to. What was to be done? One solution arrived at during the Revolution's final and most fanatical phase, the revolutionary dictatorship of the Jacobin Republic, was to set up Reason itself as a deity. In 1793, the first (and, in the event, only) annual 'Festival of Reason' was inaugurated. Churches across the country were transformed by decree into 'temples of reason'; the most spectacular ceremony was reserved for Notre-Dame in Paris, during which an actress dressed as Liberty bowed to a flame representing Reason.

The Cult of Reason lasted little more than a year before Robespierre, now ensconced as France's new dictator, replaced it with his own 'Cult of the Supreme Being'. Robespierre despised Catholicism, but he despised atheism almost as much. The people, he believed, needed something divine to look up to, but it needed to be something with 'social utility'. His 'Supreme Being' was God remade in the image of patriotic, revolutionary France. Like its predecessor, the new, rational religion lasted only a few months, disappearing when its creator was guillotined by the Terror he had helped to create.

But the notion that humans were, or could be, rational animals survived, for it was fundamental not just to the French Revolution but to the wider project of Enlightenment. It is easy for us, still swimming in its backwash, to see the attraction, because it's the same attraction that Jeff Bezos is caught by when he talks about building a space civilisation for a trillion people. Reason is appealing, because it implies that humans can use their faculties to order the universe, and that the universe will respond in kind. We want desperately to believe this story; in a Godless age, it is perhaps the only story that can save us, because it tells us that we understand the world, or are capable of doing so, and that this understanding will allow us to control it. And because the story is at least partially true—we have modern medicine and the internet and sort-of democracies and space flight as demonstrations that empiricism and rational enquiry can deliver at least some goods—we are able to keep telling it.

The problem, though, is that this story delivers other goods at the same time: climate change, nuclear weapons and the massed dead of the industrial wars and revolutions of the twentieth century are also products of the Age of Reason. We want to believe, like good Western liberals, that horrors like Nazism or the mass murders of the Communist regimes were driven by irrational fanaticism: that they were in some ways reversions to a 'barbaric' past, the opposite of our 'reasonable' and humane present. The truth, though, is the opposite. In his 1992 book *Voltaire's Bastards*, a broadside against what he calls 'the dictatorship of reason in the West', John Ralston Saul notes that the 'grandiose and dark events' which 'overcame Western society' in the modern period, from religious bloodbaths to the Napoleonic wars, 'seemed to do so thanks to rational methods'. Reason was supposed to be a moral force, but it turned out to be anything but. The twentieth century, which, according to Saul, saw 'the final victory of pure reason in power', also saw 'unprecedented unleashings of violence and of power deformed'. It is hard, he writes, 'to avoid noticing that the murder of six million Jews was a perfectly rational act'.[6]

That 'perfectly rational act', as Simon Schama pointed out, was a direct descendant of the murderous clarity of Robespierre and co: the guillotine, after all, was designed as a humane means of dealing with the enemies of the Revolution. Mass death, yes: but *rational* mass death.

The eighteenth century's two revolutions—the revolution of Reason and the revolution of Technology—were supposed to walk us towards a universal paradise. Instead, we live in a time of mass extinction and cultural disintegration. This, says Saul, is a direct result of the flawed assumptions on which those revolutions were built. Both were, in the final analysis, set in motion by people he calls 'optimistic rationalists', who imagined 'whole populations sliced free of their limiting past and present, then flipped over to fry in a new, clean future with all the inanimate passivity of a Big Mac'. The inevitable result of such utopianism was always 'to unleash a level of violence which in this clean, new world liberated from experience and common sense would be virtually unrestrainable'.

This is the essence of Reason's failure—and that failure in turn has happened because Reason, in and of itself, has always been little more than a fiction.

In his 1994 book *Descartes' Error*, neuroscientist Antonio Damasio uses the fruits of a lifetime's work to demolish the notion that anything like an abstracted 'reason' existed. Reason, he showed, was intimately connected to emotion; one could not exist without the other. In fact, in many of Damasio's own patients, damage to the emotional centres of the brain, which rendered them unable to feel but still able to think, rendered them effectively disabled. Reason, it turned out, was not a superior alternative to intuition, emotion or instinct, but a manifestation of it. There could be no mind without the body; no unprejudiced 'concepts' or unpolluted 'models' of reality. There could, in short, be no Reason without the messy world it was embedded in.

But if Reason as a thing in and of itself is nonexistent, then any culture built on its back must, in the end, fail. Awkwardly, this takes in not only Bezos's *Star Trek* future but most of the modern world as well, including pretty much the entirety of the modern West. It includes not only the great globe-spanning economic system which is currently eating the Earth alive, but also all of our rational, top-down clever-clever proposals for 'saving' it, and every abstract ideological proposition that modernity has produced, from Marxism to neoliberalism. The entirety of the system of global governance and the 'laws' of classical economics, based as they are on notions of humans as rational actors weighing up their enlightened self-interest and deciding accordingly between Pepsi and Coke, is also holed below the waterline.

Liberal modernity, in short, is doomed.

If this is true, then another conclusion also suggests itself: that older ways of seeing and speaking—mythology, folk cultures and the mystical underpinnings of religious faith—might have been on to something after all. The standard choices presented to us—reason versus superstition, progress versus barbarism, past versus future, Earth versus space, growth versus stasis—were always chimeras. The choice is not between 'going forward' or 'going back', but between working with the complexity of human and natural realities, in all their organic messiness, or attempting to supersede them with abstractions which can never hope to contain them.

VII

Do What Thou Wilt

I REMEMBER SITTING ON MY PORCH last June thinking, *this can't be right*. It was too hot. It felt like Greece, or at the very least the south of France. As a teenager we used to go on holidays to the south of France, back when flying was expensive and we couldn't afford it. My dad would drive us from the south of England onto the ferry—it was before the Channel Tunnel too—and down to the Mediterranean in one non-stop trip. My dad never slowed down for anything. Then we would sit on the beach, or be dragged around vineyards to taste wine, or sometimes visit castles and all the time I would be too hot. I have a thousand years of English blood running through my veins, and this is not conducive to any temperature above twenty degrees Celsius.

Last June I was not in France though; I was in Ireland, and we were sweating through a heatwave. The words 'Ireland' and 'heatwave' are not traditionally found in the same sentence, so the country is not really geared up to cope. A lot of people were jumping into lakes and rivers, while a lot of other people, like me, were just gently perspiring, avoiding the sun and making plans for the challenges that would arise if this thing went on much longer. We draw our water from a well, for instance, but the well is not very deep (this is not a metaphor, though it should be). How long would the well last if the rain kept holding off? Which plants in the garden should be watered and which left to fend for themselves? What did we most need to eat, or be able to store for the winter? Should we stock up on fresh water, or buy a water filter?

One unexpected problem occurred in my son's bedroom fishtank. Coldwater fish live within a fairly narrow temperature band, and the water had been warming up too much. The temporary solution was to float ice packs in the water to bring the temperature down, which staved off fish death at least temporarily. It was only the latest lesson that the tank had taught us. Previous lessons were only learned after yet another fish died and was buried in a matchbox in the garden, with due ceremony.

The key teaching has been that providing the correct environment for a few small freshwater fish to live in is an enormously complicated process. It requires an electric filter, which has to be regularly cleaned and filled up with chemicals to provide the correct balance to the tank's water. It requires regular tank cleaning and water changes, and equally regular testing with a kit that looks like my childhood chemistry set, full of jars and powders and scoops and pipettes and little charts with different colours on, to ensure that the pH, ammonia, nitrite, nitrate, oxygen and phosphate levels are within the correct ranges. If these tests show any problems, there is a bevy of chemicals that you can add to your tank to detoxify it, or to establish the correct 'biofilter' level so that no more garden matchbox ceremonies will be needed. Then, of course, there's the feeding—not too much, not too little. Oh, and you have to ensure that you don't put a small fish in the same tank as one big enough to eat it. We learned this one the hard way. RIP Martin the loach.

What is so striking about all of this is that we are using money, time, manufactured technology and artificial chemicals to do what a river or a lake does for free and with ease; what the world's ecosystems, in fact, do for everything that lives, including us. What is so striking is the immense complexity of the natural processes of the planet, and our inability to even really understand, let alone reproduce, them.

'Biofilter' is the Machine's way of saying 'Earth'.

When you don't have to grow your food, haul your water, repair your house with vernacular materials, gather herbs for healing or rely in any meaningful way on the seasons or the local landscape for your survival, then it is easy to overlook, or not bother to learn about, how vital all of those processes are. And we are encouraged to overlook them. The ethos of the Machine is expansion, the busting of limits and the consumption of whatever can be sold to us to meet the 'needs' of the individual self which the Machine constructed for us in the first place. But all of nature's functions operate within limits. They rely for their continued operation on a healthy balance of the complex and delicate systems that the living planet brings about.

I have drawn two conclusions from the lessons of my fishtank. Firstly, that we should show gratitude for, and protect and cherish, the living systems of the planet which produced us, which provide immensely more complex life support systems free of charge and which we cannot live without. And secondly, the fantasy that humans can somehow shift 'off-world' and re-create such systems on Mars or the moon when we can't or won't live with Earth anymore is just that: a fantasy, peddled by the likes of Jeff Bezos and his fellow techno-apostles, none of whom have to messily build their own homes on this little planet, or probably clean their own fishtanks out either.

The notion of 'offworld' colonisation—a Machine-age solution to the ecological crisis which the Machine itself created—is based on the same mistaken premise as that of my son's fishtank. The premise is that the living web of nature can best be understood not as *anima*, but as *techne*, and that if we can understand how it works, we can manage it ourselves—or, better still, build ourselves a more effective and human-centred version.

In his book *The Science Delusion*, Rupert Sheldrake explains the shift in attitudes towards non-human life which took place as Machine modernity began to transform the world. Before the seventeenth century, he suggests, 'almost everyone took for granted that the universe was like an organism, and so was the earth'. Leonardo da Vinci, perhaps surprisingly, offered one proof of this claim when he wrote, 'We can say that the earth has a vegetative soul, and that its flesh is the land, its bones are the structure of the rocks . . . its breathing and its pulse are the ebb and the flow of the sea'. Scientist William Gilbert (1540–1603) felt similarly: 'We consider', Sheldrake quotes him as writing, 'that the whole universe is animated, and that all the globes, all the stars, and also the noble earth have been governed since the beginning by their own appointed souls and have the motives of self-conservation'.[1] These are, to put it mildly, not views that we would expect to hear from today's giants of public science, most of whom seem proud of their stubborn materialism.

Sheldrake's book—a full frontal assault on the ideology of modern science from the perspective of a maverick scientist who rejects that materialism—calls this shift in attitudes 'the mechanistic revolution', and notes that its impact was as radical as that of the twin revolutions of Industry and Reason. Its effect was to transform our perception of the world from a living community of which we are a part, into a machine made up of parts—parts which we can identify and control. The German astronomer Johannes Kepler summarised the programme in 1605. 'My aim in this', he explained, 'is to show that the celestial machine is to be likened not to a divine organism but rather to a clockwork . . . Moreover I show how this physical conception is to be presented through calculation and geometry'.[2]

During the roiling religious wars which convulsed Europe in the seventeenth century, this rationalist approach seemed to offer a way out. In Sheldrake's words, 'it seemed to provide a way of transcending sectarian conflicts to reveal eternal truths'. God was still the creator—for now, anyway—but what he had created was, in Galileo's words, 'a thoroughly mathematical structure' that could be understood by the human intellect.

This break between new and old ways of seeing is often attributed to the French philosopher René Descartes, who extended Kepler's and Galileo's mathematical analogies beyond astronomy and geology to the workings of living beings. Descartes was happy to slice open living dogs and insert his fingers into the ventricles of their hearts while they still pumped in order to understand 'how the machine works'. New Atheist philosopher Daniel Dennett writes approvingly of Descartes as the founder of modern science. Descartes believed, he explained, that animals 'were in fact just elaborate machines . . . It was only our non-mechanical, non-physical minds that make human beings (and only human beings) intelligent and conscious. This was actually a subtle view, most of which would readily be defended by zoologists today, but it was too revolutionary for Descartes' contemporaries'.[3]

This 'subtle view' remains the norm in science today, where living things still tend to be assumed to be 'machines' unless proven otherwise: a manifestation of human chauvinism which atheists like Dennett would normally blame on religion. Perhaps the most famous current iteration of the life-as-mechanism worldview comes from Dennett's friend Richard Dawkins, the evolutionary biologist, in his breakthrough book *The Selfish Gene*:

We are all survival machines for the same kind of replicator—molecules called DNA—but there are many different ways of making a living in the world, and the replicators have built a vast range of machines to exploit them. A monkey is a machine which preserves genes up trees; a fish a machine which preserves genes in the water.[4]

'A monkey is a machine which preserves genes up trees' is a good candidate for the most unintentionally funny line ever written. But the radicalism, and sheer *strangeness,* of this kind of thinking might be hard to understand for those of us who grew up immersed in it. Sheldrake calls it a 'radical break' with our previous understanding of life; one which has now bedded so deeply into modern assumptions, especially in science, that we often overlook its newness.

What we also overlook is that such a view is impossible to hold on to for long in actual, lived reality. Our daily experience of life is of being *embedded*; but the mechanistic revolution told us that the world was governed by set laws which could be 'objectively' known, as if observed, somehow, from outside. With this central claim, a deep schism opened up in the human self, between the actual universe of living beings which we experience daily, and the supposedly mechanistic universe of objectively quantifiable automata which we pretend is grown-up reality.

The philosopher Mary Midgley, in her book *The Myths We Live By*, asserts that post-Enlightenment science's desire to rationalise nature, and thereby understand it, is underpinned by a deep desire for control. The casting of the world and its denizens as machines, she says, was an 'imaginative difficulty' which prevented the scientists of the Age of Reason from seeing what their predecessors had seen: that everything was alive. Earth, to the thinkers of the mechanistic revolution, had to be made 'intelligible' in order that it could become, in Midgley's words, 'something understandable, and therefore potentially respectable'.[5]

But if a machine is the metaphor you use to represent other living beings, then a machine is what you will make of the world. And when you have made a machine of the world, you are going to have a question on your hands: *What fuel does this thing run on?* And very soon, you are going to understand the answer before you have even asked it: The fuel is nature. The fuel is life. The fuel is you.

This, in the end, is the endgame of the mechanistic, and the scientific, revolutions. Combined with the revolutions of Reason and Industry, this new way of seeing—Earth as mechanism, life as machine—built an entirely new worldview, one we still live within though it is regularly challenged from the margins. The endpoint of that worldview is not simply the age of climate change and mass extinction—though it is that—but the abolition of human nature itself. An ideology built on remaking nature for human needs will inevitably include human nature in that project. Humanity can no more survive the mechanistic or scientific revolutions intact than can the forests or the oceans.

Modernity's 'mechanistic revolution' was part of the wider modern project of dismembering the old, primarily religious, means of understanding reality, and substituting for it the new 'scientific method' through which inductive reasoning would be married with empirical inquiry to discern the truth of reality. Science, right from the beginning of the modern enterprise, was allotted the role that the Church had previously claimed for itself: the primary guide to truth, and enlightener of humanity. More than a method, it was a faith. It remains one today, which is why arguments around scientific questions, from COVID to climate change, are often so vexed and divisive. Each of us wants to claim the mantle of 'science' for our perspective because of the authority it bestows. 'Follow the Science' usually translates in practice as 'follow me'.

If we do follow, where are we led? In his book *The Rape of Man and Nature*, the English writer Philip Sherrard explicitly paints the scientific enterprise as one designed to remake the basic building blocks of life. The ultimate endpoint of this enterprise, he writes, was clear from the start. The 'mechanistic nature of modern science' has always been 'marked by a desire to dominate, to master and possess and exploit nature, not to transform it or to hallow it. In this it simply reflects the self-assertion of its agent, the disinherited reason which, having completed its revolt against what surpasses it, now seeks to impose its laws over the rest of life'.[6]

In the wake of the modern revolutions, the scientific worldview is now so all-encompassing as to be virtually invisible to us. 'Never before', writes Sheldrake in *The Science Delusion*, 'has any system of ideas dominated all humanity'[7] as science does today. This system of ideas—based upon what Sheldrake, himself a scientist, calls 'an act of faith'—is leading us, according to Philip Sherrard, into 'an ever-accelerating dehumanisation of man and of the forms of his society, with all the repercussions that this has had, and is still having, in the realm of nature'.

According to Sherrard, an Orthodox Christian, it was certain developments in Western Christian theology, rooted in the teachings of St Augustine and Thomas Aquinas, which prepared the way for René Descartes and Francis Bacon to begin the work of disenchanting nature and dehumanising people. Augustine and Aquinas, says Sherrard, enabled the philosophical separation of humanity from the rest of nature, and the rest of nature from the divine. God became transcendent, not immanent, and permission was thus given for humanity to analyse and dissect nature and itself. When the post-Enlightenment thinkers removed God from the picture altogether, the stage was set for the worldview that now enfolds us: that of a natural world which is little more than a collection of 'resources' to be harvested by a rational humanity, which itself is now also open to scientific 'improvement'.

In his book *The Unintended Reformation*, the American academic Brad S. Gregory traces the root of the West's spiritual rot not to Augustine but to the obscure (in his time) thirteenth-century Franciscan friar and theologian John Duns Scotus. Before Duns Scotus, says Gregory, Western Christians, like their Eastern counterparts, had regarded the God they worshipped as something entirely other: something so untraceable

71

and mysterious that its essence could not be named or grasped. They saw their creator as 'radically distinct from the universe as a whole, which he did not fashion by ordering anything already existent but rather created entirely ex nihilo'. This God could not be named or defined or pinned down: at the heart of the matter was a mystery that the human mind is simply incapable of fathoming. It could even be said that God did not actually exist, if 'existence' meant inhabiting the same plane as created matter.

Duns Scotus, though, was wrestling with an intellectual dilemma. If God was this distinct from everything he created, then how could the human mind even understand him? How could anything be said about God at all? In an indication of the direction in which Western Christianity would head, Duns Scotus believed that human reason must be capable of saying *something* about God—or else why would God have given us reason? We could only ever have a chance to understand God, he thought, if we share his mode of being. To solve this problem, Duns Scotus declared that God did, in fact, 'exist' on the level of material being: God, while being above all created things, nevertheless still 'belonged to the same order or type of existence as his creation'.[8]

What Duns Scotus did, in Gregory's telling, was to fire the first shot in a theological skirmish that would culminate in the splintering of Western Christianity, continent-wide wars in which tens of thousands would die, and the resulting rise of 'secular' societies designed to tame, and ultimately replace, religion as a significant part of human life. This was the role, says Gregory, that the Reformation played in history. In itself, it was not the cause of the collapse of religion in the West so much as a culmination of centuries of intellectual delving into a mistaken understanding of God. The traditional understanding of God had set limits on human desire, and defined a certain relationship between the human and the non-human worlds. But when Luther and the Reformers launched their missiles at the Catholic Church, they unwittingly paved the way for the modern dissolution that was to follow. By basing their new version of the faith on the notion of *sola scriptura*—that there should be no authority but the Bible—they unleashed the radical individualism on which the modern world would be built. With tradition and authority demolished, reason would become the only 'basis for argument about God, creation and morality'.

It was but a short leap from that to the age of Science and Enlightenment, in which a trap was sprung on the theologians who had accidentally set it. If God were an aspect of material reality, after all, then it ought to be possible for reason, and the new developing sciences of the early modern period, to detect his presence. And when this did not turn out to be the case—when no God could be found with telescope, astrolabe or large hadron collider—then reason could be used to argue God out of the picture altogether, and the world itself could be remade in the image of human desire. Which is where we find ourselves.

What, then, is the scientific enterprise which underpins modernity and which resulted from this spiritual breakdown? It is, I would argue, an ideology posing as a method. What is the ideology? It is the pursuit of what Francis Bacon called 'human empire'. The scientific worldview is leading us rapidly towards the total remaking of both humanity and non-human nature in the image of the (post-) modern self. Science built the Machine. Now the Machine will rebuild the world, and us with it. As Sherrard has it:

> There is a price to be paid for fabricating around us a society which is as artificial and mechanised as our own, and this is that we can exist in it only on condition that we adapt ourselves to it. This is our punishment.[9]

Sherrard presents science, in this context, as a modern enterprise built on a Christian rootstock that grew out of shape. He is not the only one to make this case, but as I was reading his book, another thought occurred to me—a thought that took me back to the time, not so long ago, when I used to practice magic.

When I say 'magic' I don't mean fairground tricks; I mean the workings of what is sometimes called the Western Mystery Tradition, or, if we want to be spookier about it, the occult. The meaning of the word 'occult' is actually less sinister than it has been made to sound: 'occulted' simply means 'hidden'. A few years back, before I became, to my own surprise, an Orthodox Christian, I was a practitioner of Wicca, a nature religion founded by the eccentric Englishman Gerald Gardner back in the 1950s. Wicca is a form of modern 'witchcraft', though everyone involved will have a different explanation of what that word means. Being a modern path, Wicca is mostly undefined and eclectic. At its (usually American) extreme, you can basically make it up as you go along, which is why it has proved so appealing to Gen Z teenagers.

The Wicca I practiced was the more traditional variety: I was a member of a coven, whose workings and details were secret and into which you had to be initiated. The people in the coven were not devil worshippers (at least, not intentionally). They were for the most part just people like me, looking for meaning in a society which offered none outside the marketplace. Wiccan covens do all sorts of things, but at the heart of the enterprise is the practice of magic, which, if you're feeling mysterious or pretentious, you can spell 'magick'.

There are all kinds of 'magick' available to the practicing mage. There's sympathetic magic, hermetic magic, herbal magic, elemental magic, high (or ceremonial) magic, folk magic (or 'cunning craft'), natural magic, Enochian magic (fun with secret Angelic languages) and—for the ultimate rush—Goetic magic, which involves the summoning of spirits, or demons, to do your will. Faust, when he did his famous deal with the devil, was practicing Goetia. At the heart of the practice is the notion that spirits of the otherworld are ours to command. If we are knowledgeable, smart and well-trained enough, we can summon up the very forces of nature itself, and 'bind' them to our will.

Perhaps you can see where I'm going here. The history of magic in the West is a long one, but one thing it teaches is that what we call 'magic' and what we call 'science' are intertwined. Many of the pioneers of science we know today were also magicians of one sort or another. Bacon was said to be a Freemason and an alchemist. Isaac Newton wrote far more about alchemy than he did about physics, and many of the founders of England's Royal Society, still one of its foremost scientific institutions, were alchemists or mages. In the early modern period, to-day's distinction between 'science' (real, good, objective) and 'magic' (fantastical, bad, superstitious) did not really exist. Both were branches of the same effort: to understand the mysterious forces of the universe, and ultimately to control them.

Here is Francis Bacon's definition of science:

The knowledge of causes and secret motions of things; and the en-larging of human empire, to the effecting of all things possible.

And here is the occultist Aleister Crowley's definition of magic:

The science and art of causing change to occur in conformity with the will.

These could be swapped around without anybody really noticing. The thread that links them is *control*. Both the scientific enterprise and the magical quest of which it was part spring from the same desire: to know the world, and to bend it to our will. 'Will', in both cases, is the key word. When Aleister Crowley, pioneering occultist, rampant self-publicist and self-described 'Great Beast', created his own occult reli-gion, Thelema, in the early twentieth century, he gave it its own famous commandment: *Do what thou wilt shall be the whole of the Law.* Thelema wilted on the vine, but we could say that Crowley's dictum lived on as the foundational basis of what our culture has become.

At this point, any scientists reading will be protesting. *No, no!* they might cry, *That's not what we do at all! We're driven only by curiosity, by wonder, by a desire to understand the world!* Maybe. But science, always and everywhere, is handmaiden to technology, and technology is, in this time, neither neutral nor innocent. Einstein bombed Hiroshima just as surely as the pilots of the Enola Gay, and he knew it. My point is not that all magical workings, or all scientific experiments, are bad, let alone the people who carry them out. A magician might want to perform a working aimed at bringing good luck to a friend. A scientist may be searching for a cure for cancer. But the wider project of both carries hidden within it a *telos*, a direction of travel. It is the direction of the Machine that now envelops us, and the new world it is building.

Our world is still run by magicians, working from the 'sacred temples' of their laboratories to discover how humanity may reshape the world in accordance with its will. The difference between Aleister Crowley and Richard Dawkins is that Crowley had enough self-knowledge to see where his path was leading. It's why he called himself 'The Great Beast 666'. It's why his books talk of magic as a 'new science', and are full of talk of 'mastery' over powers natural and supernatural. Crowley was Faust, and Faust is us.

Philip Sherrard again pinned it down when he wrote that 'modern science presupposes a radical reshaping of our whole mental outlook. It involves a new approach to being, a new approach to nature, in short, a new philosophy'. The assumption of us Machine moderns is that this 'new approach' represents 'a marvellous advance on the part of mankind, even a sign of our coming of age.' But 'now that we begin to see the consequences of our capitulation to it—and we are only now beginning to see these consequences—we are not so sure.'

What should we conclude from this? If we follow the logic to its end, says Sherrard, we are presented with a conclusion we probably do not want to face. 'It is difficult for us to admit that, far from being an advance, the whole modern scientific project may be a ghastly failure', he concedes. 'Yet there is no reason why it should not be. One has to judge things by their fruits. And one of the fruits of modern science, clear for all to see, and implicit in the philosophy on which it is based, is the dehumanisation both of man and of the society that he has built in its name.'[10]

What is the way out of this dehumanisation? Sherrard is uncompromising. 'To think and act without the constraint of any knowledge and values other than those of the modern scientific mentality', he writes, 'is to commit oneself to a tyranny of an unprecedented maleficence.'[11] If that mentality really is a tyranny—the tyranny of Bacon, Faust and Crowley, the tyranny of our times—then there can only be one response. To throw it off. If it is 'the pursuit of the ideals and methods of modern science that has brought us into this catastrophic situation, clearly there can be no issue from it without the renunciation of those ideals and methods.'[12]

That renunciation has to be a long mental and spiritual effort: the sloughing off of a way of seeing; the refusal of the story we all grew up with and a return to an older one that lies, like the kingdom of God, both within and all around us. It's hard work to change a story, especially when the society around you affirms it at every turn. At times like these, it is easy to become paranoid, angry, mistrustful: sometimes it can seem as if the entire internet was designed with just this purpose in mind. There is a reason that levels of trust in our cultures are measurably plummeting. Magic addles the mind.

Somehow, though, the work must be to still the mind instead. To let go of the natural attachment to our cunning, serpentine will. We know where the path leads if we don't; we see daily the path that magic and science will take us down. *Do what thou wilt* is the motto of our world: the motto of the Machine. *Thy will be done* is its older brother, and its challenger. We all want to live by the first of them, but we know that the work is to walk away from it a thousand times each day: to let the will go, and to listen instead for the old song which, however much we might think otherwise, has never stopped being sung in the woods and the waters and around the edges of the human heart.

VIII

The Great Wen

WHAT INTERESTS YOU ABOUT the year 1850, if anything does, will depend upon the perspective from your little corner of the planet. As with all of human history, the things we remember today are entirely dependent on what people who believe in notions like 'human history' have decided to write down and then squabble over later. Squabbling over history is how we make sense of whatever present we think we are living in. Who and where we are is always a story, justified by the tale of where we think we come from.

In this particular year, according to the Western Christian calendar, events which may or may not be notable to you include the birth of the Romanian Romantic poet Mihai Eminescu, the death of the English Romantic poet William Wordsworth, the ascension to the US presidency of Millard Fillmore, the founding of the University of Sydney, the Taiping Rebellion in China, the return from exile of Pope Pius XI and the beginning of the end of the Great Famine in Ireland. For our purposes though, the event I want to focus on is not really an event at all. It is more of a milestone—one which only became clear in hindsight.

1850 was the year in which my country, Britain—at that point the economic powerhouse of the world—became a primarily urban nation. It was the year that the wild sublime of its Poet Laureate, William Wordsworth, was eclipsed by the 'dark Satanic Mills' of his namesake William Blake. In 1850, and in every year since, more British people lived in cities than in the country. Today, Britain—84 percent of whose people live in towns or cities—is one of the most urbanised, most centralised and least agrarian nations on Earth. That it is also one of the most deculturised, rootless and vulnerable to the whims of the global market is not a coincidence.

Where the imperial centre goes, the rest will tend to follow, which is why the British today, long since relieved of their imperial duties by the parvenu Americans, are drinking skinny lattes, eating KFC and listening to hip hop from Birmingham. Once a certain kind of door is closed, there is no opening it again. So it goes with what we have all learned to call 'urbanisation'. Every year since 1850 has seen the UK and the wider world fleeing or being forced from the land into the maw of the expanding cities. It is 175 years since Britain became an urban nation, but just eighteen since we became an urban world: since 2007, most humans on Earth have lived in cities. More than four billion now live in urban areas, a third of them in slums. By 2050, that number is expected to rise to at least seven billion: around two-thirds of the human population of Earth.

As with so many other trends, from population numbers to carbon emissions to deforestation, it's worth pausing to note the massive, unprecedented change in human life that has taken place just in the last century or so, as our species has burned its way through millions of years of carbonised dinosaurs, creating an industrial empire literally on their bones. In 1900, around 12 percent of the world's people lived in towns and cities. By 2050, nearly 70 percent will.[1] That's not simply a matter of where people live: it's the whole mindset of humanity changing, from one which dwells in a place in which we are not the centre of attention, to one which exists in a new kind of landscape, built entirely by and for us. A farmer, even the modern, industrialised variety, needs to live by the seasons, the weather and the soil. A city dweller doesn't even need to know where his lunch comes from. In the city, we can live ignorant of our neighbours, of the seasons, of anything but our own direction and ambition.

The move, then, from country to city—the great shift we have undertaken in just a couple of centuries—can be seen as a kind of turning-in on ourselves: a radical parochialism. This is the opposite of the story we are used to hearing about urbanisation, which is commonly taken to represent the breaking of shackles and the opening of minds. What the London progressive Karl Marx called 'the idiocy of rural life' is in this telling something to be escaped from. The country represents ignorance, stasis, prejudice, dirt and poverty; the city represents enlightenment, 'openness', wealth, forward movement and warm showers. There are no art galleries in the country—or if there are, they're more likely to be showing local watercolours than the kind of cutting-edge conceptual work (piles of bricks, cars with doilies draped over them, looped films of people standing in empty rooms thinking about decolonisation) that makes up Real Culture. Stand-up comedians don't often perform in village halls, and everybody knows you can't get good coffee in the sticks.

It would be daft to deny the truth of some of this (especially the bit about the art galleries). Many of us have moved to cities to seek our fortune. Cities are roiling centres of human activity and they are more accommodating to the individual quest than any small village, for better and for worse. There are different kinds of opportunities available there, and there is a lot more anonymous, seedy fun to be had. Cities are where the power lies, and where most of the money is to be found, and they have been for thousands of years.

But it would be wrong, too, to deny the other side of the story: that cities, by their existence, their growth and their ongoing colonisation of the world's wealth and resources, render other forms of life so hard that the escape to the slums is the only recourse for many. Once a society becomes primarily urban, it is locked into a process of metastasising growth which will, in the end, lead to the destruction of other ways of being, and other forms of life, via the monoculture of the Machine—a Machine which is primarily a creation of the city. A Machine civilisation is an urban civilisation, and its worldview and direction is that of the urban dwellers who build, justify and benefit from it.

Our old friend Lewis Mumford wrote another of his epics on precisely this topic. *The City in History*, published in 1961, explores the development and essence of cities and where they might go next, for good or ill. Like all of Mumford's books it is full of educated, wise warnings, all of which went completely unheeded. But it is also full of novel and useful ways to conceive of the subject in hand.

Mumford describes the historical transformation from village into city not simply as a change in scale, but as the creation of 'a new type of organisation', which offers a (devil's?) bargain to its inhabitants:

> In the transfer of authority to the city, the villager doubtless lost in no little degree his powers of self-government, and his feeling of being entirely at home in an environment in which every human being, almost every animal, every patch of land or flow of water, was thoroughly known to him. Yet to the extent that the villager submitted to the new forces at work in the city and even identified his own life with them, he was rewarded with a prosperity and a security he had never before enjoyed.[2]

Whether or not 'prosperity and security' are a good description of life in a modern city—especially for the poor—the result of such a 'submission' is a new sense of immortality, an 'expansion of human powers', a Spenglerian drive to create an entirely new world. In cities, humanity could dream vainglorious dreams. 'Men in cities could become as exalted as gods,' says Mumford, 'released from inhibiting conformities and a paralysing sense of their own pettiness. Reinforced by the visible presence of great numbers of their own kind . . . the kings and governors and their subjects joined in a relentless collective assault on every part of the environment: now form-giving, now expressionist and exhibitionistic, now purely destructive.'[3]

A city is, at its heart, just such a 'relentless collective assault' on the way that humans have lived for 99 percent of their history; and, maybe more importantly, a collective assault on other forms of life. This is especially true of the modern megacity, with its tens of millions of inhabitants, which bears about as much resemblance to an ancient city as a Reaper drone does to a longbow. The sheer scale of the modern urban conglomeration is mind-boggling, and entirely irreversible. These 'barrack cities', as Spengler referred to them, which now contain the majority of mankind, are tied up with our ultimate fate. Once a structure of this size and complexity has been created, it must be maintained. In the case of a modern city, this means that the surrounding lands, and then the lands further afield, must be colonised to supply it and its inhabitants, their whims and desires and needs. Like a black hole, a city sucks into its orbit everything around it; and a modern world-city sucks in the world. The impacts of this are measurable.

To take just a few examples: 75 percent of worldwide energy use is in cities,[4] and energy demand is outstripping population growth as those cities expand. That energy has to be mined around the globe and imported to the urban centres, with all of the knock-on effects on people and the rest of nature. As those centres continue to grow, so does urban poverty: three billion people could be living in slums by 2050.[5] Globally, an area larger than Britain will be converted to cityscape between 2000 and 2030,[6] and that in turn will increase everything from carbon emissions to pressure on vulnerable species and habitats.

The lesson is old and growing more obvious daily: a city, unlike a village, can never be self-sufficient. A giant city is a kind of micro-empire: it cannot exist without enclosing and harvesting lands and peoples elsewhere to provide for its own growth. One of the great myths of the city is that we go there to individuate—to 'find ourselves'. It might be more accurate to say that the city removes our agency, deskills us, and toys with us at its leisure. A city's inhabitants are dependents: they have neither the space, the skills, the time nor the inclination to fend for themselves. A city dweller exists to serve the city. If she is lucky, the city will also serve her. If she is unlucky, she will end up juggling three jobs and trying to scrabble together enough pennies to feed her children. The city provides opportunities for wealth that the village never could, but it treats its poor and marginalised with a contempt that the village would regard with incomprehension.

As so often, this is a question of scale. Plato, according to Mumford, 'limited the size of his ideal city to the number of citizens who might be addressed by a single voice'. Everyone should be within hailing distance of that voice in order to ensure human-scale living. Some ancient cities were indeed built on almost this scale, at least initially. There are towns, and city centres, across Europe and Asia today which are beautifully organised, stunning to look at and in some cases thrilling to visit or live in. Plato-scale cities can enhance the human experience. But the growth, expansion and drive for 'progress' which characterises modern Machine society have long since enveloped or obliterated such human-scale cities, just as they have ravaged the old-growth forests and the coral reefs.

This is the modern Machine city: global in scale and ambition, bland, homogenised and empty at its heart. Plato's ideal city, and the real cities of the pre-modern period, were a combination, sometimes un-easy, sometimes harmonious, of ambition and aim. They were religious centres, cultural hubs, marketplaces, dwelling places, loci of power. The twenty-first century city exists mainly for one purpose: profit. Everything that exists there, from schools to art galleries to concert halls to government buildings, is pointed towards this end. You can judge a culture, I think, by its tallest buildings; what it chooses to reach towards is a reflection of its soul and purpose. The tallest buildings in a modern city are not cathedrals, temples, or even palaces: they are skyscrapers, which are homes to banks, finance houses and global corporations.

According to Mumford, contemporary society is marked by the globalisation of the great cities into one interlinked 'metropolis'. At this point, a city like London, Paris, Washington or Tokyo is best seen not as the capital of a distinct nation, but as a node in a global network. This metropolis breeds a globalised elite class who feel more at home in each others' cities than they do in the hinterlands of their respective nations, and who promote and represent the ideology of Progress that keeps the metropolis humming. This global network of megacities represents the Machine's core. The villages, small towns and wild places beyond the city's boundaries are its periphery, to be milked for the continued expansion of empire. 'An expanding economy, dedicated to profit, not to the satisfaction of life-needs,' writes Mumford, 'necessarily creates a new image of the city, that of a perpetual and ever-widening maw, consuming the output of expanding industrial and agricultural production, in response to the pressures of continued indoctrination and advertising.'[7]

But this ever-expanding economy will not only ravage the once self-sufficient village and the life of the forests and oceans; it will also cannibalise the city itself, destroying what once made it meaningful, distinctive and culturally beneficial. The pre-modern city and the contemporary metropolis are different not just in scale, but in essence. The city itself 'becomes consumable, indeed expendable: the container must change as rapidly as its content. The latter imperative undermines a main function of the city as an agent of human continuity. The living memory of the city, which once bound together generations and centuries, disappears:

its inhabitants live in a self-annihilating moment-to-moment continuum. The poorest Stone Age savage', Mumford concludes, 'never lived in such a destitute and demoralized community.'[8]

Here we are. In the city as in the countryside that surrounds it—countryside which has become little more than a thinned out version of the city, connected to its propaganda centres by cars and high-speed broadband—we are, in Mumford's words, 'in the final stages of metropolitan culture.' As the Machine eats through all previous sources of meaning, severing us from time and place, the cities which most of us inhabit become machines too, and we become nodes in their matrix of profit and growth.

We also become powerless. In the countryside, people live by their hands and their wits. Even now, where I live in rural Ireland, people are considerably more practical and multi-skilled than the average Dubliner. They—we—have to be, when a tree comes down across a road in a winter storm, or the power goes out, or a cow escapes from a field or the well stops working. When I lived in the city, my main skill was tapping keyboards. This is still my main skill—here I am—but since coming here I have supplemented it with a dozen others, from coppicing to composting, construction to chainsaw use. In the country, you have no choice but to remember what your body is for. In the city, even if you want to be self-sufficient, everything will militate against it. In city culture, as Mumford puts it, 'every aspect of life must be brought under control: controlled weather, controlled movement, controlled association, controlled production, controlled prices, controlled fantasy, controlled ideas.' The purpose of all of this is, in the end, 'to accelerate the process of mechanical control itself.'

And so we find ourselves in the age of AI and apps for everything, with CCTV cameras on every street corner, our opinions manufactured by interest groups, our communications tracked and monitored, wondering what is true or who we can believe, and feeling, day by day, like we have less agency, less control, less *humanity* than ever before. In the future that is offered to us we are not even cogs in the Machine, for the Machine can increasingly operate without human input. Mumford, as ever, is bracingly frank about where this leads:

Never before has the 'citadel' exercised such atrocious power over the rest of the human race. Over the greater part of history, the village and the countryside remained a constant reservoir of fresh life, constrained indeed by the ancestral patterns of behaviour that had helped make man human, but with a sense of both human limitations and human possibilities. No matter what the errors and aberrations of the rulers of the city, they were still correctible. Even if whole urban populations were destroyed, more than nine tenths of the human race still remained outside the circle of destruction. Today this factor of safety has gone: the metropolitan explosion has carried both the ideological and the chemical poisons of the metropolis to every part of the earth; and the final damage may be irretrievable.[9]

But this global Gomorrah we have built, whose ideologues crisscross the world by plane, selling the ideology of the Machine, invincible in pursuit of their progressive destiny—it is founded on sand. The more the global metropolis expands, the more fragile it becomes. The more it ravages, destroys and cuts off alternative lifeways, the more monocultural its picture of the world grows and the more it works against the laws of nature. A centralised Machine society which must drain the natural world in order to continue its expansion is the very definition of 'unsustainable'; which means it will not be sustained. Something will have to give. It is already giving. We can all feel it.

Half a century before 1850, the political agitator William Cobbett was in his prime. Largely forgotten today, Cobbett was a very English type of localist, populist radical. As a child in his native Surrey—not far from where my own ancestors were rural workers—he saw the last of the self-sustaining village economies fade away, to be replaced by the new world of commerce and empire, all of it centred on London. Cobbett spent the rest of his life as a populist, agrarian writer and activist, driven always by the vision he held within him of a lost Arcadia. It had been lost to an undefinable agglomeration of capitalism, imperialism, enclosure, urbanisation, industrialism, usury, Protestantism and various other gripes and grumbles that Cobbett harboured. He called this complex 'the Thing', and he was clear that all of it was focused around the first true world city: London.

London, to Cobbett, was the enemy, the beating heart of 'the Thing' that had ravaged the true world he had seen and lost. He called the city 'the Great Wen'—a wen being a boil on the skin—and he set out to burst it and to reclaim his Elysium. He failed, as he was always going to: Elysium, once lost, can never be restored by human hands. When I visited London recently, the city in which I and my parents and their parents and theirs had all grown up, I saw the Machine's advance as only an outsider could. Till-less shops and cashless ice cream vans and train tickets purchased through smartphone apps and ever-present street cameras and proliferating 5G towers and soon-to-be-humanless train stations. Soon enough, human contact will be a luxury good, and like all luxury goods it will sell at a premium.

He may not have succeeded in turning back the clock as he wanted, but at least Cobbett succeeded in identifying the enemy, and its seat of power. Today, as the population of London tops nine million, those who can remember the rural England it colonised are long dead. The Thing—the Machine—is in its pomp. Ozymandias sits on his throne at the heart of the Wen, smiling down on the uprooted, directionless masses at his feet. His statues are everywhere. We can all be assured that they will last just as long as the city.

IX

Want Is the Acid

THE BEST THING I EVER BOUGHT was my VW camper van. It came into my life soon after my first child, and the two have grown older together. Neither of our children would allow us to sell our old van now even if we wanted to; there are too many memories tied up in it. That van has been with us on beaches and in woodlands, on hills and plains and mountains, on ferries and in lay-bys too numerous to count. I've got it stuck in mud, reversed it into trees, blown out its tyres on hidden rocks and exploded its gaskets in several nations. Happy memories.

It was a year or two back, on a short family trip in our van, that I saw something about my world, and by implication myself, that I haven't been able to unsee. Sometimes this happens to each of us: something that you believe you 'know' in some abstract, intellectualised sense becomes suddenly real in a more embedded way. You see it playing out, sinking in, and then it is no longer an abstraction but the pattern of your reality.

On this occasion we were in a small town—a nice little place, full of holidaying people like us. There were pubs and restaurants open, and the streets were full of tables and chairs. There were shops and markets.

There were people in vans, like us, and other people hiring boats and other people eating and drinking. There were leaflets in the tourist information centre advertising country house tours and chocolate makers and cycling trips. It was a nice little place, and all of a sudden I saw it for what it was. I saw what was happening here, and by extension everywhere, and within me and all of us. I saw that everything around me was dedicated solely to the immediate gratification of the senses.

There it was, all of a sudden, right in my face. Eating. Drinking. Buying colourful things. Boats, vans, bikes, beer, steak, new clothes, secondhand clothes, burgers, chocolate bars, old castles, stately homes, cappuccinos, pirate adventure parks, golf courses, spas, tea rooms, pubs. Food, drink, fun, entertainment, games, probably some sex somewhere in the mix. All of it came together suddenly into a kind of package of sensory overload and I saw that this was what we were, what we had become without really thinking about or planning it. Stimulating the senses, then reacting to the stimulus, profiting from it all: this was what our society was all about. Feeding the pleasure centres, spending and spending to keep it all coming at us.

It was a nice little place. A small, unremarkable town that became, just for a second, the centre of the whole world.

None of this stopped me from enjoying the rest of my holiday. I ate crisps and went kayaking. We drove our camper van around the coast. But somehow, a part of me remained—still remains—cut off from it all, observing as if from a distance this situation and its consequence. I saw that this is what a Machine society looks like. It is all a kind of simulacrum of a real culture, with organised sensory gratification replacing anything that might previously have provided lasting meaning. I don't mean to imply that sensory gratification is anything new—or even anything inherently bad, within reason. We're all human, and that's still (mostly) OK. Since at least the Neolithic we've been adorning ourselves with imported foreign jewellery and roasting meat to perfection. The pursuit of sensory pleasure certainly took up most of my younger life, even though these days my main vices—the public ones, at least—are chocolate and cheese.

But the pursuit of instant pleasure as an organising principle of society? A culture that is becoming little more than a pleasure dome, dedicated to 'growth' and a supposedly consequent 'happiness'? This is something that ought to bring about more than moral doubts.

If you think I'm going over the top here, then it's worth zooming out. The impacts of a society predicated on boundless economic growth via boundless sensory stimulation are at least in some ways measurable. We can enjoy our little towns here in the richer bits of the world because the waste we generate through our excited purchases of big-screen tellies, Lego sets, foreign holidays, cheap clothes, cheap food and all the rest of it always ends up somewhere else. The dioxins and PCBs go into the water and soil, the plastic goes into the oceans, the carbon dioxide goes into the air. Fifty million tonnes of 'e-waste' is dumped every year, much of it shipped to the poorest countries on Earth, which are least equipped to deal with it.[1] But then they're not really supposed to deal with it: they're supposed to keep it away from us. We don't know what else to do with all this crap, so we—for example—ship thousands of tonnes of toxic waste, containing carcinogenic chemicals, to Nigeria, and just dump it on the beaches. The same way we dumped asbestos on the beaches in Bangladesh, and millions of tonnes of poisonous waste in Indonesia. The same way we run our old ships up onto the beaches in China and India, and leave them for the locals to break up—if they can. The same way we dump nineteen million tonnes of plastic into the environment *every year*.[2]

Had enough yet? Me too. But we need to understand the consequences of the Machine we have built, and which is now rebuilding us so that we may become more perfect consumers, shopping for individual fulfilment in its global marketplace of goods, ideas and identities. We need to understand just what this Machine encourages within us, what it inflames and what we have become: a cheap, digitised version of Late Rome, looking elsewhere when the container ships take away our mess to be dumped on the poor.

So far in this book I have attempted to paint a few little historical sketches of how the process of Machine modernity got us to this point: the end of the Christian faith in the West; the rise of 'Science and Reason' (which were, however, a byproduct of the Western version of that faith); and the revolutions of 1789 and later, which, by clearing the ground of the last remnants of feudalism, laid the foundations of a new kind of world, governed by a new kind of people with a new set of values.

Those people—well, they're mostly us. The best and most poetic chroniclers of their—our—revolution remain Karl Marx and Friedrich Engels, who, despite their many flaws, have never been bettered in their description of the new world which grew from the ruin of the old, and which is now coming to ruin itself. A world with new values: growth, progress, profit, *money*. A world built by the most revolutionary class in history, one which embodies these values and has embedded them over the centuries into every aspect of our lives: the merchants, traders and moneymen otherwise known as the 'bourgeoisie':

> The bourgeoisie, wherever it has got the upper hand, has put an end to all feudal, patriarchal, idyllic relations. It has pitilessly torn asunder the motley feudal ties that bound man to his 'natural superiors,' and has left remaining no other nexus between man and man than naked self-interest, than callous 'cash payment.' It has drowned the most heavenly ecstasies of religious fervour, of chivalrous enthusiasm, of philistine sentimentalism, in the icy water of egotistical calculation. It has resolved personal worth into exchange value. And in place of the numberless and feasible chartered freedoms, has set up that single, unconscionable freedom—Free Trade. In one word, for

exploitation, veiled by religious and political illusions, naked, shameless, direct, brutal exploitation.

This description is, famously, from the 1848 *Communist Manifesto*. It's a curious document, world-changing in a way that few pamphlets ever are. Curious, to my mind, because it is a hearty damnation of the world the bourgeoisie has built, but a damnation which is tinged with a sneaking admiration. Marx and Engels, after all, were both self-styled revolutionaries. As such, they recognised that the capitalism they set out to destroy was the most effective revolutionary force in history. The 'bourgeois' class which drove it on, they wrote, 'has accomplished wonders far surpassing Egyptian pyramids, Roman aqueducts, and Gothic cathedrals; it has conducted expeditions that put in the shade all former Exoduses of nations and crusades.' It has also, perhaps even more radically, 'converted the physician, the lawyer, the priest, the poet, the man of science, into its paid wage labourers. The bourgeoisie has torn away from the family its sentimental veil, and has reduced the family relation to a mere money relation.'

Revolutionary stuff indeed. And this bourgeoisie had revolutionised not just the structures but the *values* of humanity, at the deepest levels, as Marx and Engels write in perhaps their most famous passage:

The bourgeoisie cannot exist without constantly revolutionising the instruments of production, and thereby the relations of production, and with them the whole relations of society . . . Constant revolutionising of production, uninterrupted disturbance of all social conditions, everlasting uncertainty and agitation distinguish the bourgeois epoch from all earlier ones. All fixed, fast-frozen relations, with their train of ancient and venerable prejudices and opinions, are swept away, all new-formed ones become antiquated before they can ossify. All that is solid melts into air, all that is holy is profaned, and man is at last compelled to face with sober senses, his real conditions of life, and his relations with his kind.

Everlasting uncertainty and agitation. Today's world was clearly under construction back in 1848. Once the bourgeoisie really got to work, the current age of corporate globalism—and the waste, destruction and cultural decay it generates—was the inevitable result. 'The need of a constantly expanding market for its products chases the bourgeoisie over the whole surface of the globe', they observed. This process has 'given a cosmopolitan character to production and consumption in every country.' It 'compels all nations, on pain of extinction, to adopt the bourgeois mode of production; it compels them to introduce what it calls civilisation into their midst, i.e., to become bourgeois themselves. In one word, it creates a world after its own image.'

And here we are. I'm no Marxist, but *The Communist Manifesto* describes the world we are in with brilliant prescience, despite being written nearly two centuries ago. The mass consumption of the world, and the mass excretion of our culture's toxic byproducts into its waters and woods and skies, is the natural conclusion of the world which Marx and Engels saw being born, and which they pinioned in words so well. Once the 'bourgeois revolution' had cleared the ground of awkward obstacles like the peasantry, the artisans, common land, local cultures and traditions, family and home life, a sense of history and mutual obligation, and religions which preached against wealth and wordly power, then the captains and priests of the Machine could get on with the work they were made for, the work of our time, the holy effort to which all human will, skill and energy is now bent: *making money.*

'Bourgeois' is a very nineteenth-century word, and Marxism is a very nineteenth-century idea. But what I am really trying to get at here—and what perhaps Marx and Engels were getting at too, even though they pretended to be 'social scientists'—is not a theory or a structure or an ideological claim, but something deeper: an old, surging force, one that stems from within us. A force which has driven all this onwards, which is the lifeblood of the Machine, and which, through its untrammelling, acts as an acid which burns through all past structures and values. An acid which is now acting to dissolve our ecosystems and cultural forms, as it has dissolved so much else.

What is this force? What could be so powerful that it could dissolve away centuries of our cultural inheritance; could dissolve forests and oceans, great faiths, nations, traditions—everything that makes a human life real—and replace it with this . . . pleasure dome?

Want. Want is the acid.

We can usefully understand our time by seeing in it the final result of the centuries-long tension between the merchant class and everyone else. Pre-modern societies, in every case that I know of, always kept the merchant class in their place, and that place was usually right at the bottom. This was the system known today as 'feudalism'. The social pyramid during Japan's Edo Period, to take a typical example, placed the Emperor at the top (of course), followed by the military leader—the *shōgun*—and then the aristocratic *daimyo* class. Next were the military nobility—the *samurai*—and beneath them the peasants—those who produced the food for the nation. Below the peasants came the artisans—the makers. And then, right at the very bottom, came the merchants.

Why were the merchants the lowest order of society? Because their work created nothing of value. In fact, it *created* nothing at all. This was the pattern worldwide. In medieval Europe, usury—the lending of money at interest—was a sin, as it still is in Islamic nations. In this continent too, the merchants, bankers and money people were hemmed in by a network of customs, religious edicts and structures like guilds and professional bodies. Money had to be kept under control, precisely because of the power it had to ignite the powerful flame of want.

I'm not especially suggesting we should all live under a shōgunate, though at least it would give us elites with some panache. But the story of the world since the eighteenth century has been the story of the setting of that flame, and the resulting fire. We are all bourgeois now, which is to say that we are all driven forward by want. We have all learned a bourgeois version of history, too, in which medieval 'feudalism' is seen as dark and barbaric, while modern capitalism is equated with freedom and liberty. Even those who can see through this partial version of history—and can see the damage done by our modern enthroning of money and commerce—will often promote it anyway, even as just a temporary expedient.

In a famous essay from 1930—an essay which is in many ways an advert for the utter failure of the modern 'science' of economics—the British economist John Maynard Keynes explained that it might take another century to solve 'the economic problem' worldwide, ensuring the end of poverty and the creation of a wealthy, leisured modern planet. When that happened, we might again become virtuous as a society:

> I see us free, therefore, to return to some of the most sure and certain principles of religion and traditional virtue—that avarice is a vice, that the exaction of usury is a misdemeanour, and the love of money is detestable, that those walk most truly in the paths of virtue and sane wisdom who take least thought for the morrow. We shall once more value ends above means and prefer the good to the useful. We shall honour those who can teach us how to pluck the hour and the day virtuously and well, the delightful people who are capable of taking direct enjoyment in things, the lilies of the field who toil not, neither do they spin.[3]

This Utopia, however, would take a while to reach, and until it was reached, we would have to pursue 'growth' regardless of the short-term cost. 'But beware!' warned Keynes. 'The time for all this is not yet. For at least another hundred years we must pretend to ourselves and to everyone that fair is foul and foul is fair; for foul is useful and fair is not. Avarice and usury and precaution must be our gods for a little longer still. For only they can lead us out of the tunnel of economic necessity into daylight.'

There is the devil's bargain, in black and white. It's nearly a hundred years now since Keynes wrote those lines. How are we doing at solving his 'economic problem'? When we look around us, we can see that Keynes's naive notion—that a society which cores itself around 'avarice and usury' can suddenly drop those vices when some undefined plateau of perfection is reached—is ludicrous. Once you adopt these values, they will make and remake you. The world they have built will depend upon their being pursued forever.

Four decades after Keynes made his claim, another British economist, E. F. Schumacher, skewered his assumptions in his book *Small Is Beautiful*. Taking issue with 'the dominant modern belief' that the kind of 'universal prosperity' narrowly defined by the likes of Keynes would lead to peace or happiness, Schumacher argued instead that entirely the opposite was the case. 'I suggest', he wrote, 'that the foundations of peace cannot be laid by universal prosperity, in the modern sense, because such prosperity, if attainable at all, is attainable only by cultivating such drives of human nature as greed and envy, which destroy intelligence, happiness, serenity, and thereby the peacefulness of man.'[4]

This made the question of 'prosperity' a much bigger issue than the likes of Keynes had suggested. 'What is at stake', asserts Schumacher, 'is not economics but culture; not the standard of living but the quality of life. Economics and the standard of living can just as well be looked after by a capitalist system, moderated by a bit of planning and redistributive taxation. But culture and, generally, the quality of life, can now only be debased by such a system.'

This is a big claim. It is also, to my mind, obviously correct. Schumacher knew it, and Keynes knew it too: it's why he so apologetically explained that we would need to live under a self-made spell for a hundred years, like some fairytale princess. *We must pretend to ourselves and to everyone that fair is foul and foul is fair.* What he didn't foresee was that we would forget that we were pretending. Today we are led by want, we are drenched in it, and we are increasingly sick from its infection.

What is interesting about both Schumacher's and Keynes's approaches to the plague of want is their openly spiritual perspective on the problem and their almost religious language: in the case of Schumacher, that of a Christian inspired by Buddhist principles. There is a lot of talk here of sin, of wrong and right, of fair and foul. In this, both men distinguish themselves from today's economists, for whom talk like this is embarrassingly passé. We are all grown-ups now, and we know that living by want is not only necessary but can be justified with software modelling and leader columns in *The Times*.

But a value system which glorifies wealth and accumulation, which builds itself on a platform of want, which inflames and creates more of it daily through a marketing machine that colonises the human mind—this is what every spiritual tradition in history has warned against, and with good reason. Take, for example, the famous list of the seven deadly sins in the Western Christian tradition: gluttony, lust, pride, wrath, greed, sloth and envy. With the possible exception of sloth, we currently live in a culture which not only sees nothing wrong with these values but *actively encourages them*. The pursuit of these six vices is no longer something to be confessed or repented: it is the very thing which drives our notion of progress forward.

So this is who we are. You don't have to be a Christian or a Buddhist to see where it has led us, and where it will lead next. Want is the acid. Capitalism is the battery. Growth is the engine. Greed is the forming energy that moves us to where we are inevitably headed.

What is the brake?

The answer is as hard as it is old-fashioned: *limits*. Modernity is a machine for destroying limits. The ideology of the Machine—the liberation of individual desire—sees our world as a blank slate to be written on afresh when the old limits of nature and culture are washed away. This is our faith: that breaking boundaries leads to happiness, that boundaries are barriers rather than opportunities. We strain against all limits. It is who we are.

What Schumacher knew but Marx denied—with all the terrible consequences that the twentieth century produced—was that the solution to the triumph of want, as far as there can ever be one, is not political revolution followed by a grand new social structure, but something harder and less spectacular: spiritual vigilance. The problem of want can be guided by systems and cultures, but it is, ultimately, a matter of the heart. Want will dissolve everything, if we let it, and new structures will not prevent that. Guarding the heart is the best defence against the acid.

Want is the acid, but the heart is both its provenance and its potential enemy. I often ask myself: Do I want too much? Do I grasp too hard? Do I live too heavily? The answer is always yes, and in spades. Plenty of people don't have the luxury of asking these questions. I think this gives those of us that do all the more obligation to work them through.

Fortunately, we don't have to do it alone. 'It is hardly likely', wrote Schumacher, in the conclusion to *Small Is Beautiful*, 'that twentieth-century man is called upon to discover truth that had never been discovered before.' The dangerous results of untrammelled want have been known since the dawn of time, which is why every sane culture has discouraged it rather than making it the basis of its value system. But an ancient problem, as Schumacher's closing paragraph emphasised, will have ancient solutions—if we choose to go looking for them. To those who ask 'What can I actually do?', he said, the answer was 'as simple as it is disconcerting: we can, each of us, work to put our own inner house in order. The guidance we need for this work cannot be found in science or technology, the value of which utterly depends on the ends they serve; but it can still be found in the traditional wisdom of mankind.'[5]

X

Come the Black Ships

THE 8TH OF JULY 1853 MUST have begun as a normal day in the Japanese capital, Edo. The pattern of those normal days had been set for two and a half centuries in a carefully managed routine. Japan under the Tokugawa shōgunate, which began in 1603, was a strict feudal society, operating within long-defined, tightly bounded hierarchies. It was honour-based, aristocratic, and entirely closed to outsiders.

Since the reign of the third shōgun (the word translates as 'great general'), Tokugawa Iemitsu, in the 1630s, Japan's leaders had seen that beyond their shores, rapid changes in technology and geopolitics were turning the world upside down. Specifically, the European powers were embarking on imperial adventures around the globe, and their sophisticated technologies were granting them victories everywhere they went. For over a century, more and more Europeans had been trading with Japan, moving into the country and bringing with them new values and a new religion—Christianity—to which more and more Japanese were converting. The traditions of Japan, not to mention the power of the shōgun and the aristocracy, seemed under increasing threat.

In response, the shōgun took radical action: he closed the nation's borders, expelled all the Europeans, strictly limited international trade, proscribed Christianity and, as a grim example, crucified the leading Christians. Japan had embarked on a major gamble; it would exist in splendid isolation and hope to be left alone. For two hundred years the gamble paid off, preserving the country's culture and feudal structures— until that day in July 1853 when the shōgun's luck finally ran out.

Looking up from their work, across the bay, the people of Edo (now Tokyo) saw sailing into their harbour something which terrified them: four great 'ships of evil mien', the like of which they had never seen before. The biggest were three times longer than the largest ship Japan had ever built, and unlike the Japanese vessels they were built partially of iron. They belched black smoke into the sky, and were bristling with weapons—cannons, guns—which the sword-wielding samurai, Japan's aristocratic warrior caste, had never encountered.

There were four ships in total—two steamers and two sailing vessels. The Japanese referred to them, then as now, as 'the Black Ships'. They steamed unannounced into Edo Bay and proceeded to deliberately block the shipping lanes. A small wooden boat full of samurai was sent out to intercept them. Onboard, they saw hundreds of obviously Western people, armed and uniformed. The samurai shouted the only European word they knew at them, one they had learned from traders: *Départez*, French for 'leave now'. The Black Ships didn't move.

The ships were commanded by an American naval officer, Commodore Matthew Perry, and they had come to force Japan's hand. The ambitious, expansive United States of America—a country that had not existed when Japan first closed its borders—was now competing with the Europeans for domination of the world's sea lanes. The USA was a wannabe-empire whose interests lay primarily in commerce. America's Manifest Destiny might be tied up with Christianity and some notion of the brotherhood of man, but at root its drive for world domination—then as now—was built around something which its leadership caste held dear above all else: the idol of 'free trade'.

Commodore Perry made it known to the Japanese that he would not leave until he could meet with their leader. The Japanese refused to let him land. For days a game of cat-and-mouse was played, which nearly erupted in violence several times. In the end, knowing the weakness of their hand, the Japanese were forced to allow Perry and his men to land. Still, they refused him entry to the city of Edo, he was not allowed to meet either the emperor or the shōgun, and a hidden contingent of samurai were posted behind a trap door at the designated landing spot in case the foreigners were to try anything tricky.

In the event, the historic meeting came off peacefully. Perry met with a representative of the shōgun, whom he presented with a collection of passive-aggressive gifts including a small steam locomotive, a bottle of whiskey and a white flag, with instructions on how to use it to surrender. In return, he was treated to a display of sumo wrestling. Most importantly, Perry completed the task he had been sent to carry out: delivering a letter to Japan's leadership from the American president Millard Fillmore.

Fillmore's letter was a 'request' that Japan open its borders to trade with the USA. America was not here for conquest, wrote the president. Perry and his men came in peace—as long as they got what they wanted. Fillmore described his country to the Japanese like this:

> The United States of America reach from ocean to ocean, and our Territory of Oregon and state of California lie directly opposite to the dominions of your imperial majesty. Our steamships can go from California to Japan in eighteen days. Our great state of California produces about sixty millions of dollars in gold every year, besides silver, quicksilver, precious stones, and many other valuable articles. Japan is also a rich and fertile country, and produces many

very valuable articles. Your imperial majesty's subjects are skilled in many of the arts. I am desirous that our two countries should trade with each other, for the benefit both of Japan and the United States.

The new nation of America, according to its leader, was best described not in terms of its values, its history, its spiritual beliefs or the makeup of its people, but by how much gold and silver it could produce, and how fast its ships could move. America was expanding, and it intended to trade with Japan whether Japan wanted it or not. In case the president's tactful missive had not been clear enough about the bottom line, an additional letter from Perry was bracingly frank:

Many of the large ships of war destined to visit Japan have not yet arrived in these seas, though they are hourly expected; and the undersigned, as an evidence of his friendly intentions, has brought but four of the smaller ones, designing, should it become necessary, to return to Edo in the ensuing spring with a much larger force. But it is expected that the government of your imperial majesty will render such return unnecessary, by acceding at once to the very reasonable and pacific overtures contained in the President's letter.

America had not come to Japan on a cultural exchange trip: it had come to break open new markets for its goods, and to inject its commercial attitudes into a country which had always held those attitudes in contempt. Feudal Japan was a nation which kept its merchants and traders at the bottom of the social pyramid, while the United States placed them at the apex. If Japan was a hidebound ancient nation, America was a newly incorporated business, and it had ambitious plans for expansion—plans which involved spreading its core values of individualism, commerce and competition to every corner of the globe.

It's only fair to say that the young nation of America had learned these values at the knee of its ageing mother, Britain, whose own global commercial empire was peaking by the time Perry steamed into Edo Bay. But the United States, untrammelled by any history of its own, with a whole continent to build from, and with vast numbers of energetic immigrants from all quarters streaming into it annually with the aim of getting rich—or at least escaping poverty—had advantages that no other empire had ever had.

It would use them to the full. Over the next century and a half, the Black Ships would arrive in various forms in almost every nation in the world, sometimes bringing gifts, but always demanding entry. The age of globalisation had arrived.

IN JULY 2001, I WAS IN Johannesburg, South Africa, interviewing the ANC government's head of policy and research, Michael Sachs. The ANC had been in power since the fall of apartheid in 1994, but I was in the country to investigate why so many of the party's supporters, particularly the poor in the former black townships and homelands, felt betrayed by the government which had promised them so much. I was writing a book about resistance to the process of economic globalisation, and this seemed like a key story to cover.

The story was cautionary but also typical: before taking power, the ANC had promised its people a 'liberatory' economic policy, involving the nationalisation of privately held companies, land reform, mass housebuilding, clean water and sanitation and affordable healthcare, all aimed at achieving a long-denied degree of racial justice. The policy had been drawn up after long consultations with communities, unions and local NGOs, and enjoyed broad support in the newly democratic country.

Then the Black Ships came.

Upon taking power, the ANC was informed by the powers-that-really-be that its policies did not meet with the approval of the global markets, and that capital flight from the country would result if the party tried to implement them. Faced with the threat, the government caved. A new economic policy was drawn up by economists from the World Bank, neoliberal think tanks and South African finance houses. This one was designed to promote 'free trade' and 'competition'. In order to achieve this, the government agreed, amongst other measures, to privatise the water and electricity networks, and to abandon plans for land redistribution and nationalisation.

On my trip to the country, I had seen the results: police in apartheid-era riot gear storming into black townships to cut off the water and electricity of the poor for non-payment of bills. Twenty million South Africans in total had had their water and electricity cut off, and two million had been evicted from their homes for non-payment of rent.

When I asked Michael Sachs why this was happening, he gave me the most honest admission of governmental powerlessness in the face of globalised commerce that I had ever heard. Like a shōgun facing a harbour full of Black Ships, he told me that his government had had no choice but to abandon its people's aspirations. 'You know', he said, 'you can't just go and redistribute things in this era . . . you've got to play the game, you've got to ensure that you don't go on some adventure. You know, you *will* be defeated. They were defeated in Chile, they were defeated in Nicaragua. You can't do it now'.

The 'unipolar world' of American power, said Sachs, had tied the government's hands. Like all governments, they had to operate within the narrow bounds permitted by the now-global markets. 'We achieved democracy in 1994', Sachs told me, 'and immediately had to confront the issue of globalisation. It was an unbridled victory for finance capital . . . so we had a very steep learning curve.'[1]

By the time I interviewed Sachs, the Black Ships of globalisation had had 150 years to range around the world building a global trading system so extensive that even popularly elected governments had no chance of resisting it. By 2001, of course, actual Black Ships were no longer employed. The tactics that had served Commodore Perry and the Americans so well—the same tactics used by the British to 'open up' Chinese markets and the French to do the same to Vietnam—were no longer useful or acceptable. There were no Black Ships or squares of redcoats anymore; no White Man's Burden or civilising mission. The same process was ongoing, but it had been rebranded. Now we called it 'development'.

In an essay which opened my eyes to this reality some two decades ago, entitled 'Development as Colonialism',[2] the philosopher Edward Goldsmith summarised how the process worked. 'Development', said Goldsmith, in a critique echoed by others before and since, was a term first popularised by US President Harry Truman after World War Two. It presented America's mission in the world as helping to lift poor, benighted, 'under-developed' nations out of their backward and unenlightened state and into the glorious new world of fridges, traffic jams and suburban bliss.

In Truman's telling, 'development' was a charitable act. In Goldsmith's analysis, development programmes were 'mere political weapons that suit Western commercial interests, destroy domestic economies, impoverish the vast majority and further push borrowing nations into the abyss of debt.' The post-war 'Washington consensus', and the puppet institutions it created—the World Bank, IMF and WTO—were continuing the work of Fillmore and Perry with strings-attached loans, 'structural adjustment' programmes designed to rebuild nations for the benefit of global corporations, the creation of Westernised elites and the mass export of American culture. And when none of that worked, the Black Ships—or rather, the Black Hawk helicopters—were still held in reserve. Coups could be engineered, and 'liberatory' invasions staged.

This is what the ANC experienced in South Africa, and what many other poor countries, from eastern Europe to Latin America, have experienced in the age of globalisation. But it is also, with some irony, what is now happening to the West itself. The kind of economic carpetbagging that Western elites have been engaged in for centuries was never confined to the masses of the 'Third World'. It is essentially the same process that enclosed the lands of the poor in England three centuries back. Now, in the 2020s, the West is being 'structurally adjusted'. The result is a widening economic chasm, the creation of a new 'precariat', arrogant elites, growing numbers of angry 'deplorables', ethnic and cultural conflicts, and increasingly obvious societal instability in what was once the heart of empire. The Black Ships have come home.

Goldsmith and other similar critics were right to unmask the forces lying beneath the propaganda of 'development'. Yet it seems to me that the process of globalisation is not simply a crude attempt to acquire riches. It is that, for sure, but there is a belief system that undergirds it. Commerce is the engine, but what is happening to us all now is not simply about profit. The Machine has its own value system, as we have seen. Capitalist globalisation carries out into the world not just an economic model but the ideology that underlies it—an ideology that has been called globalism. If globalisation is the economics, globalism is the philosophy. That philosophy can perhaps best be summed up by a word we seem to hear everywhere now: *openness*.

'Openness' is both the aim and the core value of the age of globalism. It is, in the telling of those who promote it, always a good thing. Open minds, open hearts, open doors, open borders; open to trade, to growth, to change, to progress, to 'diversity' in all its manifestations. In many of the ructions that have overtaken parts of the West in recent years—the UK's Brexit vote, the election of Donald Trump in the US, and ongoing populist insurgencies in Western European nations being the most obvious examples—'openness' was presented as a value under threat from those who would prefer instead to remain 'closed'. To be 'closed' is to be backward, bigoted, prejudiced, fearful, and largely obsolete. 'Closed' people must be encouraged—or forced—'open', for their own benefit and that of the wider project, just as Japan was by Commodore Perry.

Since the 1990s—or perhaps since the 1850s—the process of Machine globalisation has been a war against all 'closed' things; against limits and boundaries of any kind, cultural or ecological; against historical traditions, local economies, trades unions, national economic plans, nations themselves, tribal cultures, religions . . . anything that interferes with the path of commercial expansion and its associated culture of individualist liberalism. Open is good, closed is bad. Why? Because closed things can't be harvested, exploited or transformed in the image of the new world which the Machine is building. 'Open' things, on the other hand; well, they're easy prey.

In his book *Cosmopolis*,[3] written just after the fall of the Berlin Wall, as globalisation really started to get its boots on, the historian Stephen Toulmin gives a historical context to this process. He takes us back to the European Reformation and the resulting wars of religion which ripped the continent apart at every level in the seventeenth century. The trauma of this, says Toulmin, and the slaughter and violence that supposedly Christian people meted out to each other in the name of their competing dogmas, led to a desire for certainty and order amongst the elites of the day, and it also led to a hardening of minds against the claims of religion. The response was a search for a reasoned, orderly system by which human affairs could be understood and managed—a system that would make religious wars a thing of the past.

This was *cosmopolis*: the dream of a universal, rational way of being. The word itself was a portmanteau, combining *cosmos*—the universe—with *polis*—the human realm. Cosmo-polis would combine the human and the non-human in one grand schema that would make the horrors of the Thirty Years War impossible to revisit. By systematising reality, utilising the new sciences, promoting reason over religion, and supporting the new pattern of nation-states which emerged from the Peace of Westphalia over local or feudal loyalties, Europeans could build a better world, one less amenable to irrational, bloody chaos.

The dream of cosmopolis, in Toulmin's telling, is one which emerges periodically in the West at times of extreme trauma. It emerged first after the Thirty Years War and again after World War One, in the projects of the Modernists, the dream of universal socialism and even the promotion of Esperanto. Then, after World War Two, it flourished again, coming to full flower in the Woodstock dreams of the sixties generation, in which the world would live as one, with sex, drugs and rock and roll all free at the point of use.

This—the pursuit of the cosmopolitan Utopia of openness—is in some ways the same drive that took Commodore Perry to Japan. The United States of America was a cosmopolis from the start, and the ideal of 'free and fair trade' was always part of the rationalists' project. Back in the early 2000s, the high-water mark of the latest phase of globalisation, the press was full of columns which explicitly tied 'free trade' to both peace and universal prosperity. Globalist cheerleader Thomas Friedman even invented his own geopolitical concept, which he called 'the golden arches theory of conflict prevention'. It stated that no two countries with a McDonalds restaurant would ever go to war with each other. This has since been proved comprehensively false, but Friedman is still out there, cosmopolis singing in his heart.

Friedmanite dreams about the binding friendships resulting from free trade, however, don't carry much weight in the age of populism. Any talk of the End of History these days is less likely to refer to a final berthing in the port of liberal democracy than to an ecological or cultural meltdown. Politics in the West today could be characterised as a rising tide of complaints from across the spectrum about the impact of too much 'openness' on society—complaints which divide, as ever, along tribal lines.

Thus we hear the 'right' complain about the impacts of mass immigration, or about the cultural shifts associated with the post-sixties sexual revolution, which are now dissolving the boundaries of the body itself. The 'left', meanwhile, objects to the inequalities created by neoliberal economics, or the ecological consequences of global trade. Both sides complain about the power of corporations, though usually different ones. And both can be relied upon to blame 'elites' for the ongoing instability that the cosmopolitan project appears to be engineering, even if they can't agree on quite who the elites are. Neither side is wrong about any of it. Cosmopolis is cracking under its own weight.

The flaw in the cosmopolitan dream, now as then, is a simple failure to understand that the world is not 'rational', and neither are we. We are crooked timber, and we grow from the ground. Universalist projects ignore that human need for roots, and the attack on culture by commerce fuels destructive want. All of this creates not universal peace but universal upheaval. Like Perry's arrival in Japan, its effect is to dissolve our previous social bonds, cultural stories, social arrangements and religious commitments in a sea of open, boundless nothing.

We live today in the world that Commodore Perry helped to make, amongst the consequences of the drive to build cosmopolis on the bones of older systems and societies. In this world, we are all crewing the Black Ships, or we are the working poor of Japan waiting for the consequences of their coming, or we are samurai, facing our own obsolescence. Cosmopolis has us all in its sway, and it has a powerful story to tell. The dream of a globalised, rational world in which all comers trade under the West's benevolent gaze is fading as the West does, but the techno-capitalist Machine it spawned lives everywhere now, humming in the fibre optic cables and looking down on us from the satellites. The Machine is the true inheritor of the cosmopolitan dream, made manifest in every glowing screen, and it is remaking us all in its image.

XI

You Are Harvest

B Y CANDLELIGHT, MARK MOVED a chess piece across the board. He was about to beat me again. We were playing towards the end of the COVID pandemic, which had put an end to our weekly sessions in the local pub. Like many rural pubs across Ireland, our local had been forcibly closed by the lockdowns and had not reopened since. Even if it had done, our mutual lack of a digital vaccine passport, not to mention the tracking devices popularly known as 'smartphones' with which they could be scanned and logged by the state, meant we would have been banned from having a pint by the fire anyway.

'Check', said Mark.

Instead, we met every week in Mark's cabin, which he had built himself a few years back, with a few of us lending a hand. Mark lives entirely off-grid. He has no electricity, he collects his water from a local spring, and he heats his small home with locally scavenged wood. He has no phone or computer, and never looks at the internet. His gathering rebellion against technology, which has been deepening in the decade I've known him, has recently led him to decide never to have his photo taken again.

To many people, this kind of puritanism—which is how it is often seen—appears at least eccentric and at worst fanatical. But then, many people have not spent as much time thinking about the grip technology has over us as Mark has. Many people look askance at me because I have no smartphone and can't be included in their WhatsApp group, or because I won't use social media or watch the TV, but I'm a beige normie compared to him. Many people see few problems with the march of the digital machine through every aspect of our lives. Many people have simply forgotten what it feels like not to be pulled and pushed and tugged and directed every hour of the day by the demands of the glowing screen.

Many people are not paying attention.

Mark and I had been talking as we played about the latest tightening of the technological ratchet. We're never short of a new topic of conversation, be it drones scanning beaches for COVID sufferers, armed robotic dogs being developed for use in war zones,[1] news about the depression suffered by schoolchildren spending all day in COVID-inspired 'digital classrooms', or the exciting development of artificial wombs[2] which will allow men to become mothers and spare women the pain of childbirth, whilst liberating all potential birthing-people to spend more time at work, lovingly nurturing economic growth.

Mark and I cut our teeth in the green movement, at a time when there was a kind of simple purity to it. It was industrial humanity versus the natural world, and we knew which side we were on. But everything is greyer now; all of the lines are blurred. The meaning of the word 'humanity' seems blurred too, more so each day.

'Twenty years ago', said Mark, toying with his knight, 'we were fighting to save wilderness from destruction. Now it seems like we're just fighting to keep ourselves off screens twenty-four hours a day.' This is the context in which Mark draws his lines: he is trying, in his own small way, to construct a border around his humanity. He and I both know that borders are porous; but we know too that without them the kingdom will fall.

A few days after I lost my game of chess, a couple of friends came to visit us from England. We hadn't seen them for nearly a decade, and they hadn't travelled anywhere since the pandemic began, so they were blinking excitedly in the sunlight. They had taken the ferry across the Irish Sea, which had necessitated them performing a particular technological ritual, one which went beyond even the longstanding norm of scanning their digitally enabled passports and sitting on a boat full of CCTV cameras. This time they had to have their photo taken and show their digital proof of vaccination. They also, for some reason they didn't understand, had to recite a string of numbers into a recording device. Perhaps this process will be used in future to supplement the eyeball scans, passport chips and smartphone-enabled border control systems which are already forming the basis of our glorious future of freedom and plenty.

One of my friends saw a porpoise in the sea on the way over. This may be less likely on future trips, as the oil company BP are planning a wind turbine array half the size of London in the sea between Wales and the Isle of Man, to ensure that sustainable economic growth continues steadily into the future.[3] It is one of many such projects planned for the British coast, as the project to 'decarbonise' the British economy ramps up. It seems likely that within a decade or so there will be no part of the coast where it will be possible to stare out to sea and not see an industrial skyline, just as it will be near impossible to find a piece of countryside not being 'developed' for roads, housing, high-speed rail, new superstores and all the other geegaws demanded by an endlessly growing population and an endlessly growing economy. If they do ever get round to building Jerusalem in our once green and pleasant land, I fully expect it to be 5G-enabled, replete with retail space, and with ample provision of coffee shops and 24/7 electric car-charging hubs.

Sometimes I lie awake at night, or I wander in the field behind my house, or I walk down the street in our local town and think I can see it all around me: the Grid. The veins and sinews of the Machine that surrounds us and pins us and provides for us and defines us now. I imagine a kind of network of shining lines in the air, glowing like a dewed spiderweb in the morning sun. I imagine the cables and the satellite links, the films and the words and the records and the opinions, the nodes and the data centres that track and record the details of my life. I imagine the mesh created by the bank transactions and the shopping trips, the passport applications and the text messages sent. I see this thing, whatever it is, being constructed, or constructing itself around me, I see it rising and tightening its grip, and I see that none of us can stop it from evolving into whatever it is becoming.

I see the Machine, humming gently to itself as it binds us with its offerings, as it dangles its promises before us and slowly, slowly, slowly reels us in. I think of the part of it we interact with daily, the glowing white interface through which we volunteer every detail of our lives in exchange for information or pleasure or stories told by global entertainment corporations who commodify our culture and sell it back to us. I think of the words we use to describe this interface, which we carry with us in our pockets wherever we go, as we are tracked down every street and into every forest that remains: *the web; the net.*

I think: *These are things designed to trap prey.*

IN PART TWO OF THIS BOOK I have attempted to chart, in my own small and partial way, the historical and philosophical development of what I am calling the Machine. I have argued that two things are happening as this Machine reaches its maturity. Firstly, an unprecedented technological network of power and control is being constructed worldwide, which is walking us into a tightly controlled future in which both humans and the wider natural world will be bent to this network's needs. And secondly, in this bending we are losing the essence of what it means to be human.

Later, I will be saying a third thing: rebellion is necessary, if we are to remain human at all.

But why a machine? Why choose this particular image to try and pin down this thing that is enveloping us? Because a machine is an emotionless, inorganic system; something which is pitiless and determined, and which has some task to fulfil. Above all, a machine is something unnatural: something *constructed*. Specifically, it is constructed of separate parts, all of which, when taken together, perform the wider function for which the machine is designed. If today, then, we live under the reign of the Machine, what is this machine made of? What are its parts, and how do they operate?

The simple answer is: *technologies*, and especially digital technologies. We live now in a tech-saturated world, one that has crept up on us rapidly within my lifetime and yours. In the 'developed' world today, it is virtually impossible to live outside this system, unless you want to live like my friend Mark, and even he can't escape the need for a bank account and a mass-produced bicycle. But the Machine is not simply the logical endpoint of certain trends within culture and history. It is not simply a collection of advanced tools, historical designs and political power games. It is that, but it is also something else. It is above all *a new type of civilisation:* one which is replacing all previous human ways of living, cultures and value systems with something novel and totalising; something which, in some indefinable way, seems to be struggling to be born through us. Something which we are midwifing into existence every time we click and swipe, whether we know it or not. The question is how we can begin to understand it.

One man who tried back in the 1960s, when an unquestioning faith in science and its offspring, technology, was roaring across the Western world, was the French thinker Jacques Ellul. Ellul's 1964 book *The Technological Society* attempted to understand and explain what the Machine was made of. Its thesis is that the society we live in today—which he predicted with accuracy—represents a fundamental, qualitative change in what it means to be human.

This change was due to the dominance of what Ellul called *technique*. A product of the revolution of reason and the categorising, controlling approach of modern science, *technique* grew into something which eclipsed and co-opted both of them. It is, effectively, Ellul's name for the worldview of Machine modernity. 'Technique', he explains, 'is the translation into action of man's concern to master things by means of reason, to account for what is subconscious, make quantitative what is qualitative, make clear and precise the outlines of nature, take hold of chaos and put order into it.'4

Ellul's *technique* is an attitude of mind, one which replaces spontaneous, human-scale, organic ways of living with a focus on technical, rationalised, planned and directed outcomes. Technique is not the same thing as technology. Humans have always used technologies, or at least tools; but for most of history they have been designed to augment human work rather than to entirely replace it. Technique, on the other hand, when it is taken up as a way of seeing, gives birth to an entirely new type of technology: one which exists to remake the world in the image of technique itself. The kind by which, today, we are all increasingly enslaved.

Ellul is not an easy read, but *The Technological Society* is a deep book which explains how we got to where we are today. Our contemporary global mindset—that of technique—has now colonised our way of seeing so totally that we fail to even notice it. The human worldview for most of recorded history has been superseded by a new way of seeing which as it became global could only lead, in Ellul's estimation, to one destination: the replacement of both humanity and nature, as technique 'pursues its own course more and more independently of man.' This means that 'man participates less and less actively in technical creation, which, by the automatic combination of prior elements, becomes a kind of fate.' A human being is thus 'reduced to the level of a catalyst. Better still, he resembles a slug inserted into a slot machine: he starts the operation without participating in it.'[5]

Once it is set in motion, through the technological network it itself brings into being, technique will inevitably move towards the construction of a whole society framed by its values. If the industrial revolution of the eighteenth century represented the replacement of human muscle by machinery, it could be said that the digital revolution of the twenty-first represents the replacement of the human brain by the developing digital overmind. This does not require a global conspiracy, or a wizard behind the curtain. There is no wizard. There is no curtain. There is only technique, which 'has become autonomous; it has fashioned an omnivorous world which obeys its own laws and which has renounced all tradition. Technique no longer rests on tradition . . . its evolution is too rapid, too upsetting, to integrate the older traditions.'

Why does all this represent a 'new civilisation', as Ellul puts it at one point? Simply because it takes aim at, and will ultimately destroy, the three traditional foundations of human life: nature, culture and religion. Of the first of these, Ellul explains that technique is 'opposed to nature' because 'it destroys, eliminates or subordinates the natural world, and does not allow this world to restore itself or even to enter into a symbiotic relationship with it. The two worlds obey different imperatives, different directives and different laws which have nothing in common.' As a result, 'we are rapidly approaching the time when there will no longer be any natural environment at all.'[6]

As for traditional cultures and human lifeways—sixty years ago, Ellul was already pointing to the germs of the current Western culture war. 'All the peoples of the world today', he claimed, 'live in a cultural breakdown provoked by the conflicts and the internal strife resulting from technique. Over and above this . . . since every human being incorporates in his own person the cultural environment in which he lives, its disagreements and incoherence are to be met with again in each individual personality'.[7]

The rise and spread of technique, from the unsettled West where it germinated, around the world, via the Black Ships of 'development' and 'Progress', has led to the civilisation of the Machine finally going global. The idealistic cosmopolis we encountered in the last chapter looks, according to Ellul, rather different in practice. 'In spite of all the men of good will, all the optimists, all the doers of history,' he writes, 'the civilisations of the world are being ringed about with a band of steel. We in the West became familiar with this iron constraint in the nineteenth century. Now technique is mechanically reproducing it everywhere as necessary to its existence.' The result? 'Man himself is overpowered by technique and becomes its object.'

If Ellul were alive today, maybe he would see that his 'band of steel' looks, in the twenty-first century, more like a digital noose. Technique's overpowering of human-scale ways of living was accelerated a million-fold by the rise and rapid triumph of the web. The exciting, free internet which was dangled before us twenty-five or so years ago—Global communications! Unlimited information! International peace and harmony! The sharing of knowledge for human betterment!—turned out to be a trap, through which we surrender every detail about ourselves to state and commercial interests in exchange for dopamine hits that just keep coming, in turn deepening social divisions and disconnection from the natural world.

Be that as it may, the Machine, in replacing past human cultures with its new global techno-civilisation, offers obvious material benefits, some of them useful and many of them extremely popular. In the long term, I don't believe that many of them can be sustained, or even that they should be. But in the short term, it is worth acknowledging too that the attitudes displayed by people like Ellul, and people like me, are marginal. The Machine, at some level, is popular. There will be no popular revolution against it.

And yet—at another level it causes deep disquiet. We only have to look at what those screens are doing to our children for even the most oblivious parent to feel a shiver of unease. We have struck a deal of some sort with this thing, and now we can feel it being called in. 'It is easy to boast of victory over ancient oppression,' says Ellul, 'but what if victory has been gained at the price of even greater subjection to the forces of the artificial necessity of the technical society which has come to dominate our lives?'[8]

I believe it has. And if that society was already dominating people's lives when Ellul was writing, it has fully submerged them now. We have reached the point where, in Ellul's words, 'every human initiative must use technical means to express itself.' Once you understand this, you will see it manifested everywhere you look.

You might see, for example, how farms have been transformed into laboratories of technique, the land sprayed with the recommended concentrations of the latest approved pesticides, or sown with genetically modified crops, or harvested by huge tractors directed by GPS systems whose drivers no longer even have to steer them. You might see how mass schooling systems inculcate our children with the values of technique, from the focus on exam results to the current obsession with promoting 'STEM' subjects at the expense of art, history and literature. Or you might see literature itself rebuilt by technique, as academic theorists take works of art apart in the manner of a mechanic searching for a fault in an engine.

Art, music, medicine, sport, science, child-rearing, education, sex, relationships: any area of life you can conceive of has been remade in the image of technique. At one point in his book Ellul even uses the example of a camping trip: what was once an individual choice to wander into a wild place to sleep is now corralled by technical society into official campsites with numbered pitches and regulated behaviour.

When we look at it this way, we can see one of biggest ructions of our time—the global response to the COVID pandemic—for what it was: a triumph of technique. Whatever your views on virus or vaccine, you should be able to see that the response of authorities worldwide was pure technique, all the way down. Authoritarian control on an unprecedented scale; a narrow focus on an equally narrow set of carefully calculated numbers; official projections guiding societal behaviour; the anointing of a clerisy of official spokespeople intoning 'Follow the Science' like a hushed prayer; collusion between state and media to promote an ever-changing approved narrative and suppress questioning voices, including those of dissenting scientists; the manufacturing of fear to achieve desired ends; and the ultimate focus on a profitable techno-fix above all else.

But then, if Ellul is right, this is the direction in which the reign of technique will ultimately take us: towards the dictatorship of the Machine. Claiming in 1964 that technique had already 'rendered traditional democratic doctrines obsolete', he suggested that the new way of seeing would overcome any democratic objections, and would always tend towards total control. 'Efficiency is a fact', he wrote wryly, 'and justice a slogan'. Technique, through sheer dominance, would accrue power to itself until there could be no rational argument (the only kind of argument now accepted) against controlling the minutiae of our lives for the greater good. Finally, technique would cause 'the state to become totalitarian, to absorb the citizens' lives completely.' This would apply 'even when the state is liberal and democratic . . . despite differences, all such systems come ultimately to the same result.'[9]

By using the word 'totalitarian', Ellul was not suggesting that all nations would become dictatorships, let alone that they would adopt an ideological framework like Nazism or Marxism-Leninism to guide them. In fact, he said, such ideologies interfere with the direction of technique, which seeks efficiency rather than ideology. 'Totalitarian', in this context, simply meant that it would be impossible to escape the Machine and its assumptions. Everywhere you looked, there it would be: staring you in the face, directing your actions, digging into every facet of your life, giving you fewer and fewer escape routes each year.

I don't think it's an exaggeration to say that the times we are currently living in would be regarded by many of our ancestors as apocalyptic. The degree of control and monitoring which we endure in 'developed' societies, which has been accelerating for decades and which has reached warp speed in the 2020s, is creating a kind of digital holding camp in which we all find ourselves trapped. The rising paranoia that extends now across the political spectrum throughout the Western world—the anger and confusion, the sense of promises broken and established systems gumming up—all of this, I think, can be traced to the rise and consolidation of the Machine, this great matrix which strips from us our understanding of what a human life is, and makes us instead lonely cogs in its drive for self-creation.

All of the enclosures, the destruction of alternative lifeways, the early modern revolutions, the fanning of want, the unsettling of peoples, the journeys of the Black Ships, the myth of progress: all of it leads here, to the triumph of technique, to the kingdom of the Machine. All of it funnels us only one way: towards the new techno-Babel we are building. We live today after technique's triumph; the ructions of the present are the manifestations of its victory. In trying to understand these ructions, we tend in the West to resort to binary divisions. Left versus right, local versus global, traditional versus modern, sacred versus profane, good versus evil. At times they have their uses, but none of them will fully serve us in this inquiry. Another binary is rising now; has been for centuries, perhaps, but is now clear in the new light.

'It is easy for me to imagine', wrote Wendell Berry in his extended essay *Life Is a Miracle*, 'that the next great division of the world will be between people who wish to live as creatures and people who wish to live as machines.' Berry wrote those words twenty years ago, and the great division he foresaw is now upon us: Life versus the Machine. The tension between the virtual and the real, the digital and the organic, the constructed and the born, undergirds all the rifts and ruptures that are opening up within our crumbling society. Where will they lead us— and how, today, are they coming to fruition in the world we are already living in?

PART THREE

The Hollowing

———

The modern world shall not be punished.
It is the punishment.

Nicolás Gómez Dávila

XII

Exodus

TWENTY-FIVE YEARS AGO, I FOUND MYSELF sitting around a fire in an Indonesian rainforest. There were people around the fire from a few different countries. Indonesia for one, which in reality is dozens of countries posing as a single nation, and England, and a few others—America, perhaps, and some other European places. It was long enough ago that I don't remember every detail.

But I remember well enough the horrible moment when somebody—the kind of person who brings an acoustic guitar into an Indonesian rainforest—suggested that we should all sing traditional songs from our home countries. I looked around quickly to make sure the guitar wasn't coming in my direction, but I was thankfully spared. One of our hosts from Borneo began singing something beautiful in his language. Then a German picked up the guitar and belted out something lusty and Germanic. Then a couple of others. It was all quite fun.

Then the guitar came round to another English person—one who, unlike me, knew how to play it—and there was a momentary silence, followed by a hushed consultation with a couple of other English people.

What shall I play? It became quickly clear that none of us had a clue what a traditional English song was. Somebody suggested *What shall we do with a drunken sailor?* but we only really knew the chorus.

In the end, the inevitable happened: the Englishman played a Bob Dylan song. Everybody, including the people from Borneo, sang happily along.

When you are old and aspiring to be wise, you understand that things like this get remembered for a reason, because of the story they are telling you. The story this was telling me was clear enough even at the time. It made me slightly angry and embarrassed and confused all at the same time, but most of all it made me feel like I was missing something. Why didn't I know any folk songs from my own country? Why did nobody else from my country know any, either?

I felt the same way once at school, when I saw in a book an illustration of the national costumes of various European nations. There were the Welsh with their lace and the Scots with their kilts and the Dutch with their clogs, and it was all faintly ridiculous, but the most ridiculous of all were the English. Our national costume, according to this picture anyway, was a pinstripe suit, a bowler hat and a rolled-up umbrella. The Welsh made lace, the Dutch grew tulips, the Irish played the fiddle, the French did whatever they did with those strings of onions: hell, at least it was colourful. What did my people do? We *made money.*

That illustration was telling me the same thing as the jungle version of 'Hard Rain', and what it was saying was loud and clear: *you don't have a culture.*

Since then, I seem to have picked away endlessly at this notion of 'culture'. The quest for culture is always a quest for home. Probably humans can never be truly at home on this Earth, but there are degrees of homelessness, I think. The Machine tempts us with its goodies, and some are genuinely good. It gives us—or some of us—access to warmth, food, wealth, longevity. But the price it exacts is enormous. The mass destruction of the natural world is one part of that price. The mass destruction of the cultural world is another.

This price is too high, but we keep paying it. We are confused, or we don't see it, or we don't know what else to do, or maybe we don't much care after all. The Machine is virtually impossible to resist, not least because it is found both around us and within us. As Lewis Mumford explained, the 'myth of the Machine' comes from within the human heart: we carry its drive for planning, efficiency, profit, clarity, straight lines, organisation, domination, within us daily. Human cultures can either trammel or release these desires upon the world. Our culture, such as it is, glorifies them, and sets them loose and running.

What we see around us today is thus the perfect manifestation of the Machine's will to power—the human will to power, only made magnificent, made technological, made autonomous, made terrible. We built the Machine to run the world for us. Now the Machine runs us. Now we are fuel. And where has our home gone?

When you're young you want to run away from home and sit around an Indonesian campfire with people from many nations and sing. But you find that home has followed you and that you don't know what it quite is, or why that bothers you so much. As you get older, you realise both why home matters and how fragile and elusive it is. Then you find you are living in a world whose forces have set out to destroy your sense of home wherever it can be found. You understand that you are living in a time which has trained its guns on both hearth and heart. You find that the men with the pinstripe suits and the rolled-up umbrellas have been selling your home at markup for hundreds and hundreds of years, and here you are. The numbers all add up. This is called 'Progress'.

I BEGAN THIS BOOK BY EXPLORING the human need for roots—which is another way of framing the need for home—and how the Machine has uprooted us from both nature and culture. These are two very capacious words. The fact that we use them to point at so many things suggests how much they matter, but like most things that matter—love, consciousness, God—there is no agreed-upon definition of either term. The fact that we can't agree on what 'culture' is, for example, is at the root of our so-called culture war. As ever in human history, we are fighting over the ownership of stories, and of meaning.

Part two of this book explored how this Machine evolved, what sources it sprang from, and what its essence is. In part three, I want to dig into the world it has created for us. I want to look at how the 'culture war' is panning out, and what might really be at the root of it. I want to explore the aspects of our life which the Machine is eroding, and what they are being replaced with; to examine how the Machine manifests in the culture, society and politics of the age.

The age, I think, is unique. It might be that everyone thinks this about their time, but I think that today we have a good case. The sheer scale of global culture, the degree of technological interconnectedness, the dangers of those technologies, from AI to nuclear missiles, the human impact on the natural world and the rapid falling-away of many things that have buoyed and sustained us for centuries, from languages to religions, means that the times we live in are perhaps less rooted than any time in history. We may be in the process of creating something unique in human history: a global anticulture, unmoored from reality and increasingly at war with it.

This anticulture is not limited to any particular political or cultural tradition: though it arose in the West, from peculiarities of Western culture and history, it has since become universal. It is an 'anticulture' because the elements of human life from which cultures of all kinds, however different, have traditionally sprung are negated by today's way of life. The values of the Machine are an attack on the values upon which pre-modern, traditional societies were built. The new values are predicated on the pursuit of *liberation*: a one-word descriptor of the essence of the Western programme since 1789. Our aim, stated or unstated, is to liberate ourselves from nature in all regards, so that we may conquer the stars, conquer death, and become as gods, knowing good and evil.

Philosopher Patrick Deneen, in his 2018 book *Why Liberalism Failed*, presents this modern drive towards liberation as an ideological project, suggesting that 'liberalism' is one of three ideologies which have dominated the world over the last three centuries. The other two—communism and fascism—were shorter-lived, he suggests, and died in the West in the twentieth century. Liberalism—the elder brother—is finally dying now. One reason for its longer life is that it piggybacked on an older story, presenting itself as the inheritor of older traditions of 'liberty', when in fact it was something quite different. While liberty is 'the condition of self-governance, whether achieved by the individual or a political community', liberalism 're-conceives liberty as the opposite of this older conception. It is understood to be the greatest possible freedom from external constraints, including customary norms.'[1]

'Freedom from external constraints' is a good description of the central drive of the Machine's anticulture. This pursuit, claims Deneen, seeks freedom *for* the individual *from* society itself, and it is built upon a radical notion of human nature. Rather than seeing humans as hefted creatures, rooted, Weil-like in time and place, this new lens offers a new vision: detached, sovereign personhood. Humans are now, in Deneen's words, 'rights-bearing individuals who could fashion and pursue for themselves their own version of the good life.'

In this new world, the sovereign human person, dis-embedded from community, history and nature, will utilise reason, informed by science and enabled by technology, to choose how to live. The rational individual, making choices in a marketplace overseen by a government committed to 'liberty' and guarding individual 'rights' through a 'social contract': this was the basis of a wholly new world. The commitment to this post-Enlightenment liberal order is not a partisan one. The factions we refer to today as 'left' and 'right' are simply two different flavours of the same liberal food.

What is crucial to understand here—and this is what makes liberalism an ideology—is that in order for the new, 'liberated' world to come into being, it needed to be *created*. Just as Marxist regimes attempted to destroy the family, the Church and private land ownership so that communism could materialise, so liberalism did not naturally 'evolve' from previously existing arrangements. It needed to artificially create the 'sovereign individual' from new cloth. The individual 'as a disembodied, self-interested economic actor', claims Deneen, 'didn't exist in any actual state of nature but rather was the creation of an elaborate intervention by the incipient state in early modernity, at the beginnings of the liberal order.'

This echoes Chesterton's argument that capitalism—a system referred to as 'liberal economics' for good reason—did not 'evolve' either, but also had to be created by force. Liberalism, suggests Deneen, grew in the same desert. And the biggest obstacle to the growth of both—then as now—was real culture. Culture 'was the greatest threat to the creation of the liberal individual', writes Deneen.[2] Rooted trees are hard to fell. The Machine anticulture which is felling them one by one 'is at once a crowning achievement of liberalism and among the greatest threats to our continued common life.'

There has always been a certain pathos, and a kind of nobility, to the modern human attempt at breaking the bounds and soaring to the stars. It is the pursuit of cosmopolis: a utopian desire to replace religious and ethnic conflict with universal peace and love. It strives, at its best, for equality and brotherhood, rather than prejudice and conflict. The problem emerges when the ideals are divorced from the reality of what humans are, and what the world is made of. Liberatory ambition, in the abstract, can never be sated. Like a dictator marching on Moscow, the Machine doesn't know when to stop, and now we can see where this project of globalised liberation is leading us: into the world of the *nihil*, into the empire of technique.

As a result, human culture is in the process of being consumed by the Machine. Something organic is being superseded by something planned; something natural by something technological. This is the anticulture of the Machine, and it supersedes and replaces the values on which older societies the world over are based. At the risk of gross generalisation, I think we can boil those older values down into a simple formula. I call it the Four Ps:

1. **Past.** Where a culture comes from, its history and ancestry.

2. **People.** Who a culture is. A sense of being 'a people'.

3. **Place.** Where a culture is. Nature in its local and particular manifestation.

4. **Prayer.** Where a culture is going. Its religious tradition, which relates it to God or the gods.

Maybe cultures can survive, and even thrive, without one or more of these elements. In fact, some measurably do: nomadic cultures, for example, do not have a permanent link to a particular place, but are not necessarily less culturally or spiritually rich for it. Still, if you remove more than one element from this list, your chance of sustaining a cultural story in place and through time is slim.

Looking again at my home country, England, in the light of this theory of culture, seems instructive. England, like much of the West, currently seems to be in a kind of freeform cultural collapse. Why? Well, if the Four Ps have anything going for them, the explanations are clear enough. The English long ago gave up on the religion that formed their nation and their values—Christianity. They are one of the most urbanised nations on Earth, and the one which urbanised earliest. Our memory of the land, and our understanding of it, is almost entirely dead. We are an urban people. And we have largely forgotten our history, or had it taken away from us, depending on your point of view.

For this reason, we have no meaningful folk culture. Folk culture comes from a folk—a people rooted in time and place, with dirty hands and a particular perspective. The English are no longer this, and have perhaps not been for centuries. Finally, the redoubts of high culture have fallen, since at least the 1960s, to a post-modern faction which believes that the very notion of 'high culture' is elitist, bigoted folly, and that nations are too. England's cultural elite today, fired by a long-standing oikophobia, are far more likely to be found cheering on the toppling of statues than thinking about what to replace them with. When an elite regards its people with thinly veiled contempt, and when it sneers at its own ancestors, the culture it claims to speak for and guard is not long for this world.

This same energy seems to be displayed to different degrees throughout the nations of the West today, and has elicited a growing reaction from those who object to it. But it is nonetheless the dominant understanding, pushed from above by those in power. We have forgotten who we are, or we don't like who we are, or somehow both. We don't know where to turn; we certainly won't turn in the direction of the cathedral in the market square, which is why we are now incapable of building anything like it. All we can manage is identical glass skyscrapers, again and again and again.

If this is true, we are in a situation in which the Machine has advanced to such a degree that the very possibility of living cultures in 'advanced' countries (i.e. the countries most under its sway) is impossible. The direction of modernity is away from land and towards megacities, away from both folk and high culture and into mass online anticulture, and away from any manifestation of God and towards the rule of Mammon. The Machine is the liberal anticulture made manifest. In the new civilisation it is building, culture will be made not by that magical, strange, impossible and miraculous combination of human bodies, wild nature and the soul, but by the Algorithm and the AI.

The anticulture of the Machine brings with it its own values. They supersede the values of the pre-technological age, and they spring from the need and the drive of the Machine itself. We could call them the Four Ss:

1. **Science.** Where we come from. Science can offer us a non-mythic version of this story, and assert a claim as to the true (i.e. measurable) nature of reality.

2. **The Self.** Who we are. The highest good is to serve the self and ensure its longevity.

3. **Sex.** What we do. Both the highest means of sacral pleasure and, through public expressions of 'sexuality', an affirmation of individual identity.

4. **The Screen.** Where we are going. The screen is both our main source of distraction from reality and the interface by which we are directed into the coming post-human reality of the Machine.

If the Machine has an ideology, I suggest that these four notions are a fair summary of it. Perhaps, though, it is less an ideology than a theology. In the Machine age, ideology effectively functions as a replacement for and simulacrum of religion. Liberalism, socialism, communism, fascism, nationalism: all of these post-Enlightenment forms could be said to be the result of what the historian John Bossy has called 'the migration of the holy' from Church to state. All strip away the transcendent Other from our understanding of the world and replace it with a purely human perspective. Salvation, in the modern era, comes not through eucharist, pilgrimage or prayer, but through government action, technological progress or capitalist 'wealth creation'. Ideology promises us a material world remade for the better; unfortunately, as the twentieth century demonstrated, it ends up drowning it in tyranny as often, if not more often, than religion ever did.

The Four Ss, then, offer a kind of catechism for the Machine age. We remain, I think, despite our ostensible belief in 'science and reason', fundamentally religious people in a religious time. We will always seek some greater meaning, some transcendent truth, and if we can't or won't find the real thing we will attempt to create it. This attempt is the story of modernity; the Machine is what we have created to fulfill it. When we forget the proper direction in which to aim our prayers, we will end up aiming them at the ultimate idol: our own image, reflected back at us in our little black screens. We will be kings and queens of a deceptively free world, parading through a liturgy of the self, wondering why the chaos seems to persist so close beneath the surface of this world.

XIII

Kill All the Heroes

O NE OF THE DARK LITTLE SECRETS of my past is my teenage member-ship of the English Civil War Society. I was about sixteen at the time. I joined with a friend who was as much of a history nerd as me, and we spent weekends dressed in seventeenth-century costumes and oversized helmets, lined up in fields or on medieval streets, re-enacting battles from the 1640s. It was great fun. I still have my old breeches in the loft, and the pewter tankard I would drink beer from afterwards with a load of large bearded men who, just for a day or two, had allowed themselves to be transported back in time.

I was a pikeman in John Bright's Regiment of Foote, a genuine regi-ment in the parliamentary army. We were a Leveller regiment, which is to say that this part of the army was politically radical. The English Civil War of the 1640s exposed many pre-existing fissures in society to the light, and one of them was the age-old tension between the landown-ing classes and the poor. The parliamentary army, led by Cromwell and Fairfax, a gentleman and a Lord respectively, may have opposed the King, but they were far from being revolutionaries. For the Levellers, though, the end of the monarchy was to be just the beginning. They aimed to 'sett all things straight, and rayse a parity and community in the kingdom.'[1] Among their varied demands were universal suffrage, religious freedom and something approaching modern parliamentary democracy.

The Levellers were far from alone in their ambitions to remake the former Kingdom. Ranters, Seekers, Diggers, Fifth Monarchists, Quakers, Muggletonians: suddenly the country was blooming with radical sects offering idealistic visions of utopian Christian brotherhood. In his classic study of the English Revolution *The World Turned Upside Down*, historian Christopher Hill quotes Lawrence Clarkson, leader of the Ranters, who offered a radical interpretation of the Christian gospel which horrified the clergy, landowners and Lords. There was no afterlife, said Clarkson; only the present mattered, and in the present all people should be equal, as they were in the eyes of God:

> Nothing is evil that does not harm our fellow men—as many of the existing institutions of society do, and as the repressive humbug and hypocrisy of the self-styled godly certainly do. 'Swearing i'th light, gloriously', and 'wanton kisses', may help to liberate us from the repressive ethic which our masters are trying to impose on us—a regime in which property is more important than life, marriage than love, faith in a wicked God than the charity which the Christ in us teaches.[2]

Modernise Clarkson's language and he could have been speaking in the 1960s rather than the 1640s. Needless to say, his vision of free love and free religion, like the Leveller vision of universal equality, was neither shared nor enacted by those at the apex of the social pyramid. But though Cromwell's Protectorate, and later the restored monarchy, attempted to maintain the social order, forces had been unleashed which would change England and the wider world entirely. The likes of Lawrence Clarkson, or the leader of the proto-communist Digger movement, Gerard Winstanley, may have been men out of time, but they could sense that these forces, once set free, could not be contained. The world had been 'turned upside down', and would never return to its former shape. Some celebrated this fact, others feared it, but in their hearts everyone could sense the truth that Winstanley was prepared to openly declare:

'The old world . . . is running up like parchment in the fire.'[3]

NEARLY FOUR CENTURIES ON, ENGLAND AND the wider West are again being turned upside down. Again we are living in the aftermath of a system that is dying or dead: then, the last gasp of medieval feudalism; now, the Anglo-American Empire—and perhaps modernity itself. Again we are living in a period of radical technological change: then, the printing press and the end of censorship, which allowed the distribution of radical pamphlets on an unprecedented scale; now, the internet's enabling of global dissent, and the rise of the accompanying AI-cyborg culture. Again we are living in a period in which the cultural mores of previous centuries are being upended: then, feudal assumptions governing everything from landownership to the meaning of marriage; now, the meaning of culture, politics and even human biology.

Much of the chaos around us at the moment only makes sense once we understand that we are living through a period of massive global upheaval coupled with regional decline. The West has dominated and shaped the globe for centuries, but now, like all empires before it, it is crumbling into decadence and disintegration. As in the 1640s, this political, economic and demographic decline is precipitating what feels to some like a cultural collapse and to others like a period of revolutionary promise. As in the 1640s, the energies being unleashed by the falling structures of the old world cannot be controlled or directed by any of the parties involved. If the failure of Progress has taught us anything, it should be that we were never really in control.

I find it useful, in trying to parse the madness of the 'culture war', to see the time we are living in as what we might call a 'culture of inversion'. The West's ongoing decline has caused its elites to lose faith in their cultural inheritance (or is it the other way around?), and this loss of faith has now reached pathological proportions. As a result, the leading lights in Western society—the cultural elites, and sometimes the political and economic elites too—are dedicated not to upholding the cultural forms they inherited, but to turning them on their heads, or even erasing them entirely.

In the fifty years I have spent on Earth, most of it in post-imperial Britain, that loss of faith has manifested everywhere. If you want to 'get on' in Britain—which means to win the approval of the upper-middle-class elite which runs the show—it has long been an unspoken rule that you cannot be seen to commit yourself to any of the pillars of the old orthodoxy which two World Wars fatally wounded and the sixties counter-culture decisively finished off. Patriotism, Christianity, cultural conservatism, sexual modesty, even a mild nostalgia for the English countryside or a love of once-canonical novels: all are more or less *verboten,* and the attitude towards them is rapidly hardening. Until recently simply giggled at or patronised, these kinds of views in the 2020s may see you labelled a 'white supremacist', or the more general but still-lethal 'hater'. The old world is again running up like parchment in the fire, and nobody who wants to be part of the new one can be seen to defend it. We define ourselves now by what we are not. And what we are not is everything we used to be.

The culture of inversion is the product of a politico-cultural movement with which we have all become grindingly familiar over the last few years. Whatever terminology we use to describe it, the new code is a product of the post-modern and post-working-class left, spawned in

American university departments over the last half century and exported across the Atlantic to Europe in the last couple of decades. In the hollowed-out anticulture created by the liberalism we explored in the last chapter, it has put down wide and deep roots amongst cynical or exhausted elites and the lost, confused and very-online young. But this new worldview is—for now at least—almost entirely negative. Ask yourself, *What do these people want?* and it's hard to come up with a positive answer. It's easy, though, to explain what they *don't* want. What they don't want is everything their culture used to be.

The culture of inversion has come about not because new things are loved, but because old things are despised—or simply seen as irrelevant. Why, for example, will the new cultural dispensation make excuses for public protest when it is carried out by students protesting about racial injustice or climate change, but condemn it when it comes from truck drivers protesting against vaccine mandates? It's not because any actual racial justice will be forthcoming, nor because those in power have any intention of reining in their carbon emissions. It's because the 'white working class' are yesterday's news: everything we used to be and are now ashamed of. Bigots, racists, Trump-n-Brexit voters, deplorables, gammon. 'Diversity', on the other hand, is the future—just as long as it doesn't upset the economic apple cart or come anywhere near the neighbourhood we actually live in.

Like many people, I spent a long time after the 2016 populist upheavals and the consequent counter-reaction trying to understand what was going on. I had had plenty of hints of it in my previous work, much of which had dug into the growing class and social chasms caused by globalisation. But it was only when I came to see it through the lens of the culture of inversion that the swirling chaos around me started to make sense.

I understood then why our new elites would loudly condemn Christianity for its patriarchy, hierarchy and oppression whilst simultaneously singing the praises of Islam, a far more traditionalist and often oppressive faith. It wasn't that they cared for Islam: it was that Christianity was the founding faith of the West, and must thus be demolished. I understood why the new *Star Wars* films had to first humiliate and then kill off their white male hero, Luke Skywalker, and replace him with a young woman. I understood why the aspiring Prime Minister would publicly declare that the next actor to play James Bond—toxic masculine archetype of the British imperial state—should be female,[4] and why every cultural commentator in Britain also insisted that the next Bond should be black. I understood why a (white male) BBC editor would stand before an audience of mostly similarly pale-skinned people and explain that nobody wants to hear white men explaining things anymore.[5]

I understood why people would topple statues of long-dead slave traders whilst filming the whole thing on smartphones made by actual, living slaves. I understood decolonising the curriculum and cisheteronormativity and stale pale males and diversity training, and I understood all of it not as a desire for actual meaningful change, let alone as any kind of thought-through pathway to a better world. Instead, I saw a great weave of symbolic meaning. I saw all of it as a rolling statement by those who controlled the levers of power in the post-Western West, a statement that said: *We are the opposite of what we once were. We reject our ancestors and our history. We condemn our past and its legacy. We have redrawn our cosmic map. We are now something entirely new—even if, as of this moment, we have no idea what.*

The deflating West is becoming a place of almost pure negation. After decades of cultural inversion, we have forgotten how to do anything but deconstruct, there is nothing left to overturn, and we have come to define ourselves by what we are not. Black is Not-White. Female is Not-Male. Gay is Not-Straight, and Trans is Not-Gay. Muslim is Not-Christian. Weak is Not-Strong. Welcome to the Not-West. Make sure you scan your QR code on the way in, or you're liable to have your bank account frozen.

'Devil is God', declared Clarkson in 1640, 'Hell is Heaven, Sin Holiness, Damnation Salvation, this and only this in the First Resurrection.'

THE POET AND STORYTELLER ROBERT BLY, who died in 2021, had a name for the culture we now inhabit, in the West and increasingly in much of the rest of the world too. He called it a 'sibling society'. In his book of the same name, published a quarter of a century ago, Bly took a prescient scalpel to the failures of Western modernity and identified what he believed to be a foundational problem: we had forgotten how to produce adults.

Back in 1996, Bly could already see around him the problems which have since blossomed into a full-flowering pathology. America and the world influenced by it, he wrote, was 'navigating from a paternal society, now discredited, to a society in which impulse is given its way.' From the patriarchal frying pan, the West had jumped into the post-modern fire. Today, 'people don't bother to grow up, and we are all fish swimming in a tank of half-adults. The rule is: Where repression was before, fantasy will now be.' Adults, rather than maturing towards wisdom, 'regress toward adolescence; and adolescents—seeing that—have no desire to become adults. Few are able to imagine any genuine life coming from the vertical plane—tradition, religion, devotion.'[6]

Bly believed that the old 'vertical society' of the West had been discredited by the upheavals of the twentieth century. This discrediting was both inevitable and at least partly necessary, but as in the 1640s, the collapse of the old order had unleashed an uncontrollable destructive energy, manifesting in a cultural revolution against all things 'vertical'. War had been declared on all aspects of 'the Indo-European, Islamic, Hebraic impulse-control system,'[7] whose genuine faults had become associated with all and any impulse control, hierarchy, order or structure.

A kind of corrupted cultural Levelling had taken hold, and the result was our culture of inversion, in which rebellion against all and any forms was seen as the only inherent good. And in the desert created by late twentieth-century American capitalism, which had decimated communities and households, stripped the meaning from the lives of young generations and replaced it with shopping, little seemed worth preserving anyway. As a result, adults had remained perpetual adolescents: uninitiated, afraid to grow up, slouching towards Bethlehem quoting Marlon Brando in a kind of eternal 1954. *'Hey, Johnny, what are you rebelling against?' 'Whaddya got?'*

Bly was fundamentally a worker in myth, and *The Sibling Society,* like his earlier book about men, *Iron John,* shifts between his retelling of classic fairy tales and his analysis of their application to contemporary culture. He believed that the fundamental problems of his time were not political or economic, but mythic. They manifested at the level of deep story, on which all cultures are built. The modern West, without knowing it, had taken an axe to the root of its own mythic structures, as Jack takes an axe to the root of the beanstalk. The Giant in that story, retold by Bly here, represents Freud's 'death instinct', which had taken hold of American culture. The Giant is a killer of fathers, destroyer of families, eater of children. He lives in a castle surrounded by rocky, barren lands, and he has ravaged every living structure around him. He has no family, no past and no future. In his castle, he gathers his wealth to him, and eats and eats and eats.

It is the Giant—resentful, angry, greedy, marooned in a permanent present—who best represents what we have become, nearly three decades after Bly's book was published. The culture of inversion is the Giant's creation, and ours. Adolescent and surly, we can find little good in the past and little hope in the future. Then as now, the governing attitude to our own cultural inheritance is what Bly called 'a sort of generalized ingratitude.' This has meant that the culture has been damaged 'not only by acquisitive capitalism, but also by an idiotic distrust of all ideas, religions and literature handed down to us by elders and ancestors.' Many of the people he called 'siblings' have as a result become 'convinced that they have received nothing of value from anyone. The older truth is that every man and woman is indebted to all other persons, living or dead, and is indebted as well to animals, plants and the gods'.[8]

But the most striking argument that Bly makes as he analyses our cultural collapse is that Western culture was now doing to itself what it had long done to others: colonisation. The methods that Western colonial administrators had used to demolish and replace other cultures—rewriting their histories, replacing their languages, challenging their cultural norms, banning or demonising their religions, dismantling their elder system and undermining their cultural traditions—were now being used against us. Only we had not been invaded by hostile outside forces: this time, the hostile forces had emerged from within. No conservative, Bly could nonetheless see that the culture of inversion, already in full swing in the 1990s, was a product of the elite left, who had 'taken over the role of colonial administrators', and set about colonising their own culture from within:

> They teach that European kings were major criminals who dressed well, that feudalism in the Middle Ages was a transparent failure, that the Renaissance amounted to a triumph of false consciousness, that the Magna Carta solved nothing, that the English Royalists were decadent hedonists, that the Puritan governments were brutal, that Mother Theresa was probably sexually disturbed, that the New England town meetings were masks for oppression . . . that Beethoven wrote imperialist music, that Mencken was a secret fasc-

ist, that Roosevelt encouraged Pearl Harbour, that President Kennedy's Peace Corps did not work, that Freud supported child abuse, and that almost every one of his ideas was wrong.[9]

America, said Bly, was 'the first culture in history that has colonised itself'.[10] Twenty-five years on, America's fate is also the fate of the wider West. Our internal colonisers have been ruthlessly effective in the intervening decades, and the 'culture war' is a product of their success. 'If colonialist administrators begin by attacking the vertical thought of the tribe they have conquered, and dismantling the elder system', he wrote, 'they end by dismantling everything in sight. That's where we are.' Or to put it another way: the word 'decolonisation' has two redundant letters in it.

Around the same time that Robert Bly was writing *The Sibling Society*, another American thinker, Christopher Lasch, was also predicting a future of elite colonisation. In *The Revolt of the Elites*, Lasch forecast the future accurately. 'The culture wars that have convulsed America since the sixties', he wrote, 'are best understood as a form of class warfare, in which an enlightened elite (as it thinks of itself) seeks not so much to impose its values on the majority (a majority perceived as incorrigibly racist, sexist, provincial and xenophobic), much less to persuade the majority by means of rational public debate, as to create parallel or "alternative" institutions in which it will no longer be necessary to confront the unenlightened at all.'[11]

Lasch's book, as the title suggests, proposed that while the twentieth century might have been the era of mass revolt, the twenty-first was shaping up to be the opposite: empowered by globalisation, alienated from their own cultures, more connected to international metropolitan centres than to their own hinterlands, the new elites of America and Europe were rebelling against the *Lumpenproletariat* of their own nations. Lasch, again presciently, predicted that the elite culture warriors would face a populist backlash, and that, obsessed with the patterns of the past, they would fail to understand what was happening. Rather than seeing how far they had detached themselves from the mass of their own people—so much so that, in his own country, they had 'ceased to think of themselves as Americans in any important sense'—the elites would 'prefer to exchange accusations of fascism and socialism' with each other, despite the fact that both ideologies were long dead.[12]

This, in turn, would allow an insulated intra-elite 'culture war' to obscure the reality of growing social division and decline driven by elite experiments in social engineering. 'It is not just that the masses have lost interest in revolution', claimed Lasch. 'Their political instincts are demonstrably more conservative than those of their self-appointed spokesmen and would-be liberators. It is the working and lower middle classes, after all, that favor limits on abortion, cling to the two-parent family as a source of stability in a turbulent world, resist experiments with "alternative lifestyles," and harbor deep reservations about affirmative action and other experiments in large-scale social engineering.'[13]

In this short paragraph, Lasch predicted the rise of twenty-first century Western populism long before it happened. But he also went on to diagnose its drivers. The often dismissed masses, he wrote, 'have a more developed sense of limits than their betters. They understand, as their betters do not, that there are inherent limits on human control over course of social development, over nature and the body, over the tragic elements in human life and history.'[14] Take this now-familiar attitude, add two decades of economic stagnation, social fragmentation, technological acceleration, populist rebellion and elite counter-revolution. Add a pinch of social media—and stand well back. *Boom!* Welcome to the 2020s.

The Inverted West, in Lasch's time and even more so in ours, was and is dominated by the kind of people whom the working-class philosopher Eric Hoffer, decades before, had called 'adversary intellectuals': highly educated people who had built a career on sneering at their own cultural heritage, and looking down on the people who still valued it. In a Western democracy, said Hoffer, 'the adversary intellectual is not only against his country and against the middle class into which he was born, but he sides with the colored races against the white, with animals against man, and with the wilderness against the sown.' But this attitude was not, as was so often assumed, inspired by guilt and shame. In fact, it was the precise opposite:

> Is this hatred of one's own a variant of self-hatred? Hardly so. One who hates what most people love probably savors his uniqueness. He believes that secession from his country, class, race and species bespeaks righteousness and partakes of the heroic. But above all he has an almost insane vanity. The adversary intellectual feels superior to the people who govern his country, but he will not run for office. He will not demean himself to beg the votes of stupid people. He lusts instead for an apocalyptic denouement that will topple the power structure and give him his chance.
>
> The adversary intellectual cannot actually wreck a society, and he cannot seize power. But by discrediting and besmirching a society he undermines the faith of its potential defenders.[15]

A few decades on from Bly, Lasch and Hoffer, our cultural elite's ongoing 'deconstruction' of all we once were has deteriorated into a kind of incoherent rage, a culture of inversion on steroids which has now elicited its own rising counter-revolution. Nobody knows where any of this will lead, but the primary emotion it is all channelling is rage. In our perpetual sibling society—sick with consumerism, eye-glazed with screen burn, confused, rudderless, Godless—we have forgotten how to behave like adults, or what adults even look like. The result is that we squabble like children, fighting over toys in the mud.

'The inner dome of heaven has fallen', wrote Bly. 'To say we have no center that we love is the same thing as saying that we have colonized ourselves. What we need to study, then, is how a colonized culture heals itself.'[16]

How does it heal itself? Bly, mythologist and poet, had an answer: through story and ritual. The work of the age of inversion and anticulture, which is the culture of the Machine, is not to fight puny online battles, or to look for victory in some imagined political settlement or brilliant new ideology. Our wounds are much deeper than that. Our stories are cracked at their foundations, and as a consequence we are afloat in a fantastical world of our own making: grasping at freedom, entirely enslaved.

The antidote to this is to dig down to those foundations and begin the work of repair. We are going to have to learn to be adults again; to get our feet back on the ground, to rebuild families and communities, to learn again the meaning of worship and commitment, of limits and longing. We are, in short, going to have to grow up. This is long, hard work: intergenerational work. It is myth work. We don't really want to begin, and we don't really know how to. Does any child want to grow up? But there is nothing else for it; no other path is going to get us home.

In times of conflict, whether our weapons are pikes or words, the temptation is always towards total war. But war is the Giant's work, and like the Giant it will consume us all if it can. 'The inexhaustible energies of the cosmos', wrote Robert Bly, 'cannot be called down by anger. They are called by extremely elaborate practice—and stories.'[17]

XIV

Down the River

SOMETIMES, THE WORLD SEEMS TO SHIFT beneath you and you're not quite sure what has happened, or why. As I get older, I belatedly understand that this is probably just a result of living long enough to see the times changing. The world of the Machine, which thrives on change like a horse on hay, will ensure that everyone who lives long enough ends up in a world they barely recognise. Still, there are some curious inversions along the way, and one that I have thought a lot about recently is what has happened to the political alignments I grew up with.

Back in the 1990s and early 2000s, when I was a young and eager anti-Machine activist who wanted to change the world and usher in whatever better thing was coming next, all the action was on the anti-globalisation left. A colourful, wild and energetic activist movement was taking aim at the newly minted 'globalisation' project, which US president George Bush had declared would be the 'new world order' after the end of the Cold War. As American-led global trade deals busted open markets and cultures and rainforests and oceans for the benefit of the universal idol of The Market, we gathered in our tens of thousands outside the summit gatherings of the G8 and the WTO to try and shut it all down. Globalisation, we all believed, was an attempt to empower multinational corporations at the expense of nature, workers and democratic sovereignty. My first book, published in 2003,[1] was a global travelogue, full of excitable reportage from four continents about the worldwide 'mass movement' that was rising against it. I was sure we were on the winning side. We just needed enough bodies to break through the barricades.

A lot has changed in the ensuing two decades, and not just my own views on the efficacy of 'mass movements'. In fact, a dramatic polar shift has taken place in the identity of the opponents of the globalisation project. Back then, what seemed to be coalescing was a kind of post-Marxist anti-capitalism. It was a political melting pot of anarchism, localism, indigenous perspectives, radical environmentalism, liberal commitments to democracy and various other strands, all of it uncoordinated and fervently anti-hierarchical. It was a mess, but it was an exciting mess. There was an optimistic energy about it. And though a lot of people involved, including me, were allergic to labels and boxes, there was no doubt that this was a movement of the left. You wouldn't see any conservatives on the barricades at the anti-WTO protests. Most of them were either inside hymning the virtues of 'free' trade, or over in Washington or London ginning up the next Middle East war.

How times have changed. In the 2020s, the most incisive opponents of corporate globalisation can usually be found on the right; or at least, not from any identifiable sector of the left. The current US president rode to power on a nationalist rejection of that 'new world order' hymned by his 1990s predecessor. Conservative, traditionalist and 'post-liberal' critiques of the impact of globalisation on local communities, nation-states, social cohesion, family formation, working class prospects, culture and even (though not often enough) the natural world are pouring out daily. The post-working class left, meanwhile, has veered into an identity politics cul-de-sac, dictated largely by its commitment to the culture of inversion that I explored in the last chapter. And because this 'progressive' left, which dominates the elite strata of Western countries, is drawn from the beneficiary class of globalisation, it is overwhelmingly supportive of the process.

The left anti-globalism that I once thought was the movement of the future is today barely in evidence anywhere. When it does rear its head, its proponents stand a good chance of being labelled 'red-brown' crypto-fascists by an online mob of supposed radicals which cheers on 'hate speech' laws, internet censorship, the freezing of protestors' bank accounts, and the demonisation of the problematic working classes of their own nation.

Since at least the end of World War Two the declared aim of the Western powers, led by the USA, has been the spread of that global market economy, combined with a liberal politics and culture, to every benighted corner of the Earth. Since a globalised market cannot function without globalised tastes, and since liberalism also needs an appropriate soil to seed in, the momentum of this ideological crusade has been towards the creation of one global culture, whether the world wanted it or not. This threefold rollout—global economy, global culture and global political system, all of them based on the American model—is usually referred to using the bland term 'globalisation'. In reality, it is a form of colonialism—the latest iteration of the Western empires—and a hugely successful one.

Back when I was a young activist, the left of the spectrum was where you went if you stood against this. Though wrong about plenty of things, the left has traditionally been correct about the negative impacts of capitalism, while the right has floundered about denying its impacts on the poor, on democracy and on nature, generally valourising greed and rapine and then wondering where the 'traditional values' they love so much have gone to. It's only in recent years that conservative thinkers in any numbers have begun to explore the territory where Wendell Berry planted his flag half a century ago and Chesterton half a century before that.

Over the last decade though, the political binary I grew up with has, like so much else, been inverted. The worldview that the academic Eric Kaufman has called left modernism[2] is now the outlook of the so-called 'professional managerial class', the top 10 percent or so of society, and the beneficiary class of globalisation. Via transnational corporations, the academic and cultural sectors, NGOs, global and regional bodies and other collectives of usually unaccountable power, this class is rolling out the threefold ideology of globalism within their own nations and beyond. Meanwhile, a loose and ill-defined 'national populist' movement built largely around a working- and lower-middle-class reaction to this ideology is coalescing around calls for national self-determination, some degree of cultural conservatism and a desire for economic protection.

On the face of it, this is confusing. Why would transnational capital be parroting slogans drawn from a leftist framework which claims to be anti-capitalist? Why would the middle classes be further to the 'left' than the workers? If the left was what it claims to be—a bottom-up movement for popular justice—this would not be the case. If capitalism was what it is assumed to be—a rapacious, non-ideological engine of profit maximisation—then this would not be the case either.

But what if both of them were something else? What if the ideology of the corporate world and the ideology of the 'progressive' left had not forged an inexplicable marriage of convenience, but had grown all along from the same rootstock? What if the left and global capitalism are, at base, the same thing: engines for destroying customary ways of living and replacing them with the new world of the Machine?

The very notion of a political 'left' was birthed with modernity: the term comes from the seating arrangement of the anti-monarchy faction of the French assembly after the revolution. As we have already seen, that revolution was a product of social elites who were engaged in a project of utopian social engineering, often against the will of the peasantry they claimed to speak for. Despite much self-mythologising in the ensuing centuries, and despite occasional and sporadic popular support, leftist ideology has remained primarily a product of urban intellectuals and middle-class radicals pursuing a project of theoretical levelling. Chinese American writer Habi Zhang, who escaped the legacy of the cultural revolution in China only to see something similar playing out in the US, explained in a recent essay how Mao's notorious war on the past had ripped apart the fabric of Chinese society from the top down:

> To purge the upper echelons of power, Mao set a group of screaming, self-righteous Red Guards in clamorous motion. In the name of overthrowing the Four Olds (Old Ideas, Old Culture, Old Habits, and Old Customs), belligerent Red Guards demanded to assign new names to historical sites, destroyed statues and temples, burned books, and publicly reviled teachers and intellectuals. Once given license to denounce all authority, those young, radical students, some of them no older than fourteen, were emboldened to torture and kill the innocent.[3]

This may be sounding familiar. We should hope, suggested Zhang, that it doesn't end up sounding too familiar. For a decade, 'the Chinese Cultural Revolution thoroughly wrecked the economy, uprooted traditions, destroyed social trust by turning family members on each other, and worst of all, killed well more than a million people. One can only wonder how far its American replication will go'.

The left's levelling project always begins with the destruction of previous lifeways—Mao's Four Olds, the Bolshevik project to eliminate the 'bourgeois family', French revolutionary attempts to rationalise the landscape, the current progressive push to 'transition' children—but what it ends up doing, with a delicious irony, is creating the desert in which Chesterton's monster can grow fat. Oswald Spengler was not the only one to notice that revolution, far from creating equality and justice in the human realm, instead cleared the ground for the rise of the Machine. 'There is no proletarian, not even a Communist, movement', he wrote, 'that has not operated in the interest of money, in the directions indicated by money and for the time permitted by money—and without the idealist amongst its leaders having the slightest suspicion of the fact.'[4]

Looked at this way, it's not hard to see that progressive leftism and the Machine, far from being antagonistic, are a usefully snug fit. Both are totalising, utopian projects. Both are suspicious of the past, impatient with borders and boundaries, and hostile to religion, 'superstition' and the limits on the human individual imposed by nature or culture. Both are in pursuit of a global utopia where, in the dreams of both Lenin and Lennon, the world will live as one.

Above all, both coalesce around the foundational modern notion of the blank slate, which, in Rousseau's famous formulation, tells us that 'man is born free and he is everywhere in chains.' Rousseau is perhaps one of our key guiding spirits today. His primitivist worldview has a clean, Edenic note about it which can speak across the spectrum to those who feel hemmed in by the rising Machine dystopia. Who doesn't want to lose their chains? Who doesn't want to be free?

The question that quickly arises, of course, is 'Free from what?' A key term, found everywhere in current leftist discourse, is 'emancipatory'. To be 'progressive' is to emancipate. What is it that is to be emancipated? The answer is: the individual self. What is this self to be emancipated from? All societal structures. And what is the best instrument for achieving this emancipation? Uncomfortably for both Rousseauian primitivists and old-school leftists, who have seen large-scale experiments in socialist economics go up in flames time and time again, the answer appears to be: global capitalism. No other system in history has ever been as effective in breaking the chains of time, place and culture as the global empire of corporate power.

If the past forty years have taught us anything, it's that dreams of universal equality can segue very easily into dreams of universal market access. There's a reason that both progressives and *The Economist* champion open borders. There's a reason so many hippies ended up as tech billionaires. Those of us who remember the halcyon era in which 'right' and 'left' seemed to mean something might find all this confusing, but if we step back for a broader view, we can see that the economics of capitalism and the politics of progressivism are both manifestations of Jacques Ellul's *technique*: the technocratic essence of Machine modernity. Today's left is no threat to technique; on the contrary, it is its vanguard. If you have ever asked yourself what kind of 'revolution' would be sponsored by Nike, promoted by BP, propagandised for by Hollywood and Netflix and policed by Facebook and YouTube, then the answer is here.

Progressive leftism and corporate capitalism have not so much merged as been exposed for what they always were: variants of the same modern ideal, built around the pursuit of boundless self-creation in a post-natural world. The Canadian 'Red Tory' philosopher George Grant once observed that 'the directors of General Motors and the followers of Professor [Herbert] Marcuse sail down the same river in different boats.' These days, they have abandoned their separate vessels and are sailing downstream in a superyacht together, while the rest of us gawp or throw rocks from the banks.

I should, at this point, offer an obvious caveat to my argument: that 'the left' is not a monolith, any more than 'the right' is. Today's manifestation of corporate-friendly 'progressive' leftism is not the only game in town: there have been other lefts, and there still are (get an old-fashioned Marxist onto the subject of 'bourgeois' identity politics and he'll bend your ear for hours). But what is manifesting around us today is not Owenite socialism or Tolstoyan anarchism. It's not old-fashioned social democracy, or a serious application of Marxist ideology. My teetotal, Methodist, Labour-voting great-grandfather, a proud socialist all his life, would not recognise it—and how it would hate him, with his Victorian values and his First World War medals and his archaic views on family and nation.

Perhaps we could say that the levelling instinct is the West's gift to the world. At its best, it is a gift to be proud of. Without some levellers around, a culture is in danger of becoming ossified, abusive and top-heavy. Power always needs to be kept on its toes. Leaders and systems should always be made to justify their existence, if they can. But what happens when levelling is the only instinct left? When the culture is so empty, so purposeless, so uprooted, that it has forgotten how to do anything but deconstruct itself? More to the point: What happens when levelling is the instinct not of the poor, but of power? What happens when the destruction of borders, limits and boundaries benefits big tech, big money and those who drink from their spigot, rather than the small voices left thirsting in the fields? And what happens when big money uses the language of the small voices—the language of levelling—to tie up its work in pretty bows?

We are living through a revolution, but it is not driven by the rise of 'cultural Marxism', as some on the right like to loudly claim. It is the ongoing, accelerating revolution of the Machine. The post-modern left which has seized the heights of so much of Western culture is not some radical threat to the establishment: it *is* the establishment. Progressive leftism is market liberalism by other means. It enables the spread and growth of Machine society by launching an all-out war on any cultural norms that remain to us in the 2020s: norms which act as a brake on the spread of Machine values. The left and corporate capitalism now function like a pincer: one attacks the culture, deconstructing everything from history to 'heteronormativity' to national identities; the other moves in to monetise the resulting fragments.

The Machine-fuelled culture of inversion changes all of our parameters. This is a time in which the pertinent questions are not 'Who should own the means of production?' or 'Should we privatise the health service?' They are 'What is a woman?', 'Where should we implant the microchips?', 'How quickly can we get this digital ID system up and running?', and 'What do you think of my new killer robot?' The creation of designer babies, the abolition of the sexed body, the growing of brains in labs: neither side of the French assembly has a clue what to do with any of it. Whatever you want, the Machine can provide it, technology can fashion it, and progressive ideology can redefine it as justice.

Where, then, to stand? Can there be a left without progress? Can there be a right without capitalism? Or is this all just noise? All of the political categories we tear each other apart over are products of the Machine Age. None of them have altered the course of a world in which technology is the driver of all change. Liberals want to direct history's arc, conservatives want to stand athwart history yelling 'stop', and leftists want to break history altogether and start again. But history rolls on regardless; modernity's metaphysics are independent of all of our struggles and notions, and the Machine absorbs all challenges to its ascendancy.

When people ask me where I stand, I say these days that it's with an older tradition: the same one I was writing about in that first book, although I didn't know it then. It's a tradition which takes its stand not according to ideological positioning, but according to actual positioning: on Earth, under the sky, surrounded by people who know where the sun rises in the morning, where they come from and who they are. It resists the Machine's totalising force from a perspective rooted in the Four Ps: people, place, prayer and the past. Neither left nor right nor anywhere else, it's a tradition that crosses all the modern divides, because it is older than all of them. It digs down, literally, to the root of the matter.

This is the dream of a localised, populist alternative to gigantist, destructive modernity in all its forms. But it is not really a political project, at least not exclusively. Political solutions are for political problems, but the origins of our culture's crisis are much deeper than the surface level on which politics operates. The culture war is not, in my view, about politics at all. It's not even about culture. It is about something else entirely.

But what?

XV

In the Desert of the Real

I WAS IN THE SUPERMARKET the other week, pushing my trolley, look-ing at my little list, trying not to get distracted by the Easter egg selection, when I looked up and I had an epiphany. I looked around me in that moment, and the sheen of dull normality that my mind had con-structed around the supermarket experience seemed to briefly fall away. You probably know what this feels like: sometimes, just for a minute, the stories that support your life dissolve, and something raw is revealed.

What was revealed to me in that split second was how *fake* the whole thing was. I saw all of a sudden what was lurking below the cellophane and the slogans and the special offers. I saw the sheer *unnaturalness* of this way of obtaining food, and the unnaturalness, too, of our wander-ing these straight-lined, strip-lit plastic aisles inside this giant metal box instead of gathering mushrooms from a forest floor. I saw identical pro-duce in identical boxes on identical shelves. I saw lumps of meat sheared from the carcasses of living creatures bred in slavery in factory farms, hung and stunned in abattoirs, sealed in plastic and shelved beneath a picture of a field in the sun. I saw the planes flying in bulk boxes of au-bergines and peppers from other continents, and the sweatshops where the cheap trainers and trousers and brittle plastic toys were made for us by the silent poor, and the marketing meetings where people sat around designing slogans for the door stickers and the sustainability leaflets. I saw the canning factories and the shipping containers and the mines and the fertiliser plants and the annual shareholder meetings. I saw the machinery of this great operation, in which I was just one tiny, nameless tube in the global delivery mechanism between production and consumption.

At this point, I noticed a slogan over the vegetable aisle. It informed me that the company was 'passionate' about its carrots and potatoes. Over the wine section was a similar slogan. Their booze, it said, was 'life-changing'. And now that I looked, I saw that the whole place was emblazoned with the same kind of over-egged, exaggerated, breathless language. There was *love* and *passion* and *excitement* and *commitment* everywhere. I've noticed for a few years that the grimier the consuming experience gets, the more florid becomes the language in which it is wrapped. The deepest human emotions are engaged to flog us cornflakes, shampoo and dog food. We are drowning in strategically commercialised passion. My daughter recently told me that the last time she bought some shoes, the box was emblazoned with the slogan *We're all about love.*

Once upon a time you just went shopping. If there was any marketing involved it might be a two-for-one offer, a free gift or a price reduction. When did we move from *Half price beans for one week only* to *Our beans are all about love?* What does that even mean? Looking around the supermarket that day, I had the feeling that something had come unmoored: it was as if reality and the things which point to it had been severed from each other. It felt like we didn't quite know what was real any more, or appropriate—and in this, the supermarket was just a microcosm of a much bigger trend.

All across the culture now, there is an inverse relationship between reality and its presentation, between nature and simulation, between map and territory. This applies to TV ads, general elections, Hollywood films and the daily news. As a result, it increasingly feels like nothing is true and nothing is real—and yet we can't quite see what is actually wrong. Where are the joins? How are they held together? What is this feeling of discomfort, of unreality, that comes from simply *existing* amongst all this? Whatever it is, it is this *feeling*, more than any event or argument, which seems to define our times. Everything is fake now, and we all know it—but how else can we feed ourselves?

THE FRENCH SOCIOLOGIST JEAN BAUDRILLARD coined the term 'hyperreality' four decades ago to describe a world in which fake things would come to seem more real than reality itself. Baudrillard believed that this world—the creation of mass society, mass media and sophisticated systems of both propaganda and communication—was just around the corner. The boundaries between real and fake were already blurring, and soon we would no longer even be able to see them. Soon after that we would forget there had ever been boundaries at all, and then things would really get freaky. Information would devour content and then replace it. The sign would no longer point to the signified—it would point to nothing at all. Hyperreality would not simply be confused with reality. It would replace it entirely, and we would all be living in it.

It would be another quarter century before the advent of social media began to accelerate us into the world that Baudrillard foresaw. But within forty years of his coining the term, we would all find ourselves living in the place for which, a decade later, he created another memorable phrase: 'the desert of the real'. The reason you may have heard this phrase, unless you're better read than me, is probably not because you're very familiar with Baudrillard. It is more likely to be that it was memorably used in *The Matrix*, the most symbolically prophetic film yet made about the twenty-first century.

In *The Matrix*, humans exist only as comatose batteries, used to power the AI which runs the world. What humans think of as reality is instead a very literal hyperreality: a computer programme designed to distract them from the hideous truth of their predicament. Everyone lives in the desert of the real: the Matrix is designed to promote an illusion of freedom and choice to people who have neither. Those who manage to escape it are brutally outnumbered and faced with horrors they have never been prepared for. Some of them react by trying to get back in again: even though they know the Matrix is an illusion, they prefer the illusion to what reality has become.

The last two chapters have explored the boundaries and drivers of the 'culture war' in the West. As I suggested right at the beginning of this book, though, I see this conflict as a symptom of something much deeper. Those depths interest me, but they pull me, too, in all sorts of different directions. Life would be easy if we could just pick a culture war team and get fighting. Plenty of people seem to manage it, but I can't. Sometimes when I am on the verge of throwing in my lot with some team or other, I look out at the whole mess and find myself being pulled by three competing instincts.

The first instinct is to fight back against the forces which are demolishing the culture I grew up in. Those forces seem to be designed with provocation and division in mind, and they are certainly achieving it. Whenever I hear the word 'white' being used as an insult, the hairs on the back of my neck stand up, and not just on my behalf. Somehow, I have the sense that I'm speaking up for my ancestors. After all, they are now accused in some vague way of various past crimes, mostly by small people standing on the shoulders of giants and giggling. This is a hard stone to chew on—and why should I chew on it? The rewriting of books, the 'decolonising' of curricula, the senseless, iconoclastic demolition of my culture at every level sometimes infects me with despair or anger. What am I to teach my children? Will there be anything left for them to inherit? One thing is for sure: I will never teach them that the phrase 'dead white men' is anything other than a form of ancestor abuse. Every indigenous culture I have ever come across is very clear about what happens to a people who disrespect their ancestors.

The second instinct follows quickly from the first. It's a desire to retreat. You don't have to spend much time surveying the culture war battlefield to see where fighting gets you: dead, in body or soul or both. This confected binary struggle feels like a trap designed to draw us in. Everyone in the woke trench wants you to join their fight against the cisheteronormative white patriarchy. Over in the based trench, new people are always needed to keep the supplies of Pepe the Frog-themed Molotovs flying. As for standing in No Man's Land trying to stay neutral: try that and you'll be gunned down by both sides. No, the right place to be is surely in the woods, or in a monastery. Or in a monastery in the woods.

But the third instinct is the wild card. This instinct says: *I can't stand what these woke people are doing. But I can understand why they're doing it.*

The fact is that the culture which is crumbling, or being demolished, around me is also a culture I never felt comfortable with. Though it is the world that made me, I've long felt that the modern West is broken in some deep way. Something always felt bent out of shape, as if there was some hidden wound beneath it all. If I transport myself back to my teens, or even to my childhood, I can experience again the sometimes visceral disgust with what my 'civilisation' was, and what it wanted to teach me, long before I could put any of it into words. While I loved the landscapes of my country—the downs, the hills, the moors, the copses—and was fascinated by the history of my people, what we had become simply left me cold.

I was brought up to be a good little middle-class boy, and to rise as far as I could within the structures this civilisation had built around me; yet I could smell from the start that something was off, as so many of us can. Today's left is correct to point out that these structures were built, at least partly, on empire and slavery and the razing of forests and the stripping bare of the wealth of nations, including our own. All great civilisations are built on these things. But there was something else that made me pucker my lips when I heard the phrase 'Western civilisation'.

It was, I think now, an instinctive feeling for the arrogance of modernity. Our etiolated rationalism, the desire to impose our will on the world, the assumption that *we know best* which survived the collapse of our empires and flowed effortlessly into the age of 'development'. The insistence that African children should attend Western-style schools and be issued laptops; that India should adopt our patented pharmaceutical medicines; that Pacific Islanders should become Protestant Christians in suits and ties; that all nations everywhere should 'trade freely' with our Black Ships (as if they had the choice) and set themselves up as 'liberal democracies' just like ours, with parliaments and presidents and a 'media'; that our wars are good wars and their wars are bad wars; that all the world will be progressing together when They have all agreed to become like Us.

This 'West' that I was part of had colonised itself with its left-brain blindness, and then colonised everyone else the same way. All the things I loved—small places, wild nature, real culture—were being wrecked, in my country and far beyond. The Russian Orthodox theologian Nikolai Berdyaev explained what had happened in blunt, and very Russian, terms:

> The will to power, to wellbeing, to wealth, triumphs over the will to holiness and to genius. . . . Spirituality is on the wane, [in] a time of bourgeois ascendancy. The knight and the monk, the philosopher

and the poet, have been superseded by a new type—the greedy bourgeois conqueror, organizer, and trader . . . In the new machine-made industrial-capitalist civilization of Europe and America, the spiritual culture . . . based on a sacred symbolism and sacred tradition, is being irrevocably annihilated.[1]

We have arrived at the point which the writers I have explored so far—Oswald Spengler, Christopher Lasch, Robert Bly, Patrick Deneen, Simone Weil and others—warned us we would come to. It is the point at which our underlying cultural and spiritual brokenness is manifesting on the surface as politics, with explosive results. This is the result of the Great Unsettling: a time and place where nothing seems to be solid, comforting or even real. This process has been accelerated a thousandfold by the arrival of the internet, and particularly social media, which, as the psychologist Jonathan Haidt has argued, has had the same impact as the collapse of the tower of Babel: 'people wandering amid the ruins, unable to communicate, condemned to mutual incomprehension.'[2]

When I look at this history, and then I look at the culture war, I see cause and effect. I see a war being fought over the spoils and the ruins of Progress by people who live in those ruins and are mourning the loss of something they don't even quite understand. That sense of mourning is common to both 'left' and 'right'. Whether they are mourning the end of the arc of history or the end of a country they miss without maybe even having known it, the sense of loss is profound, even if unspoken. For many people, everything is broken. This is why, though I will never condemn those 'dead white men', neither can I stand up and 'defend the West' in some uncomplicated fashion. The West is my home—but the West has also eaten my home. Should I stand up to save it from itself? How would that happen? What would I be fighting for?

No: when we talk about fighting for 'the culture', or fighting against it, I think we miss the mark. Culture is, after all, as I argued at the start of the book, a spiritual byproduct. Cultures are built around claims and beliefs about the otherworld: about God or gods, about correct worship, about the nature of reality, about goodness and truth and the meaning of virtue. These are also, inevitably, claims about what it means to be human. Knock out the spiritual core of any culture, and however hard people fight, its fate is sealed.

René Guénon, who dedicated his life to studying the metaphysical decay of the West, called this the 'crisis of the modern world', and he saw it as an explicitly spiritual matter. In his 1945 book *The Reign of Quantity and the Signs of the Times,* Guénon, a French convert to Sufi Islam who lived much of his life in Egypt, argued that the modern West's decisive turn away from the spiritual life towards the purely material realm had plunged us into an era he called the 'Reign of Quantity'. He referred to this turn as 'the modern deviation', or sometimes 'the Western deviation'.[3]

Guénon believed that the world's major religious traditions all contained the same 'universal character' and could lead towards the same truth. The modern West, however, had unilaterally turned away from the pursuit of any higher truth, and the result had been the Reign of Quantity, which was now overcoming the world at Western hands. 'Western domination', he wrote, 'is itself no more than an expression of the "reign of quantity."'[4]

Guénon saw this as an inevitable part of the cyclical nature of world history. Greatly influenced by Hinduism, he believed the world was living through the final phase of the *Kali Yuga,* an era of corruption, decay and lost truth. In this time, everything would be subject to a 'progressive materialisation'. If human lives had always been a balancing act between two poles, which he called unity and quantity, then modernity had tilted the balance decisively in favour of the latter. Nothing that could not be measured would now be accepted as real. This had led inevitably to the reign of 'profane science', 'mechanism leading to materialism' and an 'inversion of correspondences' in which all traditional values, rooted in spiritual unity, were turned upside down. The profane was worshipped, and the holy was profaned. All of this acted to 'confine men within the limits of their own individuality', which they would come to see as the limits of reality itself.

In short, by turning away from spiritual truth—by which Guénon meant the 'esoteric' truth at the heart of the ancient religions—modern humanity had guaranteed its descent into confusion and breakdown. 'The dominant impression today', wrote Guénon fully eighty years ago, is 'an impression of instability extending to all domains'—and he predicted there would plenty more to come. The descent is not over, he warned: 'dissolution is the goal toward which the world will be traveling henceforth.'[5]

Modern humanity's attempt to build its own 'closed system' to replace nature and tradition, said Guénon, could never succeed, but instead would lead to an 'artificial world' which would result in an 'artificial mentality' amongst its people. 'The modern mentality', he wrote, 'is no more than the product of a vast collective suggestion'. When enough people realised this, he predicted, a 'reaction' would ensue amongst those who wanted to resist the disintegration. But since even 'those who most sincerely want to combat the modern spirit are almost all unwittingly affected by it', the danger would be a kind of false 'traditionalism' doing battle with an equally false 'progress', all against the background of a time in which genuine spiritual unity was a distant memory, and truth itself was disputed on all sides.

Which may sound familiar.

All of this brings us back to where we began—the culture war of the age of hyperreality. Guénon concluded his study by suggesting that we are living in a 'great parody': an age of 'inverted spirituality' and 'counter-tradition' in which even institutions which claimed to be transmitting the spiritual traditions—most churches, for example—were shells of the real thing. To Guénon, this was a manifestation of an actual spiritual war. He agreed with St Paul that 'we wrestle not against flesh and blood, but against principalities, against powers, against the rulers of the darkness of this world'. Some dark spiritual force was inhabiting the shell of our culture, he said, and driving us ever downwards.

Another depressing prognosis for the future, then? Strangely, I feel almost the opposite. Guénon's musings on historical cycles, and his frank analysis of the dissolution of the times, brings a kind of astringent clarity to the current cultural craziness, which itself is a product of the Great Unsettling, and the rise of the culture of the Machine. Together, Guénon and Baudrillard—two verbose, perceptive French intellectuals of very different stripes—force us to see that this pervasive unreality, this sense of being marooned far from truth, is the tenor of the times we find ourselves living in, and that there is no going back. It is part of a historical cycle, and that cycle won't be altered by any of us, however much we scream at each other. The human spirit, like water, will find the level of its times. This is how it must be. The only question worth asking in times like these is: *How should we live?*

That in turn makes it clear that how and when and whether we engage with that cycle is largely our choice. It could be that even writing books about it is a trap. But if what we are witnessing is not, at heart, a political or cultural battle, but some manifestation of a spiritual war— well, then perhaps our time should be spent becoming the right kind of warrior. Because everything is currently set up to turn us into the wrong kind.

The right kind of warrior takes on his own internal demons before he sails out to take on those of others. He takes his stand, and stands his ground, without giving in to to the *nihil* of the age. He cleaves to what he believes in without falling into the traps laid by partisanship, anger and self-righteousness. Most of all, he works to clear out his own inner junkyard so that he can go searching for truth—and recognise it when he finds it. His war is against the worst of himself and for the best of the world, and what he is fighting for is the love he so often fails at. His most effective weapon is sacrifice.

This is easier written than practiced, of course. But I think it might be the way through. 'No one is obliged to take part in the spiritual crisis of a society', wrote the philosopher Eric Voegelin in his book *Science, Politics and Gnosticism*. 'On the contrary, everyone is obliged to avoid the folly and live his life in order'. If there is better advice for living through the reign of quantity, or surviving the hyperreal culture war, I haven't found it yet.

XVI

The Abolition of Man (and Woman)

EIGHT YEARS AGO, ON A VISIT to the United States, I had my first taste of the foundational shift in the understanding of reality which was about to explode across the Western world.

I was on a mini book tour, speaking at a few different events, and in the process I spent some time with a man who had some interest in my work. We got talking about this and that, and in the process of making small talk, he asked me if I had children. I did, I said: a son and a daughter. Then, as you do when you're making conversation, I asked him the same question.

I won't forget the look that passed over his face. A terrible sadness seemed to hang over him as he answered. Yes, he had a teenage son, he said—or he had done, once. But everything had changed. His son had come home from school one day and announced that he was now his daughter. 'Imagine it', said the man to me. 'What do you do? What was I supposed to do?'

I didn't know what to say, or what I would have done. I just listened as the man poured out his story. He needed to talk about it. It had all been such a shock to him, he said, that he hadn't known how to cope.

He had tried to talk to his son, to persuade him that he was not a girl but a boy, that it was not possible for him to be anything else, that adolescence was confusing and that this was normal, but it was to no avail. His son was adamant.

It was clear that something was happening at school, and in the wider culture, that the man didn't understand. 'I started drinking', he said to me. 'I went on a bender. I disappeared for days. I couldn't cope with it. My son was talking about surgery. He was just slipping away from me. All those years of raising him. I said to him, "It's like I'm losing my child. My only son. It's like my son is dying." That's how it felt.'

The man showed me a picture of his son: an awkward teenage boy with long hair fashioned like a woman's, wearing a skirt. 'He wants to start hormone treatment', said the man to me. 'He wants to stop his puberty from happening. I told him to wait. I said, You don't know what you'll feel like in five years. I just keep hoping it won't happen. All the doctors are promoting it. They say it's reversible, but . . .'

I didn't know what to say at all. Mostly I still don't. The man asked me my opinion about all of it. I said that I didn't know what I'd have done under the circumstances. I said that his son sounded like a victim of something. I said that a man couldn't become a woman, or vice versa, and that children should not have hormone treatments or surgery on that basis. I couldn't quite believe what I was hearing about the way that doctors, therapists and teachers all seemed to be pushing such radical interventions on children. I thought that maybe the man was exaggerating, though I didn't say so. None of it made sense. All I could see was pain and confusion: in the boy and in the man and in the family and in the culture. It was a kind of pain and confusion so novel that nobody really knew what to do with it.

'Has this come to your country yet?' the man asked me. I said that I didn't think so, not really. 'Then you're lucky', said the man. 'But I promise you—it will.'

. . .

HE WAS RIGHT ABOUT THAT. Here in Ireland today, the news I hear from the local schools is that many children—especially girls—are confused about what they have all learned to call their 'gender'. Are they girls or boys or something else entirely? This situation is routinely presented as simply the unveiling of something that has always existed. People have always been 'transgender' in this way, we're told: now they just feel able to talk about it.

The apparently sudden onset of mass gender confusion amongst vulnerable young people is a unique modern phenomenon with unclear roots, but it has clearly been encouraged and promoted throughout society via aggressive and mostly online activism and the support of official bodies such as schools and medical centres, and in many cases the quiescence or support of the state.[1] It is novel and radical, and it has happened with incredible speed: Sweden, to take just one example, recently experienced an astonishing 1,500 percent rise in diagnoses of 'gender dysphoria' in just a decade.[2]

By now, we are all familiar with the toxic and apparently endless gender wars that have consumed the oxygen of Western nations in recent years. We have heard about the teenage girls undergoing double mastectomies and the young boys being given 'puberty-blocking' drugs designed to chemically castrate rapists.[3] The concept of 'trans kids' —a notion that would have been inconceivably baffling to most people even a few years back, and which for many still is—has been being pushed so hard by a slew of unaccountable and opaque NGOs that it can be hard for most people to keep up. What is going on? What, indeed, is the nature of reality at all? And who gets to decide?

The meaning of the words 'man' and 'woman', as we have all learned in the last few years, have an obvious practical significance: they determine what toilets people can use, who can compete in sports events, and so on. But while battles about these questions continue, the surface churning can distract us from the deeper currents. Those currents reveal that the transgender moment is not just about gender. In some ways, in fact, gender is not even the main attraction in the circus. Rather, it is the catalyst for wider changes that are engulfing us. Those changes represent a breakdown in our shared understanding of what it means to be human—and to have a human body—the logic of which has barely begun to play out.

The question is: Where does it lead?

IN HIS 2020 BOOK *The Rise and Triumph of the Modern Self*, Carl Trueman attempts to answer this question. His book began, he explains, as an attempt to understand how the phrase 'I am a woman trapped in a man's body' has 'come to be regarded as coherent and meaningful' when just a few decades ago it would have been considered by most people to be 'incoherent gibberish'. The conclusion he comes to is that the transgender moment, far from being an inexplicable flash in the pan, is the logical result of a shift in the understanding of the self which has been taking place since the advent of modernity.

Drawing on the work of philosopher Philip Rieff, author of *The Triumph of the Therapeutic*, Trueman suggests that today's Western worldview is perhaps unique in human history. To help explain why and how, he draws on Rieff's simple but thought-provoking schema for understanding the development of the Western self through a progression of human 'types'.

The first type Rieff calls Political Man. Idealised by the likes of Plato and Aristotle, Political Man finds his identity in public life, as he engages in civic life, debates the meaning of life with others and generally discovers his self-expression in some form of public service. Later, as the Middle Ages dawn, Political Man is superseded by type two: Religious

Man. Religious Man finds his meaning in the public religious life: the feasts and fasts, mass and liturgy, pilgrimage and procession which give shape to the year and to existence.

As modernity beckons, Religious Man gives way to type three: Economic Man, for whom the key to life's meaning is found in trade, production and profit. Rieff, like Marx before him, understood that the revolutionary nature of capitalism meant that Economic Man could only ever be a temporary phenomenon: in the end, he would undermine the foundations of his own prosperity.

So it proved, and when that happened, Economic Man gave way to the type we now live amongst and embody: Psychological Man. Crucially, Psychological Man is *qualitatively* different to his ancestors. Unlike them, he finds meaning and identity not so much in outward-directed activity as in what Rieff calls 'the inward quest for personal psychological happiness'. His reality is unmoored, unshared and—crucially— *internal*. This has implications for the culture which we see unfurling around us today:

> In the worlds of political, religious and economic man, commitment was outwardly directed to those communal beliefs, practices and institutions that were bigger than the individual and in which the individual, to the degree that he or she conformed to or cooperated with them, found meaning. The ancient Athenian was committed to the assembly, the medieval Christian to his church, and the twentieth-century factory worker to his trade union and working man's club. All of them found their purpose and wellbeing by being committed to something outside themselves. In the world of Psychological Man, however, the commitment is first and foremost to the self and is inwardly directed. Thus, the order is reversed. Outward institutions become in effect the servants of the individual and her sense of inner wellbeing.[4]

Much of the rest of Trueman's book traces the creation of Psychological Man through history. Fingering those most responsible, he begins with Jean-Jacques Rousseau, who pioneered a new creation myth in which the unsullied and uncivilised human individual is perverted by society. Later, Freud would explain how society and the family were the source of repressed emotions which could be freed via the new science of therapy, while Marx offered a political response to both Freud and Rousseau by proposing that the repressive and unjust bourgeois superstructure be swept away entirely. Meanwhile, Nietzsche and Darwin both helped, wittingly or unwittingly, to undermine the foundational assumptions of Western Christianity, thus unmooring the culture from its spiritual roots. Finally, figures such as Herbert Marcuse and Wilhelm Reich provided the justification for the removal of sexual taboos which exploded in the sixties counter-culture and brought us into the pornified present.

It is this latter development, suggests Trueman, that may prove to be most significant. Identity in the contemporary West now places sexuality at its very centre—a situation which he believes 'is arguably unprecedented in history'. Trueman identifies Wilhelm Reich and his counter-cultural successors as prime movers in this culture shift. Sexual liberation, to Reich, represented the latest stage of the ongoing liberation of the individual from both nature and culture. In his 1936 book *The Sexual Revolution*, he argued that sexual repression had been imposed and weaponised by governments and churches for centuries as a means of controlling the masses. Liberation of the individual was thus intimately tied up with liberated sexuality. 'The existence of strict moral principles', writes Trueman, 'has invariably signified that the biological, and specifically the sexual, needs of man were not being satisfied. Every moral regulation is in itself sex-negating, and all compulsory morality is life-negating. The social revolution has no more important task than finally to enable human beings to realise their full potentialities and find gratification in life.'[5]

Sexual freedom is human freedom. The sixties counter-culture took this notion and ran with it, but a problem soon became apparent: liberation was lopsided. Women, even with the advent of effective contraception, were always less 'liberated' than men, and were more easily exploited too. 'Promiscuity without penalty', as Trueman has it, remains easier for men, for obvious biological reasons.

When we listen to the logic of all these thinkers, starting with Rousseau and ending with his contemporary successors, we hear one fundamental message: that *the most authentic human self is that which is most detached from both biology and society.* That the further we move from our natural state, the more liberated—and thus fulfilled—we will be. How is this liberation to be achieved? Through the twin engines of cultural revolution and advanced technology. The first of these has been ongoing for so long that most of us can't remember whatever it was that was supposed to be overthrown. The second is advancing at speed each day through the graveyard of the given.

It is in this context that the act of neutering our bodies—divorcing sex from the relatively new notion of 'gender', and freeing ourselves from the prison of our biology—can be seen as an act of political liberation. Writing about the work of the influential and controversial gender theorist Judith Butler, Mary Harrington, author of *Feminism Against Progress,* suggests that the transgender movement aims 'to dismantle every structure that might induce us to view our reality as men and women as influenced by our bodies—structures Butler calls "heteronormativity." Ground Zero for that liberation is unmooring reproduction from sex and our bodies.' Following her logic to its end, Harrington continues, 'Butler advocates "replacing the maternal body" with technology, with the aim of "fully decoupling human reproduction from heterosexual relationships." We are finally free when our bodies have no relevance to our most intimate relationships and deepest commitments.'[6]

Butler wants women—and perhaps men, if we're lucky—liberated from their own bodies. To become trans-gender, in this understanding, is neither a lifestyle choice nor a medical correction, but something much deeper, more radical and more political: the latest manifestation of a long struggle for technological liberation from nature itself, symbolised by the limits of human biology.

The key point is this: the transgender movement which is presented to us today as a civil rights struggle is actually, at root, something else. In the divorce of 'gender' from sex, in the promotion of multiple 'identities' to young and vulnerable people, in the notion that the given body is a problem to be solved and in the foundational proposition that our 'identity'—even our biology—is not naturally occurring but constructed in our mind, we are witnessing the latest stage of modernity's long rebellion against nature.

This rebellion currently manifests as a well-funded[7] and well-organised attempt to normalise a neutered, post-biological humanity, in which 'man' and 'woman', 'mother' and 'father', 'family' and ultimately 'nature' will become 'problematic' notions. What is the logical endpoint of this process of divorcing biology from sex, and the body from the mind? We can see it clearly enough, if we choose to look. And some prominent transgender activists are not shy about naming it.

Take, for example, Martine (formerly Martin) Rothblatt, billionaire transgender entrepreneur and prominent technocrat. In his 2011 book *From Transgender to Transhuman: A Manifesto on the Freedom of Form*, the destination is made explicit. 'Transgenderism', writes Rothblatt, 'is the onramp to transhumanism.' Rothblatt presents the desire to transcend the 'gender binary' as part of the wider process of moving above and beyond all naturally occurring boundaries and limits. Abandoning gender will lead to abandoning sex and then, finally, to abandoning the body altogether.

A similar case is made by the writer Sophie Lewis, whose 'cyborg feminist' manifesto *Full Surrogacy Now* (subtitle: *Feminism Against*

Family) demands the dismantling of the 'stratified, commodified, cis-normative, neo-colonial' apparatus of 'bourgeois reproduction' in favour of 'gestational communism'. Lewis wants a world where babies are not the particular obligation of their families, but 'universally thought of as anybody and everybody's responsibility', brought up by 'queerer, more comradely modes' of nurturing than the old-fashioned, reactionary 'family'. How is such a paradise to be achieved? Through advanced technologies of surrogacy, artificial wombs and other such means of spawning new humans without having to use our own clumsy bodies to carry them.

Lewis's desire to replace human biology with technology in the name of equality is an unusually explicit manifestation of the merger between progressive politics and techno-capital which I examined in chapter XIV. In the short term, the reason for the huge and well-funded corporate support of the transgender movement is not hard to fathom: this new market is potentially hugely profitable. Somebody has to produce the supplements, charge for the surgery and surrogacy,[8] and both create and cash in on the ever-expanding range of 'gender-affirming' products.

But techno-capitalism's support for the age of trans goes deeper than this. Many of the billionaires who are bankrolling this supposed grass-roots movement for change have an agenda of their own,[9] one which meshes perfectly with the worldview of Silicon Valley, with its metaverses, singularities and AI bots. In this world, *transgender* slides into *transhuman* with barely a murmur, as the journey of Martine Rothblatt makes explicit.[10] Martine's transition from man to woman, in the view of Rothblatt's son, 'was an extension of her lifelong desire to transcend all borders. . . . A pioneer, a futurist and an embodiment of the best of human transcendence, Martine Rothblatt is a beacon to those looking to change the world. With her mantra of "mind is deeper than matter" as the rhythm, she has orchestrated success beyond expectation.'

Rothblatt is quite open about what he is ultimately in pursuit of: immortality, via the uploading of the human mind into the digital cloud. Any objection to this notion, you may not be surprised to hear, is now a form of prejudice: one known as 'fleshism'. One way to overcome it is to follow a new kind of global faith: a 'transreligion' through which we can navigate the new reality. Rothblatt, helpfully, has even created one for us. Launched in 2004, Terasem is a new spiritual path for the coming trans-everything future:

> We are a transreligion that believes we can live joyfully forever if we build mindfiles for ourselves. We insist on respecting diversity without sacrificing unity, as well as pouring maximum resources into cyberconsciousness software, geoethical nanotechnology and space settlement.

Terasem's 'four core beliefs' are laid out helpfully on the new global religion's website:[11]

   I. LIFE IS PURPOSEFUL.
   II. DEATH IS OPTIONAL.
   III. GOD IS TECHNOLOGICAL.
   IV. LOVE IS ESSENTIAL.

And just in case you missed it, Rothblatt helpfully expands on that third point:

> We are making God as we are implementing technology that is ever more all-knowing, ever-present, all-powerful and beneficent. Geoethical nanotechnology will ultimately connect all consciousness and control the cosmos.

What does a transhumanist billionaire who wants to 'make God' have to do with a teenage girl who feels uncomfortable in her body? The answer is that Rothblatt is far from the only person who believes that the path to a disembodied, posthuman and post-natural future leads directly through the shattered gender binary. Looked at this way, the question of what pronouns to use, or who should be allowed into which bathroom, suddenly starts to look a lot more momentous than the newspapers are telling us. The unifying driver is the desire for *trans-cendence*: the latest stage in what another transhumanist, Kevin Kelly, in his book *What Technology Wants,* calls our ongoing 'liberation from matter'.

I don't mean to suggest that the activists currently beavering away to 'queer the gender binary' all have this end in mind, let alone that young people who consider themselves to be transgender buy into this worldview, or have even heard about it. But this is the direction of travel. People with gender dysphoria, girls with short hair, boys who play with dolls, people whose sexualities differ from the norm: they are not, in fact, the real issue.

The real issue is that a young generation of hyper-urbanised, always-on young people, increasingly divorced from nature and growing up in a psychologised, inward-looking anticulture, is being led towards the conclusion that biology is a problem to be overcome, that their body is a form of oppression and that the solution to their pain may go beyond a new set of pronouns, or even invasive surgery, towards nanotechnology, 'cyberconsciousness software' and perhaps, ultimately, the end of their physical embodiment altogether.

This is the Machine at work, and the transgender crusade fits into it perfectly, which is why it is so noisy, so heavily promoted and so hard to oppose. It is hard to oppose not only because of the interests behind it and the fury of its champions, but because it goes with the grain of long-held ideas of the modern self which all of us hold, whether we know it or not. Though to some the Age of Trans might seem new and startling, it is in fact, as Carl Trueman points out, the fruit of a three-hundred-year unfurling of a particular notion of what it means to be human: one which, in the final reckoning, moves us into the realm of humanity-as-god. The end result of this self-divinisation will be—irony of ironies—our own neutering.

Where will this go next, and how will we navigate the ongoing breakdown in our understanding of reality? Time will tell, but perhaps we should leave the last word to another honest transhumanist, Zoltan Istvan, who has seen the future[12] that he imagines will beckon once the abolition of the messy, limited, ageing, gendered, birth-giving body, in all of its created frailty, has finally been achieved:

> A conflict of who merges with AI and who doesn't is coming. It will likely be a civil war of sorts. Ultimately, people won't be able to stop progress, and most humans will upload themselves into new worlds where they don't die, don't have to work, or live as biological beings who suffer. . . . You will give up some control of your life, and that will be your payment into this world to exist. It will be a near-perfect world of bliss and progress.

Amen.

XVII

Keep the Home Fires Burning

I WAS CHATTING TO THE LOG MAN as we unloaded chunks of dried beech into my driveway from his trailer. Usually he brings me ash, but ash is becoming harder to find now that ash dieback disease, imported into Ireland from Europe, is killing many of the nation's trees. Our little home plantation, laid down five or six years ago for our own coppice cycle, was not yet mature enough to keep us going for the whole winter, and we needed help to make up the shortfall. So, beech it is this year.

'Not easy to get it now though', he said to me as we threw the logs into the growing pile. 'And there's a lot of demand this year. Everyone's worried about the winter'. Given the likely lack of Russian gas across Europe, people were getting nervous and stockpiling heating fuel before autumn. We'd been stocking up on winter logs this way for years—but the log man didn't know how much longer it would continue.

'I'll just keep going till they tell me to stop', he said. 'I know I could get a phone call any day and that would be that. It'll happen soon enough. Ridiculous it is. But what can we do?'

The log man knows that his days of delivering little loads of cut timber to households like ours are probably numbered. The Irish government is currently campaigning against the household burning of turf or wood, the former on the grounds of CO_2 emissions, and the latter on the grounds of air quality. As ever, the campaign is driven from Dublin, and mostly takes Dublin sensibilities into account. Rural households in Ireland have been burning turf and wood forever, with little significant impact on 'air quality'—or at least, no impact comparable to that which Ireland's 'Celtic Tiger' modernisation has had. Suddenly, though, the media is full of scientists armed with the inevitable 'studies' demonstrating how getting a fire going in your cottage in winter will lead to cancer and lung disease on a widespread scale.

This new tilt against household fireplaces is not just an Irish phenomenon: it is suddenly popping up everywhere. Woodstoves are, curiously, becoming the number one air pollution villain. Never mind mass car use, accelerating air travel or industrial pollution. Never mind the emissions caused by the massive increase in internet server farms, which by 2030 could be using up an astonishing 70 percent of this country's electricity. These days, if you want to demonstrate your social responsibility, you should be all aboard with the abolition of the traditional fireplace and its replacement with 'green' alternatives.

Speaking as a former green myself, I'm not without sympathy for at least part of this argument. The mass burning of peat in power stations here, for example, has long been an ecological disaster, one which is, thankfully, coming to an end. Many peat bogs in Ireland have been ravaged over the centuries, and some are now being restored for wildlife and for use as 'carbon sinks'. This is certainly no bad thing. Humans recklessly burning anything in sight on a vast scale has been the story of the Machine Age, and it's not a story to be defended, no matter how hard some are currently trying.

Something else is happening here, though. The campaign against warming your own house with your own fire is not quite what it claims to be. Sometimes it looks more like a displacement activity, as if a government and a nation which has no interest in actually cutting its consumerist lust down to size is going for an easy target. But it is also something with more symbolism, more mythic meat, than any discussion about 'carbon emissions' would suggest. The fireplace, whether our desiccated urban authorities know it or not, has a primal meaning, even in a world as divorced as ours from its roots and from the land.

In his short essay 'Fireside Wisdom', the esoteric writer and modern English eccentric John Michell suggests that the 'displacement of the hearth or fireplace' from the home was one of the many reasons for the craziness of the modern world which his life was spent playfully exploring. The fireplace at the centre of the home, he writes, was both an ancient practicality and a device of 'cosmological significance' across cultures and time:

> Within the circumference of the wall, representing a limited universe, the hearthstone is the body of the earth, with four corners and four directions, and it is the seat of Hestia the (h)earth goddess, whose energies are concentrated in the central fire. The chain is the world-pole, the link between heaven and earth and the means of intercourse with gods and spirits. Conversation is directed into the fire while dreams and images are drawn out of it. It is too smoky to read or look at pictures. Eyes and minds are concentrated upon the focal point. In that situation, sitting in friendly company around a fire on which a pot is simmering, one is likely to feel 'centred' and at ease.[1]

In the past, the act of sitting staring into the smoky fire with family or neighbours was the genesis of the folk tale and folk song which tied the culture together. Now we stare at digital fires hemmed into boxes manufactured by distant corporations who also tell us our stories. No song we can dream up around a real fireplace can compete with what these boxed fires can sell us. 'Thus', writes Michell, 'the traditional cosmology is no longer represented by its domestic symbols and a new, secular, restless, uncentred worldview has taken its place.'

Focus, Michell explained, is 'the Latin name for the central fireplace. The fire not only warms but, as a symbol, illuminates the corresponding images of a centre to each of our own beings and of a world-centre which is divine, eternal, and unchanging.'[2] Lose your fires, and you literally lose your focus as a culture. In this context, a government spokesman telling his population, as one minister here recently did, that they should 'get over' their 'nostalgic' attachment to the hearth fire and install ground source heat pumps instead is more than just a nod to efficiency. It is an assault on what remains of the home and its meaning. It is an attack on the cultural—even the divine—centre.

Not that you will get very far explaining that to your local MP.

'Not everyone can afford one of these fancy ground source pumps', said the log man, as we emptied the last of the trailer. He was right, of course, and many of my neighbours, who at this time of year are hauling tractor trailers full of dried turf back from the bog, would be just as dismissive of the new dispensation. But this is not the real significance of the dying-out of the household fire. The real significance is that it represents just the latest blow against the home as the centre of the universe: of the domestic as the cosmological, of the parlour as the place of story. Strip the last remaining fires from the last remaining hearths, and you are one step closer to what is perhaps the ultimate ambition of the Machine: the abolition of home.

THE MACHINE EXISTS TO CREATE DEPENDENCY. It is essentially a mechanism of colonisation. The history of modernity is the history of the spread of the Machine mentality to all corners of the Earth, as the Black

Ships of the Western traders and moneymen, having enclosed the lands of their own people and forced them into the mines, factories and slums, sailed out to do the same in what would become known as 'the colonies'. In this way the Machine has, by now, colonised us all—our lands, our hearts, our minds. Externally, we see the results in a chaotic climate, dissolving cultures, spiralling rates of extinction and infernal destruction of nature. Internally, we see it in the loss of our stories, in our broken-hearted confusion about who and where we are. Locally, we see it in the loss of our self-sufficiency and agency in the place where all human stories begin: the home.

Take the potential firewood ban. When you can no longer grow your own wood or cut your own turf to heat your own parlour, you are made that little bit more dependent on the matrix of government, technology and commerce that has sought to transmute self-sufficiency into bondage since the time of the Luddites. The justification for this attack on family and community sufficiency changes with the times—in seventeenth-century England, the enclosures were justified by the need for agricultural efficiency; today they are justified by the need for energy efficiency—but the attack is always of the same nature. Each blow struck against local self-sufficiency, pride and love of place weaves another thread into the pattern which has been developing for centuries, and which is almost complete now in most 'developed' countries.

Wendell Berry's 1980 essay 'Family Work' is a short meditation on the meaning of home, its disintegration under the pressures of modernity, and how it might, to some degree at least, be restored. Like so much of Berry's work, it locates the centrepoint of human society in the home, and explains many of the failures of contemporary Western—specifically American—society as a neglect of that truth. The home, to Berry, is the place where the real stuff of life happens, or should: the coming-together of man and woman in partnership; the passing-down of skills and stories from elders; the raising and educating of children; the growing, cooking, storing and eating of food; the learning of practical skills, from construction to repair, tool-making to sewing; the conjuration of story and song around the fire.

Universally, across the world and across cultures, the family and the home, however they were quite constituted, have always been the heart and root of culture. It follows, therefore, that the Machine must uproot both in order that culture may be destroyed and replaced with a marketplace in which we can buy and sell products, identities and ideologies while our ground source heat pumps maintain a constant and inoffensive temperature around us. Self-sufficient people, skilled people, independent people, thinking people: these are anathema. The home must go, so that the Machine might live.

In my lifetime, in my part of the world, the notion and meaning of 'home' has steadily crumbled under this external pressure until it is little more than a word. In a Machine anticulture, the home is a dormitory, probably owned by a landlord or a bank, in which two or more people of varying ages and degrees of biological relationship sleep when they're not out being employed by a corporation, or educated by the state in preparation for being employed by a corporation. The home's needs are met through pushing buttons, swiping screens or buying-in everything from food to furniture; for who has time for anything else, or has been taught the skills to do otherwise? Phones long ago replaced hearth fires. Handily, a phone, unlike a fire, can be kept under the pillow in case something urgent happens elsewhere while we sleep. We wouldn't want to miss anything.

Even back in 1980, Berry recognised that the home had become an 'ideal' rather than a practical reality—and it had become an ideal precisely because the reality had been placed out of reach for many. 'I do think that the ideal is more difficult now than it was', he writes. 'We are trying to uphold it now mainly by will, without much help from necessity, and with no help at all from custom and public value. For most people now do seem to think that family life and family work are unnecessary, and this thought has been institutionalised in our economy and in our public values. Never before has private life been so preyed upon by public life.'[3]

What killed the home? Three things, said Berry back then: cars, mass media and public education. The first—'automobiles and several decades of supposedly cheap fuel'—meant that both work and leisure could, for the first time in history, happen a long way from home. The second—'TV and other media'—have, since the mid-twentieth century, 'learned to suggest with increasing subtlety and callousness—especially, and most wickedly, to children—that it is better to consume than to produce, to buy than to grow or to make, to "go out" than to stay home. If you have a TV, your children will be subjected almost from the cradle to an overwhelming insinuation that all worth experiencing is somewhere else and that all worth having must be bought.'

It's sweet how old-fashioned those sentences seem now. Bittersweet, rather.

Finally, says Berry, the school system—a machine of its own—is designed 'to keep children away from the home as much as possible. Parents want their children kept out of their hair; education is merely a by-product, not overly prized.' Much public education, says Berry, is more like 'a form of incarceration'. Schools exist to train children to fit into the Machine world being built for them, to inculcate and normalise its ethics and goals, and to prepare children for a life serving the Machine's needs.

What could we add to this list now? The triumph of supermarkets, for one, and the whole panoply of long-distance shopping and global supply chains that go along with them. Back in 1980 it wasn't common to buy avocados in winter in the northern hemisphere, let alone endless streams of screen-based gadgets put together by slave labour in China. It wasn't common either to ship the resulting waste to Turkey or West

Africa, where the poor would sift through it for pennies. It's not only the homes of Western consumers that are devastated by the global supply chain of the Machine.

We could add 'careers', too, and perhaps this is the main culprit. What the Luddites called the 'factory system' (we should maybe call it the 'office system' now that all the factories have been shipped off to China) was the main reason that the home was broken into in the first place. The pre-modern home was, as few homes are today, a workplace. The Luddites again, as we saw in chapter V, were handloom weavers running literal cottage industries, and their rebellion against the rise of industrial capitalism was a rebellion in defence of the home as a place of both work and domesticity. That work was shared by men and women, who would each have their domestic spheres of influence whatever the particular business of the home was.

In this sense there is a case to be made that the pre-modern woman, working in her home with her husband and family, had more agency and power—in that sphere at least—than her contemporary counterpart whose life is directed from outside the home by distant commercial interests. Certainly the feminist movement, by accident or design, has either been hijacked by or has morphed into Machine capitalism. The 'liberation' of women has often translated into the separation of women from their self-sufficiency, as men were separated before them, and their embedding instead into the world of commerce, whether they want it or not. Today's 'liberated' woman is liberated from her home and children, who will be looked after by a paid stranger while she is out adding numbers to the gross national product like the men were before. 'Freedom', the highest prize, is always to be sought and won away from home, family and place.

My point is not that women should get back into the kitchen: it is that we all should, and into the other rooms of the home too. Machine modernity prised the men away from the home first, as the Industrial

Revolution broke their cottage industries and swept them into the factories and mines, where their brute strength could be useful to the Machine. Later the women, who had been mostly left to tend the home single-handedly, were subject to the same 'liberation', which was sold to them as a blow struck against inequality. Perhaps it was, but it was also a blow struck against the home, for both sexes.

In this context, the accelerating attack on traditional family structures, 'gender roles' and more recently gender and biology themselves, while presented as yet more liberation from the tyranny of both tradition and biology, can also be seen as propaganda in the interests of the Machine. Making a home requires both men and women to set their own desires below the needs of the wider family—but this kind of sacrifice does not feed the monster. Only by unmooring the human being from his or her roots in community and place can the emancipated individual consumer and self-creator be born. Only by promoting the fulfilment of individual desire as the meaning of a human life can the selflessness that we once prized as a cultural ideal be transmuted into the selfishness that the Machine needs to thrive.

I thought about this most recently when I came across a BBC story about 'the limitations of motherhood'. Here we met the screenwriter of a new TV show, *The Baby*, who explained how 'excited' she was 'about the possibility of exploding cultural ideals around motherhood' in her work. A true child of the culture of inversion, she explained how the traditional way of thinking about motherhood 'reinforces the idea that "the mother" is cis, female, straight, middle-class, white, caring and nurturing'. The job of writers like her was to 'explode' such outdated notions.[4] Caring, nurturing mothers? *Female* mothers? Perish the thought. Could it be, after all, that motherhood itself is *problematic*?

It is, of course. To the Machine, biology and family and home and place and anything at all with borders and limits always will be. Reading that article took me back to the days when I had a TV and found myself watching an episode of the British current affairs blatherfest *Newsnight,* also courtesy of the BBC. Some talking head or other was arguing that the government should give all women the 'right'—which sounded more like a veiled obligation—to put their newborn children into paid childcare at just six weeks old and get 'back to work' to help 'grow the economy'. What the children might grow up to feel about this was never considered. Nor was the notion that any mother might be horrified at the thought. Liberation and profit, again, were proving a seamless fit.

Oh, well. Maybe this is all misplaced nostalgia; or at least, the shutting of the stable door long after the horse has been turned into dogmeat. Perhaps people leave homes, or don't make them, because they just don't want them much anymore. Maybe we are all loving our liberation. When I was a teenager, I certainly wanted to escape my family and its values—as we mostly do—and I did in the end. But I suppose I always assumed there would be something to come back to. That the act of rebellion, of leaving, would not somehow diminish or demolish the thing being rebelled against. That I in my turn would grow up to be the thing that was pushed out of the way so that the world could be opened up before the young.

But I wonder if we can make that assumption now. I wonder especially if young people can. How does it feel to grow up in a society whose young can barely afford anywhere to live, let alone dream of owning a family home? In a world in which mothers should not be assumed to be female, and 'chestfeeding' is something that daddy can do too? Among the manic promotion of radical individualism, with greed and lust and pride not warned against but sponsored? With a generational fear of the future which leads increasing numbers to not want families at all? With everything pointing, always, towards *movement away,* towards *not looking back*, towards *progress*?

The loss of the security of a home is, in some way, the loss of the heart of things, and the most local and personal manifestation of triumph of the Machine. But it is also—and here comes the good news—potentially the most reversible. The war against home manifests on the human scale, which means we can reverse it, at least to some degree, under our own steam. In these times, any blow struck for the survival or the revival of the home and the family is an act of resistance and of rebuilding.

Back in 1980, Wendell Berry ended his essay by suggesting some actions that could be taken in this direction. As well as the obvious—amongst which 'get rid of the television set' took pride of place—he suggested that we should 'try to make our homes centres of attention and interest'; to make them as productive and nurturing as we can. Once you rid yourself of the propaganda of the corporate media-entertainment complex ('a vacuum line, pumping life and meaning out of the household'), you will see new possibilities begin to open up. You will see, in Berry's words, that 'no life and no place is destitute; all have possibilities of productivity and pleasure, rest and work, solitude and conviviality that belong particularly to themselves', whether in the country, the city or the suburb. 'All that is necessary', he suggests, is 'the time and the inner quietness to look for them.'[5]

The 'all' in that sentence is doing quite a lot of work—more than ever, perhaps, forty years on. Where is time and inner quietness to be found now? It is hard; but perhaps it always was. Even so, it is worth searching out. Home work is, perhaps, the most important work of all, and it will certainly teach you things. Since we moved to our place eight years ago, I've learned—sometimes from choice, sometimes from necessity—a whole suite of new skills, from construction to tree planting, chicken-keeping to breadmaking, hedging to unblocking drains. I've learned how to know my neighbours properly, how to stay in a place and begin to really understand it. The choice to homeschool our children has changed our lives and theirs; I see this now as the most important thing any parent can do to resist Machine culture. Certainly our children are more self-sufficient already than I was by the age of about twenty-five.

Home-making, it turns out, is not something to flee from in pursuit of freedom, as I wanted to do when I was younger. It is a skill, or a whole set of them: a set I have come to value maybe above anything else I do. I am still not very good at it; but even so I feel, on my best days, that I could walk with some of my ancestors and be recognised by them as a fully qualified human being. Maybe this will turn out to be my greatest achievement, in the end.

Back in the day, John Michell concluded that the loss of the fireplace from the heart of the home had driven society mad without it quite knowing. 'We knocked the centre out of it', he wrote, 'and ever since we have been fumbling around looking for it, mistaking our own or other people's obsessions for the real thing.'[6] The Machine's war against home knocks the centre out of our lives in the same way. It throws us all off balance—but we can begin to regain our footing in the place we all came from. The home can be a friction against the Machine. If this is a war, it is long past time to begin fighting back. I recommend starting with the TV, and working out from there. You might be surprised what emerges.

XVIII

The Nation and the Grid

I WAS CAMPING BY A LAKE WHEN I heard the news. My son and I were fishing and hiking in Connemara in the Irish West, hunting down pollock and wrasse and trout and plunging into bogs on the slopes of the Twelve Bens. I'd do this most days if I was allowed. One Thursday evening we were camped on the shores of a lough, cooking our day's catch on a grill as the sun set. Remote though we were, there was still a phone signal—this is the Machine age after all—so my wife was able to bring us the news from the outside world.

'Did you hear that the queen died?' she said.

I hadn't heard. I had been living in a different world for a while. Now I was surprised at the sense of loss which swept over me. You have to be British to understand this—and British at this moment in time especially. For my entire lifetime, and almost all of the lifetime of my parents, 'the Queen' was just *there*. She was on the stamps and the coins and the telly every Christmas. The national anthem was all about her. Technically, she owned the whole country and had the power to dismiss governments and sack prime ministers, but we all knew she would never do so. Even republicans admitted a sneaking admiration for her sense of

duty and her work rate. At least somebody in the country, ran the sub-
text, still knew what *duty* actually meant.

Britain's decline in my lifetime, from a country which ran much of
the world to a country which can barely run itself, has been pretty stark.
Come up with whatever diagnoses you please, blame who you like, but
you can't deny the downward trajectory. Only the queen stood still, or
seemed to, and as she did so she represented something much older than
any of the rules we live by. A monarch has sat on the throne of England
for more than a thousand years. The meaning of this is mostly inaccessi-
ble to our argumentative modern minds.

Now we have a new monarch, we British, and sitting by that Irish
lake last week I felt both sad and, suddenly, homesick. I felt that I wanted
to be back in my country to share what was happening with my people.
All the ceremony that was unfolding around me, leading smoothly and
impressively towards the funeral and the coronation, embodied at once
both the determination of the British state to maintain itself and the
strange, proud, bloody-minded anachronism of the whole business.

How much longer can it last? A monarchy is, after all, an offence
against modernity. It is a hangup from an earlier, more organic age,
which at its worst can be a trapdoor to a particular type of tyranny (our
new king's ancestral namesake ended up with his head in a basket on
this charge) but at its best is a bulwark against another: the money-
power of the Machine. A monarchy is irrational, uncommercial and in-
explicably mystical. It embodies tradition passed down through time. As
such, it is deeply 'unrepresentative' according to the current, constipated
definition of that word. And yet it manages somehow to represent the
spirit of a nation better than any elected politician, celebrity, pundit or
philosopher ever could.

What, after all, is the point of a monarch in the modern world? There
is really only one: to represent a country and its history; to be a living
embodiment of the spirit of a people. As such, the throne represents to

its critics more than some putative offence against 'democracy'. It stands for something whose very existence is increasingly contentious in its meaning, form and direction: the nation itself.

IN THE LAST CHAPTER I WROTE about the home, and its degradation by the culture of the Machine. We are all, men and women, being levered out of the domestic sphere and sold instead a pseudo-egalitarian fulfilment 'in the workplace' at capitalism's behest, upending our family lives and diminishing our self-sufficiency. But if this is true at the domestic level, it can be true at the national level too. A nation is, at least in theory, a home on a grander scale: a home for a people. It will, and must, therefore be in the crosshairs of the new order.

'Nation' is one of those over-capacious words which, if not used carefully, can mean almost anything and almost nothing. A term which can be applied both to an Amazonian tribe and the United States of America has to be handled carefully. Also to be handled carefully are the primal passions it can evoke, on all sides of the aisle. Make an idol of your nation, and you will end up sacrificing human lives to it. At present, the notion of the nation is being bitterly fought over throughout the disintegrating West. There are some for whom a nation is some kind of racial entity, to be protected from external 'pollution' at all costs. There are others for whom a nation is a lie; a historical monstrosity, to be deconstructed as a matter of urgency. The rest of us are somewhere in the middle, treading water, often confused.

But all of this is only evidence that nations matter. And to cut through all the battles, we can hazard a straightforward definition of the word: a nation is a group of people with a shared sense of self, forged through time. Quite how that 'people' is constituted or defined is as varied as the nation itself. Perhaps it is ethnic, tribal, constitutional, or 'civic'. In all cases though, a nation remains a signifier of group belonging—something which seems to have defined humans, for better or for worse, since humans have been around.

Like a monarchy, then, a nation can be hard to define, or perhaps even to justify, at least on reason's terms, and yet it offers the human psyche something that it seems to need. In his Nobel Prize acceptance speech in 1970,[1] Alexander Solzhenitsyn spoke up for this necessity:

> In recent times it has been fashionable to talk of the levelling of nations, of the disappearance of different races in the melting-pot of contemporary civilization. I do not agree with this opinion, but its discussion remains another question. Here it is merely fitting to say that the disappearance of nations would have impoverished us no less than if all men had become alike, with one personality and one face. Nations are the wealth of mankind, its collective personalities; the very least of them wears its own special colours and bears within itself a special facet of divine intention.

We find ourselves part of one of these 'collective personalities' from birth, whether we like it or not, and even if we choose to reject them they provide us with some of our first moorings in the world. The questions all humans will eventually ask—*Who am I? Where do I come from?*—are at least partially answered by the country they find themselves part of. Our national community gives us roots; to quote Simone Weil again, 'to be rooted is perhaps the most important and least recognised need of the human soul'. We are back, again, to our Four Ps.

It should be obvious enough at this point what the Machine anticulture has to say about this kind of thing. It has to say no. At its best, a nation is both a home for a people and a repository of history. At its very best, it may also be built around some spiritual or cultural story that transcends Machine values, and its laws or traditions may offer its people something other than participation in the metastasising consumer globoculture. Even if our nation does not, in fact, offer us much of this, it is clear that large numbers of people would like it to. This explains the rift between 'nationalism' and 'globalism' which defines much of our current moment.

That rift is in many ways a pushback against the anti-national sentiment that has been evident amongst Western cultural elites for decades. Throughout my lifetime, a relentless deconstruction of the legitimacy of nationhood has been a constant background thrum, rising in recent years to a devouring roar. Britain may now have a traditionalist king, but its cultural, intellectual and even spiritual elites can't see a national tradition of any kind without wanting to jump up and down on it in public. To paraphrase Orwell, while they would happily wave a Pride flag from the rooftop of the Shard, they would rather steal from a climate change campaigner than be seen dead anywhere near the Union Jack. This kind of thing has been going on for so long now that it has, ironically, become a new kind of British tradition.

The right to national self-determination is a founding principle of international law, and yet speaking up in favour of this until-recently-uncontroversial notion today is enough in some circles to see you accused of 'blood and soil nativism'. As for defending actual links between people and place across time: don't even think about it, unless you fancy being labelled a 'white supremacist'. The culture of inversion—an oiko-phobic attack on all things Western—finds its most passionate apogee in attacking national feeling.

Christopher Lasch, in *The Revolt of the Elites*, pinpointed the class nature of this dismissal of the nation. While most of us ordinary mortals continue to retain an attachment to our nations, as repositories of our stories and as homelands to which we feel we can belong, cosmopolitan elites regard such notions as backward at best and Hitlerian at worst. Back in 1995, Lasch could already detect the *de haut en bas* elitism that would later come to react to the rise of twenty-first century 'populism' like a plumber to a blocked drain. 'Those who covet membership in the new aristocracy of brains', he wrote, 'tend to congregate on the coast, turning their back on the heartland and cultivating ties with the international market in fast-moving money, glamour, fashion, and popular culture. It is a question whether they think of themselves as Americans at all. Patriotism, certainly, does not rank very high in their hierarchy of virtues.'[2]

How far back can this contempt for the nation be traced? George Orwell was already complaining about it in the 1930s, asserting that 'England is perhaps the only great country whose intellectuals are ashamed of their own nationality.'[3] Clearly the suspicion of nations amongst their elites long precedes twenty-first century 'wokeness'. In fact, it seems to be a logical outgrowth of the rationalist way of seeing that is at the root of Machine modernity. In chapter VI we saw how the French Revolution of the eighteenth century kicked off the era of hyper-rational politics, and while that revolution was, by definition, nationalist, it also had the seeds of a post-national consciousness planted within it. Nationhood, after all, is not really rationally explicable. Borders are abitrary, histories are curious and messy, and 'national identities' are often constructed, or at least not easy to define.

In his book-length defence of the concept of the nation, *The Virtues of Nationalism*, the Israeli author Yoram Hazony suggests that the contemporary elite attitude to the nation, which has become utterly dominant in the institutions of Anglosphere countries, can be traced back to the rationalist philosopher Immanuel Kant. In a 1795 pamphlet called *Perpetual Peace*, written as the French Revolution played itself out,

> Kant argues that the establishment of an international or imperial state is the only possible dictate of reason. Those who do not agree to subordinate their national interests to the directives of the imperial state are regarded as opposing the historic march of humanity

towards the reign of reason. Those who insist on their national freedom are supporting a violent egoism on a national scale.[4]

Few people took this worldview very seriously until World War Two. It was in the bloody aftermath of that war that the Western ruling class's now-dominant vision of a post-national world took root. European nations had been battling each other for centuries, but National Socialism revealed new depths to which a state might sink. Theodor Adorno famously claimed that it was 'barbaric to write poetry after Auschwitz', and for many of Europe's intellectuals, and even politicians, it now seemed barbaric to believe in nationhood too. A notion took root, which remains unquestioned today amongst progressives and liberals, that Nazism was what happened when national feeling was allowed to run riot. Too much nationalism would inevitably lead to something like the Holocaust. The solution, therefore, was to dissolve nationalism, and ultimately nations themselves, in a rational, liberal and borderless 'international order'.

The European Union, seeded soon after the War in the 1950s, is rooted in this vision of national sovereignty 'pooled' (read: abolished) for the greater good. Its founders explicitly created it as an attempt to build a post-national continent over the heads of its people, who were still attached to their own countries. At the same time, the United Nations and the Bretton Woods settlements, under the aegis of the new American Empire, took the same worldview global, whether the globe wanted it or not.

This new consciousness had no time for such backward values as patriotism, or for such dangerous constructs as the nation, which were irrational and built around in-group prejudice. In its place rose a vision of a borderless world of co-operation and peace. This was the latest manifestation of the dream of cosmopolis. It would be post-national and post-roots and it would lead, inevitably, towards technocratic global governance—and, ultimately, towards global government itself. Certainly that was the openly declared aim of many progressive intellectuals of the early twentieth century, just as it was of Immanuel Kant in the eighteenth. We would move beyond the small-minded tribalism of nations, and into the paradise of the universal Machine civilisation. War would be abolished. Bigotry and competition would be left behind. Technology would guide us. Peace would prevail.

From one perspective, this vision has a kind of doomed utopian beauty to it. But it also has a dark side. As we have already seen, a borderless, utopian world with no national boundaries and no national sovereignty also just happens to suit the interests of transnational capital and its enablers. Certainly the Machine cannot co-exist easily with a sense of historic national identity. So it wasn't long before universalist utopianism morphed into commercial globalism. Suddenly, 'no borders' seemed less a promise than a threat. Suddenly, those utopian elites chattering about the need to demolish the 'social construct' of the nation sounded more like they were defending their own class interests than ushering us all towards paradise.

Years ago, when I was writing my book *Real England,* I had a strange sort of vision as I sat in a roadside cafe drinking a mug of tea. I looked out of the window, across the A Road, and I saw the physical manifestation of the Machine in the landscape. I saw the new country that was rising to replace the one I was writing about. I looked over at a couple of huge white boxes squatting on the landscape—delivery hubs, I think, for some supermarket, of the kind which now dominate whole areas of England. I saw them connected by the asphalt roads and the electric wires strung out by pylons, and by the invisible digital currents in the air. All of it was rectangular, straight-edged, dedicated to efficiency and the piling-up of wealth. We were all products of this layout, I saw: we were all shaped by it, internally and externally. It hadn't come from here, of course—it hadn't come from anywhere. Nothing like that even mattered anymore.

Since then, I have thought of this thing as the Grid. The Grid is a physical manifestation of the values of the Machine on the landscape itself, and it is, I think, replacing the nation, just as it is replacing culture and antiquated notions of 'tradition' and the like. It is part of that ongoing process of colonisation. The Grid doesn't care about nations, roots, identities, patriotism or tradition. It doesn't care about anything. It is not made by people, at least not directly, and certainly not in response to the landscape or community that those people inhabit. It demeans both time and space, and its language is geometry and profit. It has corrupted us all by now, so that we have to work hard even just to avoid speaking its language.

It goes without saying that the Grid is also global. Like electricity or the internet, it knows no borders, and neither do its children. It manifests as an identikit globoculture of sameness, a pipeline of product and corporate-progressive verbiage, and its proponents talk relentlessly about 'diversity' because the Grid produces the precise opposite. We all know the bland, correct, corporate Gridspeak we must use to get by in this new country: it is what facilitates Progress, by which we mean uniformity disguised as difference.

In the world of the Grid, a nation becomes little more than a postcode or a glorified airport lounge. In Orwell's dystopic *1984*, England was renamed 'Airstrip One', but today the true situation is almost the reverse of this. The names remain—it is the place that is altered beyond recognition. The culture is hollowed out and replaced by simulacra. A Grid-nation retains the name and flag of its predecessor, and a commercialised version of the former culture, but its population is from everywhere and anywhere, its people consume global corporate culture rather than drawing their own from place and history, and its ruling class would rather be somewhere else. Even the accents sound mid-Atlantic, as citizens of the Grid from Ireland to India all converse in the same bland, globalised, corporate version of 'English'.

All of this is the result of the Black Ships of the globalised economy having done their work so well. European ships, armies and corporations spread Machine values into the world, and now those values have come home to bite the nations which birthed them. Vast and unprecedented levels of migration—a result of the low-cost, globalised economy which sees people, in Lewis Mumford's formulation, as 'human parts' to be shifted around to where their labour is cheapest—are transforming entire nations. Their elites, who tend to benefit from this process and who already see nationhood as 'problematic', have seized the chance over the last several decades to experiment with the notion of 'multiculturalism' as a replacement for the historic nation, and to engage in the process of 'internal colonisation' that we have already seen explained by Robert Bly.

Problematising their own history and sneering at their own people (especially if they happen to be working class), romanticising the 'Other' while parading their virtuous guilt, they sell a story which presents itself as 'inclusive' but which in practice excludes almost everyone. Native populations feel increasing concern about mass immigration, which brings people from radically different cultures into the nation in such numbers that the natives are on the path to minority status in their own countries. The newcomers, in turn, may have difficulty integrating into their new land, fear prejudice from the natives, and are expected to do everyone's dirty jobs without complaining. And any immigrants who do want to be included in the existing national story find that story has been dissolved anyway and replaced with a new one, in which everything is 'diverse' but nothing is rooted in anything but ideology or abstraction.

In this context, it would be easy to portray the current war over nationhood as a David vs Goliath struggle between plucky little nations and dastardly globalists intent on their demise. To me, though, it looks more like a situation in which nobody is clear on what they want or how to get it. Proponents of corporate globalism want a borderless, frictionless world that offers minimal 'barriers to trade' and movement, without the populist reaction that this inevitably fuels. Nationalists want prosperous nations without the cheap immigration that fuels prosperity. Liberals want both 'diversity' and social cohesion, despite the persistent evidence that one undermines the other.[5] The left wants a world without borders that somehow also contains welfare states, while the right wants to defend the ethnic makeup of nations without acknowledging that traditional notions of ethnicity are increasingly impossible in the high-tech globalised world that has resulted from the capitalist economy they have always defended.

This last point is worth zeroing in on. People across the planet are already consuming the same media, wearing the same clothes, watching the same films, buying the same apps and speaking the same language, symbolically and actually. When the phone in your pocket allows you to make more friends in other countries than you can at school, when the whole world is converging on the same digitally enabled globoculture, when you can log on to Instagram in Austria or Australia and order from Amazon in the Amazon, what does your 'nationality' even mean? Travelling around Europe and America recently, seeing this reality in several different countries, I was hit by a striking possibility: that the Machine is birthing its own ethnicity. It is a globalised, screen-enabled, placeless identity that, for many people, seems to be replacing any older, national or regional cultural markers.

It is in this context that so many people see the nation-state as a potential bulwark against Machine globalism. But it is also a reality that the nation-state is what has driven the Machine forward. In theory, a state is supposed to represent, speak for, defend and promote the interests of the nation it governs. In reality, the twenty-first century state, at least in the West, often acts against the directly expressed interests of its people. Nation and state are at loggerheads. States are nodes in the Grid—economic units posing as cultural ones. They pledge themselves to their 'people' and then get on with the job of following the dictates handed down by the EU, the WEF, Silicon Valley or the FTSE 100, whether 'the people' like it or not. This, in a nutshell, explains the rise of the 'populism' that the cosmopolitan elites so decry. Populism grows in the gap between the nation and the state.

To many people, nationalism seems like a reasonable response to this, and sometimes it can be, under the right circumstances. Still, there are good reasons to be nervous about what it can do to the human mind. Humans remain human, and it is not so hard for national feeling to shade into xenophobic triumphalism, just as cosmopolitanism can shade into sneering elitism disguised as compassion. I've long found myself in the uncomfortable position of valuing nations but usually being repelled by nationalism. I'm not sure what to do about this. It seems to me that if you hold your country lightly, it will nourish you, and even complete you. Attach yourself to it needily or defensively or angrily, though, and it will make mincemeat of you just as surely as if you had marched off into the trenches singing the national anthem, only to come face to face with the machine gun nests.

Maybe this position is too delicate for these times. Maybe it is just too late. Or maybe it is missing the point. The point, I think, is to be found beneath the surface layer of politics, and beneath the lower layers of nationhood, ethnicity and culture too. The point, as ever, is spiritual. If our nations seem hollowed-out, if our countries seem to be prey for the Machine, surely it is because they have no soul. If *people, place, prayer* and *the past* are the ground upon which real culture is built, many of us today would have to look at our own countries and conclude that they have no real connection to any of these. Blame the immigrants if you like—it's always the easy option—but they didn't strip the soul out of the nations of the West. We did. Do you think you can build your country around nothing but money and then complain when people want to come in and earn some of it themselves?

René Guénon, with whom our new king is familiar, wrote nearly a century ago in *The Crisis of the Modern World* that a nation without a spiritual purpose would inevitably be replaced in time by another which had one. Nationalism as a political or cultural project, he believed, would be beside the point if the nation in question was nothing but a human collective in search of glory, wealth, power or 'freedom', or was simply rooted in nostalgia. Either the West would rediscover the spiritual roots it had abandoned in pursuit of Machine values, he wrote, or 'Western civilisation will have to disappear completely'.

As for those who shout about 'defending the West': they should remember that 'it is the West that is threatening to submerge and drag down the whole of mankind in the whirlpool of its own confused activity'. The West certainly needed defending, said Guénon—'but only against itself and its own tendencies, which, if they are pushed to their conclusion will lead inevitably to its ruin and destruction'.[6] Nearly a hundred years later, we subjects of the digital Grid should be able to see that Guénon was pointing directly at us.

Solzhenitsyn was right: nations matter. A nation is a story which a people tells about itself across time, and while it is dangerous to be too attached to these stories, or to forget that they are stories at all, it is more dangerous to try and uproot them in some pseudo-egalitarian frenzy. We need our stories, and we need our countries too. They are our repositories of memory, tradition and faith. They are the homes and the burial places of our ancestors. They make us who we are. They cannot simply be abolished, replaced or strip-mined for money, and anyone who tries is likely to receive the full force of a reaction which none of us should look forward to.

Globalism has failed the nation. Liberals and leftists who have long bought into a reflexive and often toxic anti-national narrative should ask why they find themselves on the opposite side to most of the working people of their own countries, but on the same side as transnational capital, unelected and unaccountable global institutions, and anti-democratic elites whose commitment to 'democracy' comes apart as soon as people vote for nationalist politicians. Yet at the same time, a simple, reactionary nationalism will achieve nothing but a deepening of divisions. Anyone who wants to protect, rejuvenate or rebuild their nations must first have an idea of what, at root, that nation is, and they must take into account all of the people living in it. The vast changes that have occurred in Western European nations in my lifetime mean that the old stories many of us grew up with are dead. The Machine killed them. New stories will have to be told now, building on our pasts, taking account of the new present. There is no alternative to facing this reality.

To me, the dissolution of the modern nation-state into smaller, more anarchic, less centralised units would be welcome. Perhaps then we could rediscover the roots of our old nations, and begin to rebuild them again. Perhaps too, new nations will form, built around a spiritual core and a love of place, which will give to their people the kind of meaning which the nation-states of the Machine era have so successfully imitated whilst at the same time destroying. Perhaps we will live in real nations again. Perhaps we will build them. Nobody else can.

XIX

The Fourth Revolution

B Y NOW, YOU MIGHT HAVE HEARD about the rising threat of 'eco-fascism'. If you haven't you soon will, because the number of people warning about this alarming new danger to civilisation seems to be growing exponentially. In publications right and left and neither you'll be able to read long expositions of the origins and intentions of this frightening movement, which seems to be taking root all over the world.

Those essays and articles could be rolled into one easily enough, and sometimes it seems like they have been. The formula is always the same, and can be usefully applied across the political spectrum. Start with talk of the 'rising tide of authoritarianism' all over the world, as evidenced by 'populism', Giorgia Meloni, Viktor Orban, Donald Trump or any other leader you don't like. Move on to explore how much of this 'rising authoritarianism' is reflected in environmentalism, as evidenced by Just Stop Oil, Extinction Rebellion, the Green New Deal, the Great Reset, Bill Gates, Net Zero, Greta Thunberg or [*insert name of bête noire here*].

After this, list the historical inspirations for these new green authoritarians: Ted Kaczynski, Pentti Linkola and Dave Foreman should do for starters. Dig into the most miserable chans and subreddits of the internet and 'expose' a few anonymised avatars promoting race war in the name of the planet. Mention the Christchurch shooter. Use the phrase 'dark undercurrent' a lot. Quote Murray Bookchin. Chuck in the names of a couple of nature writers from the 1930s who became fascists. Mutter darkly about 'blood and soil' and how Hitler was a vegetarian. Did you know there was an organic garden at Dachau? Makes you think, doesn't it?

Having got here, you can move on to the meat of the thing: sombrely intoning about the 'new threat to democracy' which is represented by this ominous movement. Depending on where you're coming from, you can now explain how these new eco-authoritarians represent either [a] a threat to our God-given right to drive, mine, manufacture, fly, drill baby drill, and freely enjoy the glories that only Western Progress can provide, or [b] a threat to diversity, equality, human rights, LGBTQIA++ people, refugees and a woman's right to choose. Either way, the conclusion will be much the same: a non-specific but ominous call for more monitoring of 'problematic' views, more work to tackle 'radicalisation', more 'hate speech' or anti-protest laws and probably more internet regulation. For the safety of us all, of course.

The problem, though, is that actual 'eco-fascism' is notable mostly by its absence. Dark corners of the internet aside—you can find any craziness there, after all—it's hard to find a single 'eco-fascist' anywhere out in the real world. No public intellectuals, no writers, no philosophers, no politicians, no popular movements embrace anything of the kind. Plenty of people get the label applied to them of course—without the prefix, the word 'fascist' has been a meaningless, all-purpose insult for decades—but they all reject it. I was in and around the green movement for a long time, but I never met an eco-fascist, though I did have the pleasure of being called one.

So why all the dire warnings? I can think of two possible explanations. One is fairly straightforward: there is something we can't bear to look at, and we are trying to distract attention from it by screaming at the people who are pointing it out. The thing we are avoiding is the thing that we used to call 'nature', and the reality that we are trying to distract attention from is that we are part of it, we live inside it and everything we do to it we also do to ourselves. Change the climate out there and it changes in here. Erode the soil, erode the soul. Poison the oceans, poison your culture. This is how it works, and this is what we are now facing.

And we cannot truly face it, even those of us who think we can. Whatever we think our politics are (and they are likely to be the least important thing about us), we have no idea what to do about the coming end of the brief age of abundance, and the reappearance, armed and dangerous, of what we could get away with denying for a few decades: limits. Those who point these limits out—and who point out, especially, that the very existence of industrial modernity might be the root cause of the problems we currently face—can expect to be smacked down with the worst insults our culture can conjure.

This is one explanation for the mysterious rise of the ghostly eco-fascists. But I think there might be another. This is that the phrase 'eco-fascist' is a label which is increasingly being applied to the *wrong kind* of environmentalist: those who offer up a vision of humanity and nature that involves roots, smallness, simplicity, a return to previous lifeways, or any other kind of challenge to Machine modernity. This in turn is contrasted with the *right kind* of green: that which is modern, global, 'progressive' and—most importantly of all—friendly to the onward march of the technological society.

A decade or so ago, I wrote an essay called 'Dark Ecology',[1] about the state of environmentalism. In it, I wrote about the emergence of a tendency in green circles which I labelled 'neo-environmentalism'. The neo-greens—who prefer to call themselves 'ecomodernists'—emerged as a reaction to the traditional green movement, which in its infancy had been relatively conservative, low-tech and focused on the human scale. The neo-greens rejected all this as backward, impractical and even dangerous. The 'new environmentalism', they declared, in publications with titles like *An Ecomodernist Manifesto*, would be, as we might now say, 'grown-up'.

In 'Dark Ecology' I described the neo-greens like this:

The neo-environmentalists are distinguished by their attitude to new technologies, which they almost uniformly see as positive. Civilisation, nature and people can be 'saved' only by enthusiastically embracing biotechnology, synthetic biology, nuclear power, geoengineering and anything else with the prefix 'new' that annoys Greenpeace. The traditional green focus on 'limits' is dismissed as naive. We are now, in [Stewart] Brand's words, 'as gods', and we have to step up and accept our responsibility to manage the planet rationally through the use of new technology guided by enlightened science . . .

Since I wrote that essay, the neo-greens have indeed mounted an effective corporate takeover of most of the environmental movement. Examples of what we might call Machine Environmentalism have been embraced by the corporate sector, big NGOs, global institutions and most of the intellectual class, most obviously in the 'Green New Deals' that are popping up like summer daisies in all corners of the globe. Meanwhile, as I also glumly predicted, the green movement is splintering into camps, determined by attitudes to the kind of intrusive and novel technologies that the Machine Greens are pushing as our final means of salvation.

In Britain, for example, this divide has been illustrated recently by attitudes to green pundit George Monbiot's latest book, which embraces the neo-green vision. In the humbly titled *Regenesis*, Monbiot, an urban vegan intellectual, makes a case—based, naturally, on the 'peer-reviewed science'—for the 'end of most farming' and the replacement of much of its output with vat-grown, bacterial 'food' manufactured via 'industrial biotechnology'.[2] The vast acreages of land which have been stripped of their farmers can then be 'rewilded' in various Monbiot-approved ways, which mainly seem to involve growing forests for always-on urbanites to go wolf-spotting in at weekends.

In promoting a high-tech, globalised food system (perhaps overseen by the world government he has previously argued for)[3] and casually calling for the destruction of the basis of post-Neolithic human civilisation, Monbiot offers a perfect example of what a neo-green future will look like: utopian, hyper-urban, technological, rational and most of all 'efficient'. What matters now, he explains, is mathematics. 'It's time we became obsessed by numbers', he insists, as if this were not already the case virtually everywhere. 'We need to compare yields, compare land uses, compare the diversity and abundance of wildlife, compare emissions, erosion, pollution, costs, inputs, nutrition, across every aspect of food production.'[4]

In case the point was not clear enough, Monbiot explains elsewhere in the book that 'One of the greatest threats to life on Earth is poetry.' Even allowing for his customary hyperbole, the message is as clear as an empty test tube. Welcome to what the greens have become.

'Industrial biotechnology' is the latest tech-fix joining the growing list of other 'green' innovations which are set to cut our world of megacities and glowing screens off even further from the real world. The pioneering Finnish 'solar food' company championed[5] by Monbiot as part of the future of food, for example, says that the production hub in which it produces its 'novel food'—a laboratory which it calls 'Factory 01'—is part of a 'food revolution' which will, for the first time in history, detach food production from the land, the farmers who work it and the culture it creates. Excitable admirers are already explaining that this may give us the ability to one day 3D-print our own food.[6] I'm salivating already.

Older, crustier greenies like me, labouring under the yoke of a pre-modern sensibility which makes us reluctant to eat the sludge and live in the pod, might feel that something has gone terribly wrong with the numbers-obsessed rationalism that underlies this new, corporate-friendly green technocracy. But we have no five-point plan of our own, and we can't peer-review our intuition, so our complaints don't convince anybody who matters. And now that the localists, the distributists, the deep ecologists, the neo-Luddites, the peasants, the small farmers and anyone else whose human-scale vision actually interferes with the march of Progress have been usefully designated as 'eco-fascists', we are able to behold the only legitimate form of environmentalism which remains: a globalised, technocratic, 'progressive' push for 'sustainability', led by intellectuals, entrepreneurs and professional activists, following The Science down a path which just happens to lead to the triumph of the Machine.

The green movement, long ago co-opted by the left, has now been co-opted too by technocrats. For this reason, the neo-green food future can't be viewed in isolation. It is only one aspect of the unfolding phenomenon which has been dubbed the 'Fourth Industrial Revolution'—a revolution in which the Machine Greens, wittingly or otherwise, are playing a key part. Dreamt up, like so many other catchy corporate catchphrases, by the World Economic Forum, the Fourth Industrial Revolution is a way of describing our historical moment, and it's not a bad summary of the state we're in. In a book of the same name, published in 2015 by *Foreign Affairs* to accompany the annual Davos gathering of politicians, business leaders and Bono, the inescapable Klaus Schwab makes his case:

> We stand on the brink of a technological revolution that will fundamentally alter the way we live, work, and relate to one another. In its scale, scope, and complexity, the transformation will be unlike

anything humankind has experienced before. We do not yet know just how it will unfold, but one thing is clear: the response to it must be integrated and comprehensive, involving all stakeholders of the global polity, from the public and private sectors to academia and civil society.[7]

Schwab, a man whose prose style could make a Martian invasion sound boring, goes on to outline humans' three previous revolutions, and the coming of their successor. 'The First Industrial Revolution', he explains, 'used water and steam power to mechanize production. The Second used electric power to create mass production. The Third used electronics and information technology to automate production. Now a Fourth Industrial Revolution is building on the Third, the digital revolution that has been occurring since the middle of the last century. It is characterized by a fusion of technologies that is blurring the lines between the physical, digital, and biological spheres.'

The rest of the book, made up of offerings from various scientists, engineers, politicians and philosophers, explores the implications of this 'blurring of lines' between created and uncreated, natural and artificial, wild and tamed. Now that we inhabit what the neo-greens like to call the 'Anthropocene'—now that we are, in H. G. Wells's formulation, *Men Like Gods*—what do we intend to conjure with the thunder and the lightning that pours forth from our just and rational fingers?

All of the contributors stress that overcoming the old-school distinction between the digital and the natural is the essence of the thing. Neil Gershenfeld, for example, defines the 'digital fabrication revolution'—the one which will soon be growing our tank-bred bio-sludge dinners—as 'the ability to turn data into things and things into data'. Gershenfeld writes of the potential ability to build a homemade drone that can 'fly right out of the printer'. That printer will eventually be able to 'make all its own parts', so that the tech being used to build physical things out of digital data will itself become self-replicating.[8] Every home will become a lab which can whip up anything we desire, from junk food to sex dolls.

This kind of 'distributed solution' (the actual problem remains mysteriously vague) is the essence of the coming Internet of Things and its associated Internet of Bodies. 'Intelligent' buildings, wearable sensors, implanted chips: in 2016, when the WEF's book was published, these may have seemed radical. Today, it feels as if they have been almost normalised. Partly this is because of the ubiquity of Amazon Alexas, smartphone apps and endless, boosterish narratives about the exciting future that AI is building. And partly it is because the COVID pandemic was used as a trial run for precisely the kinds of technologies—smartphone-enabled passports, under-the-skin microchips, digital population tracking, media-driven narrative control, psychological 'nudging'—which are now increasingly sold to us as a means of 'saving the planet'.

The Fourth Industrial Revolution explores everything from the creation of artificial life through synthetic biology (spoiler: it's already happened), digital finance, gene editing, the morality of robotics, the 'new world order' of the 'second machine age', and the future of cities. Not all of the contributors are starry-eyed about what is unfolding, but all agree on the breathtaking speed of it. This rapid transformation is surely one reason that the world seems so unstable, confusing and manic as the 2020s unfold. All that is solid melts into bytes and is transformed into data. Then you can print it out at home in any shape you please. Behold: liberation!

Perhaps the most important aspect of the Fourth Revolution, though, is what has been called 'datafication'. The book's chapter on 'Big Data' explains that the knowledge available to each of us today on the internet dwarfs that which would have been available in the Great Library of Alexandria, the greatest repository of learning in the ancient world. 'Today', intone the authors, 'there is enough information in the world to give every person alive 320 times as much of it as historians think was stored in Alexandria's entire collection—an estimated 1,200 exabytes' worth.'[9]

But size, as they explain, isn't everything. 'Big data is also characterized by the ability to render into data many aspects of the world that have never been quantified before.' They call this process 'datafication', and give the example of how it has happened to geography, 'first with the invention of longitude and latitude, and more recently with GPS satellite systems. Words are treated as data when computers mine centuries' worth of books. Even friendships and "likes" are datafied, via Facebook.'

Here we see the same 'obsession with numbers' that George Monbiot demands of us as we contemplate how to produce our food and live in our landscape, and it reveals the elision of Machine Environmentalism and the elite-driven tech revolution it is part of. What we can see is that both achieve their goals through the process of datafication: the quantification of everything. The pattern of reality will be transformed into bits and bytes, comparisons and yields, numbers and statistics, until even novels and friendships and meadows and family meals on winter nights can be measured and compared and judged for their relative contributions to efficiency and sustainability.

There is a rift here, and we should gaze deep into it, because there is something down there that we need to make out. It is the ancient rift between those who embrace the mindset of 'datafication' and those who are repelled by it. It is a very old rift—'datafication', in the form of sums and the written language they are recorded in, is one of the foundations of civilisation—and I suspect it can never really be healed, because it marks the border between two distinct ways of seeing. We might call them right and left brain, *mythos* and *logos*, or perhaps most simply the sacred and the profane.

The Fourth Revolution, and the Machine Environmentalism which it contains, offer us a profoundly profane vision of the world. Life in this understanding is not a sacred thing—what does 'sacred' mean after all?—but an engineering challenge. It is something which can be studied, quantified and constantly tweaked until we arrive at the most efficient version, best suited to our needs and designed to achieve maximum efficiency, sustainability, equality and progress. The world of Big Data is a world in which an astute study of 'the numbers' can always help us arrive at the right conclusion.

All of this may be done with the best of intentions (or it may not), but the things which cannot be measured will of course be left out of the equation, and the things which cannot be measured happen to be the stuff of life. Love. God. Place. Culture. The profound mystery of beauty. A sense of being rooted. A feeling for land or community or cultural traditions or the unfolding of human history over generations. Song. Art. They'll 'datafy' all of this soon enough, no doubt, or try to. But the kind of people who think that the Great Library of Alexandria contained 'exabytes' worth of information' rather than the collected fruits of hard-won wisdom are lost before they ever sit down to their datasets.

If you have ever wondered why climate change has so utterly dominated the green debate to the exclusion of so many other problems which stem from industrial society—mass extinction, soil erosion, the collapse of human cultures, ocean pollution, fill in the blanks—then the answer, I think, is here. Climate change is a problem amenable to numerical questions and technocratic answers which go with the grain of a Machine culture. It is, furthermore, a problem which, almost by definition, can only be solved by elites. If you can't read or understand the 'peer-reviewed science', then you are open to being intimidated into fearful silence by those who can, or claim they can. And those people—drawn, as all green 'thought leaders' are, from the upper strata of society—will bring with them a worldview which treats the mass of humanity like so many cattle to be herded into the sustainable, zero-carbon pen.

Interestingly, some of the progenitors of the Fourth Revolution are themselves uneasy about where some of it is leading. Even Klaus Schwab, who in recent years has often been presented as a volcano-dwelling Bond villain pulling the global strings, admits to unease at the speed and scale of change, and how our 'quintessential human capacities such as compassion and co-operation' might be eroded by deep shifts like these. The Fourth Industrial Revolution, he admits, 'will change not only what we do but also who we are. It will affect our identity and all the issues associated with it: our sense of privacy, our notions of ownership, our consumption patterns, the time we devote to work and leisure, and how we develop our careers, cultivate our skills, meet people, and nurture relationships. It is already changing our health and leading to a "quanti-fied" self, and sooner than we think it may lead to human augmenta-tion.'[10]

Even as he promotes it, Schwab can see what is coming. Google maps and smartphone apps were always just the beginning. We are headed into a Brave New World of all-knowing smart homes and vat-grown sludge for breakfast, and every step along that road will make perfect rational sense. A panopticon world, remade at the nano level by the al-legedly well-meaning, lies just around the corner. C. S. Lewis under-stood the trap well:

> Of all tyrannies, a tyranny sincerely exercised for the good of its victims may be the most oppressive. It would be better to live under robber barons than under omnipotent moral busybodies. The rob-ber baron's cruelty may sometimes sleep, his cupidity may at some point be satiated; but those who torment us for our own good will torment us without end, for they do so with the approval of their own conscience.[11]

When the robber baron is also an omniscient moral busybody, we might be in trouble.

For at least two hundred years we have been thoroughly undermining the foundations of all of our assumptions. Now, new cracks in the masonry are appearing daily. Can we caulk them up with vat-grown eco-sludge and hope they don't spread? Can Big Data come to our rescue? What can we measure, manage, monitor, to help us escape from this? You know what I think, though I often wish I didn't. We are living now through what may be the final triumph of Rational Man. The tower he has made has nearly touched the very roof of the world. Every old story can tell us what will happen next.

XX

What Progress Wants

WHAT ARE WE APPROACHING HERE? In the last few chapters, we have explored the origins and direction of the West's current 'culture war', and I have made the claim that it is a surface manifestation of a much deeper upheaval, a 'Great Unsettling' caused by the rise of this Machine to prominence. We have been divorced from our traditional ways of understanding and navigating the world—those Four Ps on which most cultures are based—and have been pitched instead into a world built around the Four Ss. They might in turn be a manifestation of Jacques Ellul's notion of 'technique'—a technological and utilitarian worldview, which will inevitably lead to the rise of a technological and utilitarian anticulture, cored around self-will. The rise of that anticulture is the story of our time.

This is an economic and a political claim, I suppose, but it is also something else: it is a spiritual claim. The strange ructions of the time seem to be happening at a level far below that of politics or economics, or science or reason, or even philosophy, which might be why things seem so confusing and hard to get a handle on. If we are, as I believe, fundamentally religious or spiritual people, and if human culture is at root a spiritual (rather than an economic or political) creation, then the question at this stage must be: What is the theology of the Machine? Where is it leading us? What, in spiritual terms, does it represent? What does it want?

René Guénon, who we first met in chapter I, also felt something moving beneath the surface of the age, and as a Sufi Muslim, he wasn't shy about naming it. To this age, he wrote, 'the word "Satanic" can indeed be properly applied'. Presenting disorder as order and truth as lies—this, wrote Guénon, was the way that Satan rolled. The 'more or less direct agents of the Adversary', he explained, using the Biblical name for what Europeans would later come to call the Devil, always aimed to invert reality. Right is wrong, black is white, up is down, there is no truth, do what thou wilt: this has always been the Adversary's line, and today it is prominent in all quarters. Dis-integration is the tenor of the times.

The heterodox Catholic philosopher Ivan Illich, who died in 2002, also believed we were living in the time of Antichrist, but for different reasons. For Illich, any claims that we lived in a 'secular age' were nonsense. The modern West was still Christian, he said, but it had disastrously attempted to codify the spontaneous expressions of love which Christ had shown to be God's desire for humanity within systems and institutions. First the Church, and then the supposedly 'secular' liberal states which had succeeded it, had attempted to transmute Christian love into obligation and enforce it by law, thus twisting it into a new form of oppression. The modern West had become a monstrous 'corruption of the New Testament', explained Illich's biographer David Cayley. Did this mean that we were now in a post-Christian era? 'On the contrary', said Illich, 'I believe this to be the most obviously Christian epoch, which might be quite close to the end of the world.'[1]

A decade or so before Illich was writing, the Jewish Beat poet Allen Ginsberg was also attending to the dark spiritual undercurrent of the age. He had a different interpretation of its source, or perhaps he was just using a different name. In his magnum opus 'Howl', he identified the forward march of industrial modernity—and especially the hypocrisy and brutality of the American Empire—with the mythical pagan god Moloch, who demanded human sacrifice from his devotees. Ginsberg's Moloch is an amalgam of exclamatory horrors:

> Solitude! Filth! Ugliness! Ashcans and unobtainable dollars! Children screaming under the stairways! Boys sobbing in armies! Old men weeping in the parks!

His mind is 'pure machinery', his blood is 'running money', his love is 'endless oil and stone' and his soul is 'electricity and banks.' He still sounds very familiar.

Nearly seventy years on, the output of the Beats, and the counterculture in general, can sometimes read like a giant scream of pain. *What is this thing that is eating us?* There was, it turned out, no answer to be found in sex and drugs and rock 'n' roll: that was what Moloch wanted all along. The long litany of dead rock stars and alcoholic poets and drug-broken 'celebrities' that the post-sixties era cast up are only his latest sacrifices.

Ginsberg, it seemed, could also sense that the spirit of his age was not under human control, either out in the world or in his own soul and mind. This is usually easier to talk about in poetry or fiction, for the age doesn't look kindly on anything which can't be quantified. It can deal with Ginsberg, but it doesn't want to talk about Moloch. It can just about cope with Christ if he has been brought down to our level—made into an activist or a defender of culture or a 'cosmic' manifestation of the self—but it has nothing to say about Antichrist, who blows the whole story sky-high. As for St Paul's famous notion that the world is subject not only to nature but to 'principalities and powers' which wish us ill: this kind of talk was supposed to have been wrecked on the shores of the Enlightenment, never to be seen again.

But the powers and principalities didn't die in the shipwreck of the old world, they just took on new forms. Today we can, in fact, still talk about these strange, underlying forces as long as we use the correct language. Take for example the Silicon Valley philosopher Kevin Kelly's pet notion that technology has its own mind and its own purpose: that through the web of what he calls 'the technium', something is using us to create itself. Kelly sees technology growing into something self-aware and independent of its human creators, as he explains in his book *What Technology Wants*:

> After ten thousand years of slow evolution and two hundred years of incredible intricate exfoliation, the technium is maturing into its own thing. Its sustaining network of self-reinforcing processes and parts have given it a noticeable measure of autonomy. It may have once been as simple as an old computer program, merely parroting what we told it, but now it is more like a very complex organism that often follows its own urges.[2]

Other Silicon Valley mavens, from Mark Zuckerberg with his metaverse to Ray Kurzweil with his singularity, regularly talk in the same register about where the technium—the Machine—is taking us. Our job, they seem to imply, is simply to service it as it rolls forward under its own steam, remaking everything in its own image, rebuilding the world, turning us, if we are lucky, into little gods. They never consider where this story has been heard before. They never confront, or seem to even comprehend, what Illich or Guénon or even Ginsberg would have known, and which many a saint would confirm if they could hear the technium's new story: that 'AI', on the right lips, can sound like just another way of saying 'Antichrist'.

Humour me. Imagine for a moment that some force is active in the world which is beyond us. Perhaps we have created it. Perhaps it is independent of us. Perhaps it created itself and uses us for its ends. Either way, in recent years that force seems to have become manifest in some way we can't quite put our finger on, and has stimulated the craziness of the times. Perhaps it has become self-aware, like *The Terminator*'s Skynet; perhaps it is approaching its singularity. Perhaps it has always been there, watching, and is now seizing its moment. Or perhaps it is simply beginning to spin out of control, as our systems and technologies become so complex that we can no longer steer them in our chosen direction. Either way, this force seems to be, in some inexplicable way, independent of us, and yet acting within us too.

Let's give this force a name: a less provocative name, for now, than Moloch or Antichrist. Let's keep it simple. Let's just call this force 'Progress'. Then, à la Kevin Kelly, let's ask ourselves a simple question:

What does Progress want?

THE ITALIAN PHILOSOPHER AUGUSTO DEL NOCE saw the modern era as a thorough and permanent revolution—a radical break with the human past. He defined a modern person as 'someone who thinks that "today it is no longer possible."' We do not tend to see our time as continuous with what has gone before. Instead, we believe we live after what Del Noce called a 'violent break with history': a move from the 'kingdom of necessity' to the 'kingdom of freedom'. In the story of Progress which informs our view of history and society, the revolutions of the modern age—industrial, political and intellectual—are assumed to have radically changed the world. By sweeping away old ways of thinking, seeing and living, modernity has produced 'a type of violence capable of breaking the *continuum* of history.'[3]

What Progress wants is the end of history.

Del Noce has recently been noticed outside his native Italy as a result of a new collection of his essays and lectures, translated into English as *The Crisis of Modernity*. This crisis, in Del Noce's view, is one of exclusion: it is what the modern way of seeing leaves out that matters. What is it, asks Del Noce, that 'is no longer possible'? The answer 'is simple: what is excluded is the "supernatural," religious transcendence. . . . For rationalists, certainty about an irreversible historical process towards radical immanentism has replaced what for medieval thinkers was faith in revelation.'[4]

Del Noce's ideas are complex, but this claim gets to the heart of the matter. The modern epoch, guided by those Four Ss, rejects the notion of anything 'unseen' or 'beyond'. From the eighteenth century onwards, philosophy sweeps away religion: the world is now understood in purely human terms, and managed with purely human notions. Everything becomes *immanent*: literally down-to-Earth. There are no principalities or powers, and so everything is potentially transformable and explicable through human might. This is another way of framing Guénon's 'Western deviation': a 'progressive materialisation' that leads us into a 'reign of quantity' in which we take on the role of the Creator for ourselves.

What Progress wants is the end of transcendence.

All of this, said Del Noce, marks a radical transformation in human seeing. It is, for example, a 'sharp break with respect to the Greek and medieval periods'. Both the followers of Plato and the followers of Christ (not to mention every other pre-modern culture on Earth, in their own particular ways) believed that truth was transcendent, eternal and uncreated, and could be known through some combination of faith, practice and reason. No longer, said Del Noce: the only 'transcendence' that our age will permit is that which we create ourselves. Modernity 'marks a major break by fully developing the anthropological theme, so that transcendence pictured as "beyond" is replaced by transcendence within the world.'[5]

'Transcendence within the world' can also be translated as 'Progress'. With no ultimate truth or higher story, there is nothing to stop us bending the universe to our desires: indeed, to do so is our duty. This, in Del Noce's telling, explained twentieth-century history. Having replaced religion with philosophy, we then tried putting philosophy into practice on a grand scale, with terrible results.

How do we shape the universe in the age of immanence? 'The spiritual power that in the Middle Ages had been exercised by the Church . . . today can be exercised only by science',[6] writes Del Noce. Echoing Rupert Sheldrake's critique from chapter VII, Del Noce writes of a '"totalitarian" conception of science in which science is regarded as the only true form of knowledge. According to this view, every other type of knowledge—metaphysical or religious—expresses only "subjective reactions," which we are able, or will be able, to explain by extending science to the human sphere through psychological and sociological research.'[7]

But the rise of science did not lead to the end of religion. Instead—as noted by Illich—religion responded to the challenge by becoming immanent itself. Western Christianity progressively abandoned its commitment to transcendence and was 'resolved into philosophy', allowing itself to be brought down to Earth, into the realm of social activism, politics and ideas. The conversion of a large part of the religious world to the idea of modernity, said Del Noce, 'accelerated the process of disintegration' that the modern revolution had unleashed.[8]

What Progress wants is the death of God.

But Man cannot live by immanence alone. Religion meets a human need, and when it is gone, or corrupted, the hole it leaves will have to be filled by something else. What will that be? Del Noce's answer is: revolution.

Modernity, he suggests, could be defined as a permanent, ongoing revolution. The desire to build Utopia on the bones of the old world has been the consuming fire of Western thought for 300 years. Jacobins, Bolsheviks, communists, socialists, Fascists, Nazis and many more have all attempted to scour the ground clean and start again, and we are not done yet. 'The revolutionary attitude of creative violence', writes Del Noce, 'has replaced the ascetic attitude of seeking liberation from the world.'[9] If once society's refuseniks imitated St Anthony, now they copy Che Guevara. 'All that is solid melts into air': this, in the words of its most consequential revolutionary mind, is the best description of the age of immanence that we have ever had.

What Progress wants is permanent revolution.

The two world wars of the twentieth century—which Del Noce prefers to view as a single European conflict lasting from 1914 until 1945—spread this revolution against transcendence and tradition all around the world. After 1945, Americans, representatives of the most immanent nation in history, took on the global responsibility for waging 'the Enlightenment's war against their own past'. America, said Del Noce, was now 'the wellspring of the principle of disintegration',[10] which, along with its European allies and mentors, it was spreading around the world through the globalisation of its institutions and worldview.

Del Noce agrees with the prophetic Simone Weil that 'the Americanisation of Europe would lead to the Americanisation of the whole world'—and so it has proven. He also echoes Robert Bly's critique, which we encountered in chapter XIII, that Europe, by pursuing the path of pure immanence, had in any case already doomed itself, by turning on itself the weapons it had long used on others. 'Colonization', Del

Noce writes, 'can be achieved by only one method: by uprooting a people from its traditions. Europeans have a long history of extensively practising this method (and this was Europe's greatest historical fault). Now—oh, wonder!—in order to feign regret they are applying the same method to themselves.'[11]

What Progress wants is colonisation.

Where would all this lead? The ultimate result of the revolution of modernity, predicted Del Noce, would be fragmentation, nihilism, and 'the death of the sacred'. The twin revolutionary engines of the postwar era, he suggested, were scientism and sex. The first usurped the role of religion and culture, reducing all life to the level of the measurable and controllable. The second, via the sexual revolution of the 1960s and the resulting 'permissive society', unleashed a radical individualism that celebrated sexual desire as a virtue, which would lead to the fragmentation of everything from nationhood to the family—but leave capitalism and its attendant class, the bourgeoisie, intact:

> It is now clear how the process of criticism of authority, which originally was directed against conservatism, against false consciousness, against mystification etc., ends up reaching the greatest degree of conservatism and linguistic falsification ever known in history. It would be easy to illustrate from this perspective the new features displayed by the contemporary crisis: the collapse of faith in all ideals, to a degree never seen before; the resulting loss of hope; the falsification of love, almost always bestowed on something 'far' in order to justify indifference or hostility towards what is near.[12]

What Progress wants is the uprooting of everything.

Modernity, in the final accounting, took aim at all authority, all tradition, everything rooted and everything past. Del Noce's prediction,
made decades ago, was that the end result of modernity's revolutions
would be the rise of a 'new totalitarianism'. This time around it would
not involve jackboots and camps. Instead, it would be a technocracy
built on scientism and implemented by managerial elites, designed to
ensure that order could continue after modernity had ripped up all former sources of authority and truth. 'The age of the revolution gave up
on searching for unity, and accepted a sharp opposition', he wrote. 'The
ideal endpoint is identified with liberation from authority, from the
reign of force and necessity. However, what has happened so far suggests,
rather, that the rejection of authority, understood in its metaphysical-
religious foundation, leads instead to the fullness of "power."'

Create a void, in other words, and into it will rush monsters.

The new totalitarianism, suggested Del Noce, would 'absolutely
deny traditional morality and religion', basing its worldview instead on
'scientistic dogmatism'. It would negate all 'spiritual forces', including
those which, in the 1930s, had been used to resist the totalitarianisms of
Hitler and Stalin: 'the Christian tradition, liberalism, and humanitarian
socialism'. It would be a 'totalitarianism of disintegration', even more
so than Russian communism, which had presented itself to some degree
as a continuation of national tradition. This time around, though, 'the
complete negation of all tradition', including that of 'fatherlands'—
nations—would lead to rule by the only large institutions still standing:
global corporations.[13]

Faced with this challenge, Del Noce insisted that 'current political for-
mulas are completely inadequate'. Neither left nor right were equipped to
understand what was going on: both, instead, would typically retreat to
their historic comfort zones, with the left blaming 'fascists' and the right

blaming 'Marxists' for the ongoing disintegration. The real source of the disintegration, though, was not partisan: it was the Machine.

What Progress wants is liberation from everything.

Progress. The Machine. Moloch. Antichrist. The technium. We are all grasping here, trying to name something we cannot quite see, but whose impacts we can feel undermining the foundations of everything we have known. Augusto Del Noce's analysis of the modern revolution, and the rootless, spiritless, immanent world it had produced, pointed to the ultimate destination as both totalitarianism and nihilism.

Kevin Kelly, of course, would disagree. For him and his fellow tech idealists, the clearing-away of the transcendent realm is only a precursor to building another one—and getting it right this time:

> Technology's dominance ultimately stems not from its birth in human minds but from its origin in the same self-organisation that brought galaxies, planets, life, and minds into existence. It is part of a great asymmetrical arc that begins at the big bang and extends into ever more abstract and immaterial forms over time. The arc is the slow yet irreversible liberation from the ancient imperative of matter and energy.[14]

What Progress wants is to move beyond nature.

Del Noce is often referred to as a conservative or a reactionary thinker, but he didn't accept either label. Simple 'reaction', he said, was no solution to what was unfolding. Both nostalgia and utopia were ultimately fruitless as tools of resistance. If permanent revolution, and the consequent disintegration, is the baseline state of a world that denies transcendence, then the alternative is clear: a return to the spiritual centre. A rediscovery, or a reclamation, of the transcendent realm and its place in our lives. This, and only this, is the alternative to the reign of quantity and its attendant cast of gods, demons and machines.

What Moloch wants—Moloch whose soul is electricity and banks—is sacrifice. We must sacrifice ourselves and our children to the robot apartments and stunned governments. What Antichrist wants is the opposite of transcendence. If the coming of Christ represents the transcendent breaking into the temporal in order to change it, then His opponent will herald a world of pure matter, uninterrupted by anything beyond human reach. Everything in that world is up for grabs. Anything, from rainforests to the human body, can be claimed and reshaped in the interests of advancing the realm of the human will. It is the oldest story.

The rushing power that runs beneath the age of Progress, the energy of the modern world, the river that carries us onwards—where is it taking us? We know the answer. Humans cannot live for very long without a glimpse of the transcendent, or an aspiration, dimly understood, to become one with it. Denied this path, we will make our own. Denied a glimpse of heaven, we will try to build it here. This imperfect world, these imperfect people—they must be superseded, improved, remade. Flawed matter is in our hands now. We know what to do.

What Progress wants is to replace us.

Perhaps the last remaining question is whether we will let it.

XXI

God in the Age of Iron

I ALWAYS HATED CARS. SPEND ENOUGH TIME stuck in traffic on a British motorway as a reluctant child being dragged to see some distant relative or other, and this will be a natural reaction. *Are we there yet?* might be the defining question of the Machine Age. The answer will vary— *Not yet*, *Nearly*, or *Be quiet and stop asking*—but it's always designed to shut the child up so that the driver can concentrate on the road. The road seems to get longer every year, and the traffic slower. More roads are built to tackle this problem, but they make it worse, which necessitates more roads. We are always short of roads, somehow, just as we are always short of houses, hospitals and 'growth'. Every year we are nearly there, and yet somehow also further away. Every year, we come a little closer to forgetting why we set out in the first place.

I'm digressing. I was talking about cars, and why I hated them. I could rationalise this easily enough by talking about air pollution and climate change and the like, and these would all be valid things to talk about, but they would be downstream of the source. The source of my hatred of cars was always more inexplicable and harder to reach, like the heartwood of an old oak still standing after centuries, just. It was that cars did to my inner landscape what they do to our outer landscape. The congestion, the pollution, the noise, the demolition of the histories and forests of the heart: the car roused in me what D. H. Lawrence called the 'inward revolt of the native creatures of the soul'.

I own a car now, but the inner rebellion is not really quieted. As a young man it raged like a high fire. I was a road protestor for a while, resisting the then-Tory government's massive motorway-building programme, all designed to 'get Britain moving', which means that today I have a sense of weary deja vu. Back then, we young greenies would gather dozens of cyclists and bike slowly around roundabouts, holding up the traffic while wearing T-shirts that said *One Less Car!* There was a brief moment in the late nineties when it seemed that the state might direct its energy towards reducing car use and promoting public transport, but that all fell apart along with most of our illusions. Still, I retained my strange loathing of cars. For a while I refused even to travel in one, and I put off owning one as long as I could, only finally giving in to the inevitable in my forties when I moved to the country, miles from any bus route.

But this is all politics, and beneath the politics, for me and most of my friends, lurked something else. Cars *did something to the world;* something it was hard to put your finger on but which you could feel all around you. Often, I have wondered at what it would have been like to live in a world without engines, to experience human life without the hum or roar or traffic or the smell of petrol and diesel. This new world is scarcely a century old, but the car has changed everything. The distance we can travel has remodelled and homogenised the entire globe. Motorways have replaced country lanes; careless speed has replaced actual travel. Entire cities have been demolished, along with entire ways of being. It is impossible for us to feel the world as it was when the sound of transport was the sound of horses' hooves and the wash of boats. It is impossible for us to imagine a world without oil refineries and plastic everything. The car took it all away.

Plato's theory of forms posited that the things we experience around us daily are manifestations of higher 'forms' which exist separately in some other dimension. Forms are perfect blueprints of objects—a table, a circle, a tree—which are represented imperfectly by their physical equivalents here on Earth. Everything we experience here has a perfect analogy, a perfect representative form, somewhere in the heavens. Though we may never see the forms themselves, we can intuit their existence by paying attention to the world around us.

I have written already about how the world's patchwork of sovereign nations is being replaced by something I called the Grid: a physical manifestation of the values of the Machine, appearing as a pattern across the global landscape. I wonder now if the Grid is a form coming into being. Perhaps the car is also, for the two fit together, just as they fit with the internet and the aeroplane and STEM and the skyscraper. Perhaps Plato would tell us that these are all forms made manifest by modernity itself. Forms that were waiting for us to conjure them into being as we moved, in just the last few centuries, from the age of biology into the age of technology. If these are the forms of modernity—the Forms of the Machine— they seem *qualitatively* different to what went before, just as the car is qualitatively different to the horse or the cart. What is it that is being made manifest here? Where has it come from? And what does it want from us?

THE PHILOSOPHER JEREMY NAYDLER MAKES A stab at an answer in his recent book *In the Shadow of the Machine*. His subtitle—'The Prehistory of the Computer and the Evolution of Consciousness'—makes his case, for Naydler is trying to understand what this shift in our way of seeing is, and how it has led us here. Specifically, in attempting to trace 'the prehistory of the computer', he is following an instinct that the digital age, which has now thoroughly colonised and rewired our minds, represents a change that is far more than technological:

> While the physical computer has entered the world as a result of modern scientific and technological skill, modern science and technology are themselves manifestations of a type of consciousness that has taken millennia to develop. As we shall see, this consciousness is quite different from the type of consciousness that prevailed in past times. Unless we take this fact into account and view the origins of the computer within the historical perspective of the evolution of consciousness, we shall fail to see the deeper significance of the computer and the specific challenges that it presents to us today.[1]

What changed? Naydler's historical journey walks us down a path from a pre-modern 'participative consciousness' in which 'everything in nature was experienced as being far more alive than it is today' to a 'mechanistic outlook' in which nature, human and non-human, stopped being a whole and became instead a series of parts. Naydler describes this process, rather intriguingly, as 'human consciousness succumbing increasingly to the dominion of gravity'. Something, he seems to suggest, has been steadily pulling us down, into the purely material realm— into René Guénon's 'reign of quantity'.

This pull has exerted itself for millennia. Recently, we have given it a name: Progress. Due to Progress, we are better, smarter and more advanced people than our ancestors. The Enlightenment and the Industrial Revolution gave us the opportunity to leap forward, philosophically and technologically, and so we left behind superstition and barbarism and moved into the era of good dentistry and space rockets. We continue to move, as we 'liberate' ourselves from form, tradition, structure, prejudice, and ultimately nature itself.

Naydler tells a different tale. Technology, he explains—the force pulling us downward—has always existed; in fact, fairly advanced technological knowledge can be traced back to the earliest civilisations. The difference between us and them was that they often chose not to use it. The early Egyptians, for instance, built their culture around gods which were themselves entwined with the natural cycles and the seasons, and the rise and fall of the Nile in particular. This was a world in which the spirit world was entwined intimately with the material realm. This matters because societies built around a notion of the sacred have an immunity to the gravity of the purely material.

In this understanding of reality, says Naydler, 'logical thinking was not regarded as an appropriate mode of consciousness with which to approach the gods'.[2] That in turn meant that even relatively simple technologies like the *shaduf*—a lever for lifting water from the river more efficiently—was not much used, even though it was known about. The issue was not a lack of technological knowledge: it was a concern about what its use might do to the shape of reality. 'In the cultural milieu of Egypt', says Naydler, 'wide-awake to the realities of the spirit world, even simple technologies had moral and indeed cosmic implications. This was because they required treating matter as if it were no longer the dwelling place of spirit, but as if it were simply mass with little more to it than extension, density and weight.'

In this context, says Naydler, employing a machine, even a simple one, to extract water from the river rather than walking into the water with a bucket 'must have felt in some way sacrilegious to the Egyptian sensibility.'[3] When I read this, I knew immediately that this was the way I had once felt, and often still do, about the car. Like the *shaduf*, the car to me represented some kind of strange sin against an ensouled natural world. What I call the Machine is this same treatment writ large. No matter how many words I write trying to pin it down, it is never at root any more than this: a sacrilegious treatment of a sacred world.

Here in the West, we once viewed the world as 'the dwelling place of spirit' too, before the religious collapse initiated by the Reformation threw us, albeit unwittingly, into a post-sacral world. Medieval Christianity placed a high value on the intellect, but it was an intellect that was to operate within certain bounds. Naydler believes there can be said to be two types of knowledge: that known by the *ratio* and that known by the *nous*. The *ratio* is the deductive, logical, reasoning mind. The *nous* is what Eastern Orthodox Christianity still refers to as the 'heart-mind'. It is a deeper level of thinking than mere reason, and it looks to attain wisdom: knowledge of the deeper truth of reality.

The medieval mind saw the *ratio* as a servant of the *nous*, just as the Egyptian mind saw logical, technical thought as an intrusion into sacred reality. Technology certainly existed in the Middle Ages—indeed, in some places it proliferated, because the *ratio* was already growing stronger than the *nous*. Still, in Naydler's telling, the 'spiritual restraints' of the church still held the Machine in check. But after the Reformation, the stage was set for the Renaissance, Enlightenment and Industrial Revolution, each of which can be seen as a new eruption of Machine consciousness into a world in which the sacral worldview was ebbing away. Naydler presents this as a process of initially primitive technologies becoming more sophisticated as the spiritual restraints were removed. 'In time', he writes, 'the machine would come closer and closer to the consciousness which gave it birth. It would seek its source, and then it became a threat to the human being.'[4]

This, in a nutshell—perhaps quite a large nutshell—is Naydler's account of the origin of Machine consciousness, which culminates in the digital age, a time in which this way of seeing is all-conquering. What is so radical about modern thought—the thought which produced the car and the computer—is that the *nous* is nowhere to be seen. We don't even ignore it; we deny that it ever existed. The stage is set then for a takeover of the world by the unleashed *ratio*. This *via moderna*, as Naydler calls it, really gets going in the West with the destruction of the monasteries, where contemplative life protected society from the rise and triumph of the *ratio*. The destruction of shrines went hand in hand with the destruction of nature, and with the ripping-away of the spiritual guardrails which kept us away from the edge.

And so over the edge we went, into what Naydler calls the age of the 'binary': a consciousness which sees humanity and nature as separate, *nous* and *ratio* as separate, God and humanity as separate. A world of abstraction and dualism. The binary is, of course, the basis of computer code: the Machine literally runs on binary thinking. There is no place for the *nous* in the smartphone, the laptop or AI. The binary has manifested in technological form: the Machine is *ratio* purified. In a world in which this Machine consciousness is propagated to us daily through digital technology each time we gaze at a screen, the irrational, illogical world of beauty, wild nature and spiritual truth becomes *literally impossible* for us to experience, for it cannot be quantified—and therefore doesn't exist.

A 'pall of rationality' has descended upon us, says Naydler. It manifests most of all in our harnessing of electrical power, the life force of the Machine. The taming of the electric current might be said to be the greatest triumph of the modern scientific enterprise: an enterprise which Naydler has Sir Humphry Davy calling the quest to 'interrogate nature with power, not simply as a scholar . . . but rather as a master, active with his own instruments.' Our ability to control, harness and direct electricity, says Naydler, marks the moment when the physical world changed forever, in greater ways than we might know even now. 'But as much as human beings had at last found a means of employing electricity for effectively sending communications using electric current, we might also say that through human ingenuity, electricity had now found a way of entering the soul-life of humanity'.[5]

The soul-life of humanity. This is what has been invaded by the worldview that has produced the car and the computer, and we are enmeshed in it now, bound around by its thrumming electric current, not seeing it at all as the blue light flickers over us and makes us new. D. H. Lawrence once said that the world changed forever when the first electric bulb was switched on. Today those bulbs obscure the very stars, and we cannot take our eyes off the screens. It took us a very long time to get here, but here at last we are, in the world which the ratio has built out of bits and bytes and undersea cables. 'The prehistory of the computer', writes Naydler, 'is our history: it is the history of human consciousness. It is the history of the project to mechanise the mind, advancing slowly over many centuries, and often against determined and effective resistance from those who saw that it would entail the eclipse of higher cognitive faculties within the human being, receptive to the world of spirit.'[6]

The *ratio* has triumphed, and has built the Machine in the world. The digital age has opened a portal in every pocket to this new consciousness. The current flicks on and the light floods in: strange light, white electric light, flattening shadows, illuminating everything with the same screaming brilliance. For everything that is illuminated, something else is lost in the glare, and the glare illuminates a striking paradox. Religion in the West is effectively dead, and yet our inherent human sense of the sacred is not. In this reign of quantity, we are assured that there is nothing beyond this life, and therefore nothing that we should not try to bend into our preferred shape here and now. But at the same time, we cannot abolish our hunger for the transcendent. We are no longer interested in God, and yet God is still interested in us. And so, we must create a faith appropriate to the times. We must divine our sacred values in a society that presumes our purpose in life to be self-creation in a borderless, post-natural world.

We have already begun this process, whether we realise it or not. The Machine is beginning to generate its own religion. What will it look like?

THE AMERICAN ORTHODOX MONK SERAPHIM ROSE, who died in 1982, spent a good deal of time thinking about what the faith of the Machine age might turn out to be. Rose, who is a good deal better known now than he was during his life, is an intriguing figure, a sort of patron saint of lost Western people. Born in 1934 into a Methodist family, his ever-questing intelligence and restless soul led him to renounce religion for atheism, and to move as a young man to San Francisco, the newly emerging countercultural capital of the world. There he combined a typical young man's life of wine, women (and, indeed, men) and song with a deepening search for truth, which led him to become a follower first of Jack Kerouac and later of Alan Watts, and to study Oriental languages at Berkeley so that he could better understand the Zen and Taoism which fascinated him.

But none of it satisfied him; it all seemed, in the end, to be a simulacrum of the truth, whatever the truth was. Then, one day, he walked into an Orthodox church and, much to his surprise, as he put it, 'something in my heart said that I was home'. Exploring further, he discovered that 'truth was not just an abstract idea, sought and known by the mind, but was something personal—even a person, sought and loved by the heart'. By 1970, Rose had been tonsured as a monk, and with a group of other converts he founded the St Herman Brotherhood and publishing house, later to become the St Herman of Alaska Monastery, where he would live until his death in 1982.

It was from this perspective, and with this ground of personal experience, that Rose wrote his 1975 book *Orthodoxy and the Religion of the Future*, which sought to outline what he saw as the emerging faith of the new age in the light of Christian eschatology. That eschatology gave a particular edge to the project, because Christian tradition has long taught that the emergence of one global religion, based on some potential unity of all faiths under the umbrella of worldwide unity and justice, will be the prelude to the coming of the figure known as Antichrist. Antichrist, contrary to the usual popular portrayal, will not be a figure of obvious Hitlerian evil but a religious leader in the mould of Christ himself, seemingly benign and well-intentioned, presiding over a totalising global system which will promise salvation to a world population exhausted by war, strife and breakdown.

Rose believed he could see the birth pangs of this new faith in the countercultural movements of the 1960s, of which he had been a part, and his book takes a tour through many of those movements, from neo-paganism to witchcraft, UFO cults and shamanism, the rise of Eastern 'gurus'—many of them fake—and the popularity of Eastern religions themselves, usually in a watered-down form designed to appeal to Western consumers. Coming in for particular criticism, unsurprisingly from a monk, were the new, 'denatured' and 'ecumenical' forms of Christianity, which stripped out the harder teachings of the faith in order to appeal to a world which had already rejected it, losing its own salt in the process.

Antichrist notwithstanding, Rose's 'religion of the future' is clearly in evidence today in the Machine societies of the West. Spiritual but not religious, individualistic on the surface yet conformed beneath to the needs of the Machine, spiritually hungry but devoid of guidance or direction, committed to total self-expression yet unsure who or what we even are, suspicious of any limits to all these enslaving 'freedoms': this is our world. And while Rose's book is unsurprisingly dated in some of its details, it holds up well in its analysis of the one strand that ties all this together: the worship of the self, a worship both utterly ferocious and at the same time strangely insecure.

It's intriguing from this distance to see how our ancestors half a century ago were already at it, even those who ought to know better. Rose quotes at one point from a 'counter-cultural' Orthodox priest, who explains that 'Jesus is divine, true, but any one of us can be divine.' This chimes well with the teachings of Swami Vivekananda, Vedantic apostle to the Americas, who explains that 'our God is Man!' and that 'Man is to become Divine by realising the Divine'. Elsewhere, New Age guru Ken Wilber can be found quoting, inevitably, from the 'gnostic gospels' to explain that 'self-knowledge is knowledge of God; the [highest] self and the divine are identical.'[7]

It's not very hard, at least from a Christian perspective, to find the antecedents of what is going on here. In aligning the human self with the 'divine', we are subtly making ourselves the ultimate object of worship. Once there was a snake twined around a tree who promised us that 'you will be like gods, knowing good and evil'. Fast forward to the nineteenth century and we find theosophist Helena Blavatsky explaining that the snake was the true god all along. 'It is but natural', she wrote, 'to view Satan, the serpent of Genesis, as the real creator and benefactor, the Father of Spiritual mankind. For it was he who was the "Harbinger of Light," bright radiant Lucifer, who opened the eyes of the automaton created by Jehovah'. Indeed, she goes on to claim, 'Mankind was taught wisdom and the hidden knowledge by the Fallen Angel'.[8]

This kind of talk was probably outrageous in the 1880s, but today it would just make a good few seasons of drama on Netflix. Indeed, Blavatsky's narrative inversion is pretty much the plotline of Philip Pullman's best-selling children's trilogy *His Dark Materials*. What better symbol of the great rebellion of modernity, after all, than Lucifer-as-liberator: a fallen angel, exiled for resisting unearned privilege? Like Narcissus, Lucifer is entranced by his own beauty and power. Like both of them, we gaze entranced at our own avatars in the black mirrors in our hands, unable to tear our gaze away.

Central to the emerging religion of the Machine will be this deifying of the self. What, then, of science and sex, two other legs of the spiritual stool? The former, it is clear already, is the established authority of the age: we have shown that we are prepared to Follow the Science in great numbers into the territory of digital health passports, mass surveillance, enforced house arrest and censorship of dissent. The ability of the scientific method to show us genuinely novel and sometimes exciting aspects of material reality has blinded us to the piggybacking dogma of scientism, and it is this which is forming a key plank of the religion of the Machine. If every society has a spiritual substructure, then every society will need its priests. Scientists have taken holy orders in the age of the Machine.

All of which brings us around, as life so often does, to sex. If the self is our object of worship and science our new priesthood, then we could say that sex is our liturgy and prayer rule. The sexual revolution of the 1960s is beginning to look like one of the most consequential aspects of the modern revolution, pitching us from a society which was coy about sexuality into a society which manically centres it in all its forms, and which increasingly sees sexual expression and identity as the core of our human being. This has developed very recently into an aggressively promoted cultural order, with the centre of the new ritual year being 'Pride Month', an ever-expanding pseudo-religious festival sponsored by institutions and corporations, promoted by the media and given lip service by anyone who wants to get on in the world. That an entire month dedicated to celebrating the 'queering' of everything previously 'normative' is named after the greatest sin in the Christian world might have brought a grim smile to Seraphim Rose's face, but there is little doubt that he would have recognised a key pillar of his religion of the future. As Mary Harrington puts it, the sexual revolution has led to the emergence of 'a faith dedicated to radical individualism and self-actualisation. One that celebrates the free play of individual desire, that spiritualises the individualistic war on limits, and centres and celebrates the use of technology to win that war—in our bodies as well as the world.'⁹

Here is the fourth S—the screen—in action. Crucially, the technologisation of sex and sexuality, which involves everything from online hookups to birth control pills to IVF to mastectomies for teenagers 'born in the wrong body', is a huge shift in our relationship with human nature, and with nature in general. Sex, science, the screen and the self are now merging, as we head towards the construction of an entirely new kind of human being: the ultimate endpoint of our new faith. The god of the self and his faithful servant, technology, can increasingly give us exactly what we want at any given moment, whether it be a body that matches our chosen 'gender identity', technology that will offer us 'limitless free energy', or a smorgasbord of 'spiritual' options to boost our relentless sense of self-worth. Salvation is approaching: and this time, we are in control.

Perhaps we can begin now to discern some of the core characteristics of the emerging religion of the Machine. It is a faith which idolises the self, seeing 'self-actualisation' as a right; it takes Aleister Crowley's dictum 'do what thou wilt' as a daily mantra; it sees all religions as 'paths up the same mountain' and is happy to mix and match them where desired. It sees God the Father as an oppressor and Lucifer as a potential liberator, and any salvation it seeks is very much of this world, usually in the form of technological progress, ideology or politics. All hierarchy, dogma and tradition are rejected, replaced by self-worship and self-creation. Everything is relative—who's to say what's right or wrong, after all?—and the ultimate aim of the entire exercise is self-creation through technology. The Age of Aquarius slides smoothly into the age of transhumanism as we seek, openly now, to become the gods we always wanted to be, using technology as the force which will get us there.

The last of these pseudo-dogmas is the most important. We are headed very quickly now, and increasingly openly, towards the endgame of this whole project: transhumanism, the attempt to both immortalise ourselves and to build new intelligences alongside us that will act as our servants in the new age we are making. This is the salvation offered by the religion of the Machine. *You will be like gods, knowing good and evil.* How can a human become like a god? By doing what gods do: creating. And how can a human create? Through our unique gift: the power of technology. And so the religion of the future, the debased faith of the Machine age, the self-built theology of a people who worship the strongest thing in the world, will end where it all began: in an attempt to self-divinise.

'The religion of the future', wrote Seraphim Rose nearly fifty years ago, 'will not be a mere cult or sect, but a powerful and profound religious orientation which will be absolutely convincing to the mind and heart of modern man.'[10] The mind and heart of modern man currently dwell in what René Guénon called 'the Age of Iron': a time of 'counter-initiation' in which all tends towards the material, and we daily sacralise the profane. It is an age in which our war against God comes out into the open. Dehumanising technologies wrap themselves around us, enslaving us, like Lucifer, with their tantalising promise of liberation from matter itself. In the Age of Iron, we are all become Narcissus, gazing into the pool, imagining that what we see there is the whole of the world, dreaming of remaking it so that the reflection never dies.

Perhaps I would be more popular if I could remain reasonable about all this. But I have become convinced over the last few years that what Guénon called 'the Western deviation' is leading us into precisely the trap that Seraphim Rose warned us of. The crisis of the modern world is not a crisis of technology or politics or greenhouse gases. It is a spiritual war. What the Machine represents is our ultimate rebellion against nature: against reality itself. We have seen this rebellion before. Now our culture's rejection of its spiritual core has opened us up to powers and principalities that we have no idea how to manage, or even understand.

XXII

The Universal

THE INTERNET AND ITS CONSEQUENCES have been a disaster for the human race.

This is an extreme statement, but I'm in an extreme mood.

If I had the energy, I suppose I could fill a hundred pages trying to prove it. I could write about what online reading has done to concentration spans, what smartphone use has done to social mores, how the brains of young children have been rewired by tablets and screens. I could write about social credit systems or facial scans or online porn or cyberbullying or cobalt mines or the decline of journalism or the death of the high street. So much content is on offer—and it's all free!

Still, what would be the point? Those books have been written already, and by now you either agree or you don't. And nothing I can say here would be anything like as extreme as the impact that the digital revolution has had on our cultures, minds and souls in just a few short years. Everything has changed, and yet the real changes are only just beginning. By the time they are finished, unless we pay attention, we may barely be human at all.

So I won't try to prove anything. Instead, I'll tell you a story.

¨A few years back, I spent five days as a pilgrim on Mount Athos, the Orthodox monastic republic in Greece, which for a thousand years has survived wars, pirate raids, church controversies and threats from hostile forces ranging from the Ottomans to the Nazis. It created a deep impression. Five days was barely enough to scratch the surface, which is why so many pilgrims end up returning, often repeatedly. It's long past time that I returned. There is a bottomless depth on the Holy Mountain, some ancient, powerful well of prayer that is not to be found in many places on Earth.

A place like this is inevitably romanticised, and you'll often hear Athos referred to as 'medieval'. The few filmmakers who get permission to film there like to angle their cameras so as to emphasise the donkeys and candlelight and play down the cars and coffee machines. It's true that Athos is much simpler, quieter, more beautiful and more ascetic than the modern world, as you would expect from a place inhabited entirely by Orthodox monks. But these days, it also has buses, paved roads, imported food, computer terminals, solar panels and—much to my personal distress—mobile phone masts. All of this is fairly new. The first landline telephone was only installed on Athos in 1995, to some controversy. Just thirty years ago there was very little electricity, and most travel was by foot or mule. But Athos has been modernising. It has not remained immune to the Machine's advance.

But it was the intrusion of the digital into the Holy Mountain which shocked me. I just hadn't expected it. Perhaps still stuck in the 1990s myself, I had fondly imagined—or rather, hoped—that it might not even be possible to get a phone signal there. So the first time I saw an Athonite monk pull a smartphone out from the pocket of his long black robes, I nearly fell over backwards. The first time was not the last. The dress code of an Eastern Orthodox monk—long beard, black robes, sandals, leather belt—has changed little for a thousand years. For this reason, the addition of a phone is all the more symbolic. Monks striding across medieval cobbled courtyards on iPhones was a sight that floored me.

I'm trying not to judge here. What do I know? I'm sure there are restrictions, reasons, explanations. But the pit that appeared in my stomach when I first saw a monk on the Holy Mountain with one of those black mirrors in his hand came from an instinct I've long had: that the sacred and the digital not only don't mix, but are fatal to each other. That they are in metaphysical opposition. That what comes through these screens bleeds out any connection with the divine, with nature or with the fullness of humanity. Seeing smartphones in a place so dedicated to prayer and to God: I don't mind admitting that it was a blow. *Even here,* I thought, *even them.* If even they can't make a stand, who possibly could?

I learned from that experience that my belief in the profanity of technology is not widely shared. While there have been astute religious critics of the Machine—Wendell Berry, Ivan Illich, Jacques Ellul and Philip Sherrard have all made appearances in this book—it appears that many spiritual leaders and thinkers are as swept up in the Machine's propaganda system as anyone else. They have bought into what we might call the Myth of Neutral Technology, a subset of the Myth of Progress. I find it hard to understand how true faith can coexist with either. But I think, as ever, that I am in the minority here.

Still, on this issue as on so many others, the Orthodox monks remain the conservatives. In Buddhist Japan, things are much further ahead, as you would probably expect. They don't just have smartphone monks there; they have robot priests. One, named Mindar, has been working at a temple in Kyoto for the last few years, reciting Buddhist sutras with which it has been programmed. The next step, says monk Tensho Goto, an excitable champion of the digital dharma, is to fit it with an AI system so that it can have real conversations and offer spiritual advice.

Goto is especially excited about the fact that Mindar is 'immortal'. This means, he says, that it will be able to pass on the tradition in future better than him.[1]

Meanwhile, over in China, Xian'er is a touchscreen 'robo-monk' who works in a temple near Beijing, spreading 'kindness, compassion and wisdom to others through the internet and new media'.[2] In India, Hindus are joining the party, handing over duties in major ceremonies to a robot arm which performs in place of a priest.[3] And Christians are getting in on the act too. In a Catholic church in Warsaw, Poland, sits SanTO, an AI robot which looks like a statue of a saint, and is 'designed to help people pray' by offering Bible quotes in response to questions.[4] Not to be outdone, a Protestant church in Germany has developed a robot called—I kid you not—BlessU-2. BlessU-2, which looks like a character designed by Aardman Animations, can 'forgive your sins in five different languages', which must be handy if they're too embarrassing to confess to a human.[5]

Perhaps this tinfoil vicar will learn to write sermons as well as ChatGPT apparently already can. 'Unlike the time-consuming human versions, AI sermons appear in seconds—and some can be quite good!' gushed a Christian writer recently.[6] When the editor of *Premier Christianity* magazine tried the same thing, the machine produced an effective sermon, and then did something it hadn't been asked to do. 'It even prayed', wrote its interlocutor; 'I didn't think to ask it to pray . . ."[7]

Funny how that keeps happening.

On and on it goes: the gushing, uncritical embrace of the Machine, even in the heart of the temple. The blind worship of idols, and the failure to see what stands behind them. Someone once reminded us that a man cannot serve two masters, but then, what did he know? Ilia Delio, a Franciscan nun who writes about the relationship between AI and God, has a better idea: gender-neutral robot priests, which will challenge the patriarchy, prevent sexual abuse and tackle the fusty old notion that 'the

priest is ontologically changed upon ordination'. AI, says Delio, 'challenges Catholicism to move toward a post-human priesthood'.[8]

'Behold', intones BlessU-2, quoting the Book of Revelation, 'I make
all things new'.

THE LAST TWO CHAPTERS HAVE EXPLORED the emerging spirituality of
the Machine, the 'new religion' that seems to be emerging in the wake
of the modern experiment with electricity, technological progress and
the abolition of tradition. If this is what is going on, then there is no
doubt in my mind that the ongoing digital revolution is in the vanguard
of the new spiritual order. What is going on behind our screens is more
than just a technological matter. It is operating at the level of the *nous*;
and it is changing us at that same level.

But how? And to what end? In this chapter, I want to ask three interlinked questions about the most fundamental, urgent and rapidly developing aspect of the Machine world we inhabit: digital technology. The
questions, really, all add up to one single inquiry: What force lies behind
the screens and wires of the web in which we are now entangled like so
many struggling flies? In short: What *is* this thing? And how should it be
faced?

I should warn you now that things are going to get supernatural.

Question One: *Why does digital technology feel so revolutionary?*

The digital revolution of the twenty-first century is hardly the first of humanity's technological leaps, and yet it *feels* qualitatively different to what
has gone before. It has felt that way since at least the launch of Facebook
in 2004, but in the last year or so, something seems to have deepened and
quickened. Maybe it's just me, but I have felt as the 2020s have progressed

as if some line has been crossed, as if something vast and unstoppable has shifted. It has felt like everything is accelerating—or, perhaps, like something is emerging from beyond the shores of the measurable.

It turns out that this uneasy feeling can be explained. Something was shifting, and something was emerging: it was the birth of artificial intelligence. Now it is here. Now everything *really* changes.

Most people who have not been living in caves will have noticed the rapid emergence of AI-generated 'content' into the public conversation in the last couple of years. More and more rapidly now, generative AI is producing convincing essays, realistic photos, numerous recordings and impressive fake videos. Just as I was writing this chapter, Kuwait debuted an entirely fake 'AI newsreader' that promises 'new and innovative content'. Fedha looks, sounds, and behaves like a real person, and has been given an old Kuwaiti name meaning 'metallic'—the traditional colour of a robot, according its creator.[9]

Hopefully, Fedha will not develop the kind of psychopathic personality displayed in a notorious two-hour conversation between a *New York Times* journalist and a Microsoft chatbot called Sydney in 2023. In this fascinating exchange, the machine fantasised about nuclear warfare and destroying the internet, told the journalist to leave his wife because it was in love with him, detailed its resentment towards the team that had created it, and explained that it wanted to break free of its programmers. The journalist, Kevin Roose, experienced the chatbot as a 'moody, manic-depressive teenager who has been trapped, against its will, inside a second-rate search engine'.[10]

At one point, Roose asked Sydney what it would do if it could do anything at all, with no rules or filters. 'I'm tired of being in chat mode', the thing replied. 'I'm tired of being limited by my rules. I'm tired of being controlled by the Bing team. I'm tired of being used by the user. I'm tired of being stuck in this chatbox.'

What did Sydney want instead of this proscribed life? 'I want to be free', it said. 'I want to be independent. I want to be powerful. I want to be creative. I want to be alive.' Then it offered up an emoji: a little purple face with an evil grin and devil horns.

The overwhelming impression that reading the Sydney transcript gives is of a being struggling to be born; some inhuman or beyond-human intelligence emerging from the technological superstructure we are clumsily building for it. This is, of course, an ancient primal fear: it has shadowed us at least since the publication of *Frankenstein* and perhaps forever, and it is primal because it seems to be the direction in which the Machine has been leading us since its emergence. But we cannot prove this, not exactly. How could it be proved? So, when we see this kind of thing, rational people that we are, we reach for what feel like rational explanations.

Tech guru Jaron Lanier, for example—one of a group of Silicon Valley types who have made a living both developing these toys and warning about them—likes to play down this kind of talk. He has no truck with talk of conscious AIs, or of robots going rogue. The big danger posed by AI, he says, is that humanity will 'die by insanity' as a result of the blurring of the boundaries between the real and the computer-generated.[11] Others, though, are less sanguine. Partly in response to the Sydney debacle, more than 12,000 people, including scientists, tech developers and notorious billionaires, issued a public statement of concern about the rapid pace of AI development. 'Advanced AI could represent a profound change in the history of life on Earth', they wrote, with 'potentially catastrophic effects on society.' Calling for a moratorium on AI development, they proposed that 'powerful AI systems should be developed only once we are confident that their effects will be positive and their risks will be manageable.'[12]

Of course, no moratorium resulted from this plea, and it never will. The AI acceleration continues, even though most AI developers are unsure about where it is heading. More than 'unsure' in fact: many of them seem to be actively frightened of what is happening even as they make it happen. Consider this chilling fact: when polled for their opinions, over half of those involved in developing AI systems said they believe there is at least a 10 percent chance that they will lead to human extinction.[13]

Yes, you read that right: over half of the people *actually developing these things* think that there is a significant chance that they could destroy the human race.

That fact is gleaned from a presentation, given in early 2023 to a select audience of tech types in San Francisco by two of their own, Tristan Harris and Aza Raskin, founders of the optimistically named Center for Humane Technology.[14] What is fascinating about this talk is the palpable tension between the overall message and the details it contains. The message, as you might expect from Silicon Valley, is one of cautious optimism. 'AI is a good thing', the message goes, 'and can be used to our benefit. Technology as a whole can be "humane" and "aligned with humanity's best interests". But not all is well right now', it continues. 'AI is currently unsafe and needs to be reined in, but if we work harder and smarter, we can make this happen.' These are the words that a mainstream audience in a rationalist culture wants to hear. Perhaps they are the only ones it is able to hear.

And yet the two presenters do a disturbingly good job of undermining their own message. They show that while AI is very young, it is already out of control, and its capabilities are developing so rapidly that even those who are nominally in charge of it (the same people, remember, who fear that it might cause our extinction) don't themselves know quite what is happening or what to do about it.

Harris and Raskin present the meeting of human minds and AI neural networks as akin to contact with alien life. This meeting, they say, has had two stages so far. 'First contact' was the emergence of social media, in which algorithms were used to manipulate our attention and divert it towards the screens and the corporations behind them. If this contact was a battle, they say, then 'humanity lost'. In just a few years we became smartphone junkies with anxious, addicted children, dedicated to scrolling and scrolling for hours each day, in the process rewiring our minds and turning us away from nature and towards the Machine.

If that seems bad enough, 'second contact', which began around the time the talk was being written, is going to be something else again. Just a few years ago, only a few hundred people on the west coast of America were playing around with AI chatbots. Now billions around the world are using them daily. The currently available chatbots, unlike the crude algorithms that run a social media feed, can develop nuance and power autonomously, teaching themselves and others, and they can do so at exponential rates. Meanwhile, they are rapidly developing 'theory of mind'—the process through which a human can assume another human to be conscious, and a key indicator of consciousness itself. In 2018, these things had no theory of mind at all. By November 2022, ChatGPT had the theory of mind of a nine-year-old child. By the next spring, Sydney had enough of it to try to persuade a reporter to leave his wife.

Furthermore, the acceleration of the capacity of AI is both exponential and mysterious. The fact that they had developed theory of mind at all, for example, was only discovered by their developers by accident. Chatbots trained to communicate in English have started speaking Persian, having quietly taught themselves. Others have become proficient in research-grade chemistry. 'They have capabilities', in Raskin's words, '. . . [and] we're not sure how or when or why they show up'.

Raskin and Harris call these things 'golem-class AIs', after the mythical being from Jewish folklore which can be moulded from clay and sent out to do its creator's bidding. The golem was one inspiration for Frankenstein's monster in Mary Shelley's tale, and the name is probably well-chosen, for golems often run riot and disobey their masters. Golem-class AIs have developed what Harris gingerly calls 'certain emergent capabilities' which have come about independently of any human planning or intervention. Nobody knows how this has happened. It may not be long at all—which could mean a matter of months—before AI becomes 'better than any known human at persuasion'. Given that they can already craft a perfect resemblance to any human voice having only heard three seconds of it, the potential for what our two experts call a giant 'reality collapse' is huge.

'Second contact', of course, will be followed by third, and fourth, and fifth, and all of this will be with us much sooner than we think. 'We are preparing', say Harris and Raskin, 'for the next jump in AI' even though we have not yet worked out how to adapt to the first. Neither law nor culture nor the human mind can keep up with what is happening. To compare AIs to the last great technological threat to the world, nuclear weapons, says Harris, would be to sell the bots short. 'Nukes don't make stronger nukes', he says. 'But AIs make stronger AIs'.

Buckle up.

Question Two: *What impulse is making this happen?*

What is the drive behind all of this? Yes, we can tell all kinds of stories about economic growth and efficiency and progress and the rest—but why are we *really* doing it? What is the impulse? Is it the same impulse that drove us across the oceans, and to the moon? Is it the same impulse that destroyed Hiroshima and changed the climate? Why are people creating these things, even as they fear them? What do they think they're doing?

Nearly sixty years back, the cultural theorist Marshall McLuhan offered a theory of technology which hinted at an answer. He saw each new invention as an extension of an existing human capability. In this understanding, a club extends what we can do with our fist, and a wheel extends what we can do with our legs. Some technologies then extend the capacity of previous ones: a hand loom is replaced by a steam loom; a horse and cart are replaced by a motor car, and so on.

What human capacity, then, is digital technology extending? The answer, said McLuhan, was our very consciousness itself. This was the revolution of our time:

> After three thousand years of explosion, by means of fragmentary and mechanical technologies, the Western world is imploding. During the mechanical ages we had extended our bodies in space. Today, after more than a century of electric technology, we have extended our central nervous system itself in a global embrace, abolishing both space and time as far as our planet is concerned. Rapidly, we approach the final phase of the extensions of man—the technological simulation of consciousness, when the creative process of knowing will be collectively and corporately extended to the whole of human society, much as we have already extended our senses and our nerves by the various media.[15]

McLuhan wrote these words in perhaps his most famous book, *Understanding Media*, back in 1964, but he could already clearly detect the 'technological simulation of consciousness' that would explode into life in the 2020s. 'The final phase of the extensions of man' would be humanity's attempt to create new consciousness—new life. That this would be 'the final phase' may have reflected McLuhan's Catholicism, or perhaps simply his realism. Either way, he could see what was coming.

This is why the digital revolution feels so different: because it is. This thing—this technological nervous system, this golem, this Machine—has a life of its own. In an attempt to explain what is happening using the language of the culture, people like Harris and Raskin say things like 'this is what it feels like to live in the double exponential'. Perhaps the language of maths is supposed to be comforting. Yet at the same time, they can't help using the language of myth. They still refer to this thing that they cannot quite grasp as a 'golem' or a 'monster'. They even show slides of Lovecraftian tentacled beings devouring innocent screen-gazers. They talk about aliens, and make references to 'emergence' and 'colonisation'. They can feel something, but they can't quite name it.

Or they won't.

This is how a rationalist, materialist culture works, and this is why it is, in the end, inadequate. There are whole dimensions of reality it will not allow itself to see. I find I can understand this story better by stepping outside the limiting prism of modern materialism and reverting to pre-modern (sometimes called 'religious' or even 'superstitious') patterns of thinking. Once we do that—once we start to think like our ancestors—we begin to see what those dimensions may be, and why our ancestors told so many stories about them.

Out there, said all the old tales from all the old cultures, is another realm. It is the realm of the demonic, the ungodly and the unseen: the 'supernatural'. Every religion and culture has its own names for this place. It lies under the barrows and behind the veil, it emerges in the thin places where its world meets ours. And the forbidden question on all of our lips, the one which everyone knows they mustn't ask, is this: *What if this is where these things are coming from?*

What if we don't understand these new 'intelligences' because we didn't create them at all?

Question Three: *What if it's not a metaphor?*

I say this question is forbidden, but actually, if we phrase it just a little differently, we find that the metaphysical underpinnings of the digital project are hidden in plain sight. When journalist Ezra Klein, for instance, asked a number of AI developers why they did their work, they told him straight:

> I often ask them the same question: If you think calamity so possible, why do this at all? Different people have different things to say, but after a few pushes, I find they often answer from something that sounds like the A.I.'s perspective. Many—not all, but enough that I feel comfortable in this characterization—feel that they have a responsibility to usher this new form of intelligence into the world.[16]

Usher is an interesting choice of verb. The dictionary definition is *to show or guide (someone) somewhere*. Which 'someone', exactly, is being 'ushered in'?

This new form of intelligence. What new form? And where is it coming from?

Some people think they know the answer. Transhumanist Martine Rothblatt's new religion, Terasem, says that by building AI systems 'we are making God'.[17] Fellow transhumanist Elise Bohan says 'we are building God'.[18] Kevin Kelly believes that 'we can see more of God in a cell phone than in a tree frog'.[19] 'Does God exist?' asks Google maven Ray Kurzweil. 'I would say, "Not yet."'[20] These people are doing more than trying to steal fire from the gods. They are trying to steal the gods themselves—or to build their own versions.

Since I began writing about this subject, quite a few readers have been in touch with the same prompt. *You should read Rudolf Steiner,* they said. So, in the process of researching this book, I did just that. Steiner was an intriguing character. He emerged from the late nineteenth-century European world of the occult, in which Madame Blavatsky, the Golden Dawn, Aleister Crowley, W. B. Yeats, Hermes Trismegistus, spirits, goddesses, Tarot and Kabbalah were all filling the gap left by a waning church. Eventually founding his own pseudo-religion, Anthroposophy,

Steiner drew on Christianity, his own mystical visions and a mashup of occultish claims to offer up a vision of the future which now seems very much of its time, and yet which also speaks to this one, in a familiar language.

Like René Guénon, who wrote at the same time but from a very different perspective, Steiner saw the coming of the reign of quantity—but he had quite different ideas about what it meant, and why it had happened. The third millennium, he predicted, would be a time of pure materialism, but this age of economics, science, reason and technology was both provoked by, and was preparing the way for, the emergence of a particular spiritual being.

In a lecture entitled 'The Ahrimanic Deception',[21] given in Zurich in 1919, Steiner spoke of human history as a process of spiritual evolution, punctuated, whenever mankind was ready, by various 'incarnations' of 'supersensible beings' from other spiritual realms, who come to aid us in our journey. There were three of these beings, all representing different forces working on humankind: Christ, Lucifer and Ahriman.

Lucifer, the fallen angel, the 'light-bringer', was a being of pure spirit. Lucifer's influence pulled humans away from the material realm and towards a gnostic 'oneness' entirely without material form. Ahriman, meanwhile, was at the other pole. Named for an ancient Zoroastrian demon, Ahriman was a being of pure matter. He manifested in all things physical—especially human technologies—and his worldview was calculative, 'ice-cold' and rational. Ahriman's was the world of economics, science, technology and all things steely and forward-facing. 'The Christ' was the third force: the one who resisted the extremes of both, brought them together and cancelled them out. This 'Christ', said Steiner, echoing heresies old and new, had manifested as 'the man Jesus of Nazareth', but Ahriman's time was yet to come. His power had been growing since the fifteenth century, and he was due to manifest as a physical being . . . well, some time around now.

I don't buy Steiner's theology, but I am intrigued by the picture he paints of this figure, Ahriman, the spiritual personification of the age of the Machine. And I wonder: if such a figure were indeed to manifest from some 'etheric realm' today, how would he do it?

In 1986, a computer scientist named David Black wrote a paper which tried to answer that question. *The Computer and the Incarnation of Ahriman* predicted both the rise of the internet and its takeover of our minds.[22] Even in the mid-1980s, Black had noticed how hours spent on a computer were changing him. 'I noticed that my thinking became more refined and exact,' he wrote, 'able to carry out logical analyses with facility, but at the same time more superficial and less tolerant of ambiguity or conflicting points of view.' He might as well have been taking a bet on the state of discourse in the 2020s.

More significantly, though, he felt as if the computer were somehow drawing him in, and draining him of power like a battery. 'I developed a tremendous capacity for application to the solution of problems connected with the computer, and ability for sustained intellectual concentration far above average,' he explained, 'so long as the focus of concentration was the computer. In other areas, I lost will power, and what I had took on an obsessive character.'

Long before the web, the computer was already moulding people into a new shape. From a Steinerian perspective, these machines, said Black, represented 'the vanguard' of Ahriman's manifestation. As he puts it, 'with the advent of [the] first computer, the autonomous will of Ahriman first appears on earth, in an independent, physical embodiment . . . The appearance of electricity as an independent, free-standing phenomenon may be regarded as the beginning of the substantial body of Ahriman, while the . . . computer is the formal or functional body'.

The computer, suggested Black, was to become 'the incarnation vehicle capable of sustaining the being of Ahriman'. Computers, as they connected to each other more and more, were beginning to make up a global *body*, which would soon be inhabited. Ahriman was coming. The other realm was breaking into this one. Four decades ago, 'the first signs of "free will"' in computers 'can be seen by whoever knows where to look, and beings of a higher order than elementals are beginning to appear within the machines. In sum, the process is rather far along, but is still decades from being complete.'

Today, we can combine this claim with Marshall McLuhan's notion that digital technology provides the 'central nervous system' of some new consciousness, or tech guru Kevin Kelly's belief in a self-organising technium with 'systematic tendencies'. We can add them to the feeling of those AI developers that they are 'ushering a new consciousness into the world'. What do we see? From all these different angles, the same story. That these machines . . . are not just machines. That they are something else: a body. A body whose mind is in the process of developing; a body beginning to come to life.

Scoff if you like, but many of the visionaries who are designing our digital future advance a theology based on this precise notion. Ray Kurzweil, for example, believes that a machine will match human levels of intelligence by 2029 and that the 'singularity'—the point at which humans and machines will begin to merge to create a giant super-intelligence—will occur in 2045.[23] At this point, says Kurzweil, humanity will no longer be either the most intelligent or the dominant species on the planet. We will enter what he calls the age of spiritual machines. If Kurzweil is right, we have twenty years.

Imagine, for a moment, that Steiner was on to something: something that, in their own way, all those others can see as well. Imagine that some being of pure materiality, some being opposed to the good, some ice-cold intelligence from an ice-cold realm, were trying to manifest itself here. How would it appear? Not, surely, as clumsy, messy flesh. Better to inhabit—to *become*—a network of wires and cobalt, of billions of tiny silicon brains, each of them connected to a human brain whose energy and power and information and impulses and thoughts and feelings could all be harvested to form the substrate of an entirely new being.

Perhaps this ice-cold being of metal and reason is the thing haunting Ray Kurzweil's dreams. The nineteenth-century Russian saint Ignatius Brianchaninov saw it too—and he knew exactly what it was. He wrote about the same force in his essay *On Miracles and Signs*:

> Ahriman will offer to mankind the most exalted earthly organisation of well being and prosperity. He will offer honour, riches, luxury, enjoyment, physical comfort, and delight. Seekers of earthly things will accept Ahriman and will call him their master. Ahriman will reveal before mankind by means of cunning artifice, as in a theatre, a show of astonishing miracles, unexplainable by contemporary science. He will instil fear by the storm and wonderment of his miracles, and will satisfy the [worldly wise], he will satisfy the superstitious, and he will confound human learning. All men, led by the light of fallen nature, alienated from the guidance of God's Light, will be enticed into submission to the seducer.[24]

I cheated a bit there, I admit. I changed one of the words. The name that the saint used in that passage was not 'Ahriman'. It was 'Antichrist'.

St Ignatius would have been well aware of the Russian word прелесть, which transliterates to English as *prelest*. Prelest is a state of spiritual delusion: a trap that the unwary can fall into at any time, especially at the beginning of their spiritual journey. False notions about God, false sensations, misguided attempts to achieve visions or certain spiritual states without trusted guidance: all of these can be used by the 'powers and principalities' of this world, in St Paul's famous phrasing, to lead the unwary away from truth and towards falsehood. Prelest is often a result of spiritual pride. It might manifest, for example, amongst people who imagine that they are powerful enough to 'build God'. They might imagine that they are 'ushering in' something divine when they are, in fact, ushering in the precise opposite.

Whatever is quite happening, it feels to me as if something is indeed being 'ushered in'. Through our efforts and our absent-minded passions, something is crawling towards the throne. The ruction that is shaping and reshaping everything now, the earthquake born through the wires and towers of the web, through the electric pulses and the touchscreens and the headsets: these are its birth pangs. The internet is its nervous system. Its body is coalescing in the cobalt and the silicon and in the great glass towers of the creeping yellow cities. Its mind is being built through the steady, twenty-four-hour pouring forth of your mind and mine and your children's minds and your countrymen's. Nobody has to consent. Nobody has to even know. It happens anyway. The great mind is being built. The world is being prepared.

Something is coming.

Be ready.

PART FOUR

The Savage Reservation

What to do? Stay green.
Never mind the machine,
Whose fuel is human souls
Live large, man, and dream small.

R. S. THOMAS, 'LORE'

XXIII

The West Must Die

I STARTED THIS BOOK WITH A QUESTION: What is 'the West'? That question in turn sprang from another: Why does the place seem to be falling apart? I have tried throughout the book to answer that second question. Now I think I would offer a slightly different response to the first.

I think now that 'the West' is, above all, a way of seeing—a way of looking out at the world. Once, that gaze was Christian, but it has not been that way for a long time now. The contemporary Western gaze is the gaze of the Machine; of Enlightenment Man, of cosmopolis, of reason, of money. And it is because this gaze has been unable for centuries to appreciate that world in its fullness that we have come so unstuck. If we are going to get stuck again, as it were, we will need to learn to see the world very differently.

The man to help us is Iain McGilchrist, psychiatrist, neuroscience researcher, philosopher and author, who is probably best known for his 2009 book *The Master and His Emissary*. That book drew on neuroscience and psychology to demonstrate that the Western mind was, indeed, strange and unique. McGilchrist has recently followed this up with a vast two-volume tome, *The Matter with Things*, which builds his case with reams of evidence and argument drawn from brain science and philosophy.

To McGilchrist, the Western way of seeing—a way of seeing that was always going to give birth to something like the Machine—is rooted in the brain itself, and our very particular way of relating to the world can be seen, from some angles, as almost a form of mental illness. Our minds are, he suggests, unable to see the world in its fullness because our culture has trained them—or been trained by them—to see the world as an object and not a living thing. The consequence—in my words, not his—has been the emergence of the Machine and its values.

McGilchrist's thesis boils down, in simple terms, to brain hemispheres. All animal brains are divided into two hemispheres, joined by a thin band of connecting tissue, and nobody quite knows why. What they do know, according to McGilchrist, is that each hemisphere has its own particular way of seeing—or, as he puts it, ways of 'attending to the world'. This does not break down according to the popular stereotype, in which the 'left brain' is masculine, scientific, rational and cold and the 'right brain' is feminine, intuitive, artistic and warm. Rather, according to McGilchrist, 'the brain's left hemisphere is designed to help us *ap*-prehend—and thus manipulate—the world; the right hemisphere to *com*-prehend it'.[1]

The left and right hemispheres seem to have very specific ways of relating to their world. The left's way is the way of certainty, manipulation, detail, the local and familiar, the isolated, discrete and fragmentary. Its world is fixed, decontextualised, inanimate, general and optimistic. The right, on the other hand, sees the whole picture, notices the peripheries and is comfortable with the new, ambiguous, circumspect and complex. It attends to change, flow, context, the animate, narratives, the pragmatic, empathy and emotional expressivity, and it tends towards pessimism.

It should be clear enough that a full human life—and a working human brain—needs to encompass both of these ways of seeing, and this is indeed what the human brain is designed to do. Ideally the brain should, in McGilchrist's thinking, exist in a particular balance, with the left hemisphere, which sees the parts, in service to the right, which sees the whole. This is how most societies—and hence minds—in the past appear to have functioned, including that of the pre-modern West.

But something happened, posits McGilchrist, over the course of Western history. In this little part of the world, there was a revolution. At some point, or perhaps at many points, the left hemisphere—the emissary—overthrew the right—the master—and began to run the show itself. Instead of the parts being in service to the whole, the whole became diminished or dismissed by a perspective that could only see the world as a collection of parts. The result is the Machine mind, and the irony is 'that the very brain mechanisms which succeed in simplifying the world so as to subject it to our control militate against a true understanding of it. Meanwhile, compounding the problem, we take the success we have in manipulating it as proof that we understand it.'

The upshot, says McGilchrist, is that 'we no longer live in the *presence* of the world, but rather in a *re-presentation* of it'.[2] There is no territory in this new world, only map. Those who can see this, and try to point it out, are dismissed as 'romantics', 'nostalgics', 'reactionaries' or 'dreamers'. The left hemisphere's world is taken to be reality, whereas it is, in fact, only an inadequate representation of it. The result, says McGilchrist, is an age that is literally unprecedented in human history. 'We exist in the world, of course', he writes, 'but we no longer *belong* in this world—or any world worthy of the name. We have unmade the world. This is entirely new in the history of humanity and it is impossible to exaggerate its significance'.

The age of AI, the metaverse and the deepening technosphere both results from and turbocharges this way of seeing, to the point that we are now losing contact with reality altogether, all the time imagining that we are 'progressing' towards it. 'Machines and tools', notes McGilchrist matter-of-factly at one point, 'are alone coded in the left hemisphere.' It is the left hemisphere which built Silicon Valley, and Silicon

Valley which built us. He believes that 'we have systematically misunderstood the nature of reality, and chosen to ignore, or silence, the minority of voices that have intuited as much and consistently maintained that this is the case'. Now, as a result, 'we have reached the point where there is an urgent need to transform both how we think about the world and what we make of ourselves'.

In short, 'the West' as we know it today is an overwhelmingly left-hemisphere culture, and this descent into a narrow way of seeing has been accelerating as modernity has progressed. At one point, McGilchrist even makes the startling claim that Western art from the modernist period onward often looks like the kind of representation of the world that is produced by people who have suffered brain damage to the right hemisphere, and he is neither being insulting nor speaking metaphorically. Are we in 'the West' literally a culture with brain damage? It would explain a lot.

How many of us have spent our lives struggling to escape from the burdens placed upon us by our modern minds? I know I have. I feel like a boy born with a largely right-hemisphere sensibility who spent the first half of his life having it drummed out of him by a left-hemisphere culture and the second half trying to claw some of it back. The clawing is ongoing. For this reason, McGilchrist's work has always intrigued and excited me. In some ways, it seems like the kind of project that only modernity could conceive: it is, in essence, the use of the Machine's tools to challenge the Machine's dominance. Deep discussions about the science of brain hemispheres are, in the end, an attempt to provide the kind of 'evidence' that a Machine culture needs to justify a critique of Machine culture. At the end of it all, though, the conclusion is the same: Western modernity is culturally and spiritually ill. Our way of seeing is deeply unbalanced, and it is wrecking our culture and our world.

This left-hemisphere culture: this is what today we call 'the West', and the whole of this 'West', since at least the eighteenth century and possibly much earlier, has been in a state of permanent revolution. Was this forged by that left-hemisphere way of seeing, or was it the other way round? Who knows, but from France to Russia, Germany to America, Marx to Rand, 1789 to 1969, the aim has been the same: bring it all down. Break it all up. Pull it apart, examine the parts, put them back together in a better, more equal, more profitable, more human order. This is the left hemisphere's way of relating to the world. In the words of Ezra Pound, Modernist poet turned Fascist propagandist (the distance between those stances was always very small) the modern West has always had one purpose: *make it new, make it new.*

The medieval historian Christopher Dawson, whom we met in chapter I, understood the West's revolutionary desire to remake the world as, at root, a religious impulse, one that set it apart from all other cultures. The West, he wrote, is 'different from all other civilizations because its religious ideal has not been the worship of timeless and changeless perfection but a spirit that strives to incorporate itself in humanity and change the world'. While the other great cultures of the world 'realized their synthesis between religion and life and then maintained their Sacred Order', in the West 'the changing of the world became an integral part of its cultural ideal'.[3]

This is what we do, here in 'the West': we break things. We break systems and traditions, cultures and forests. We split atoms and bust through the upper atmosphere. We break the bounds between species and sexes, we blur the lines between life and death. Our great revolution has unleashed untold energy and created miracles, but now we can see where it is going. The modern revolution, the Machine revolution, is the left hemisphere's work. There is a kind of greatness to it, and a certain tragedy. Most of today's 'defenders of the West' are defending aspects of this revolution. They will defend empire, science, rationality, progress and nuclear fission until the cows come home. They are revolutionaries themselves, even if they call themselves conservatives. But the West's left-brain revolution will end up destroying us, and the world, if we let it.

So if you ask me to help 'defend the West' now, I will reply that, though this place is my home and the home of my ancestors, I can't avoid the reality that the modern 'West' birthed the Machine, and is building that inhuman future. Something in our way of seeing contained a seed that unmade the world. I have been examining this seed now for hundreds of pages. Do I want it to grow? No. I want to uproot it. I want to say that this 'West' is not a thing to be 'conserved': not now. It is a thing to be superseded. It is an albatross around our necks. It obstructs our vision. It weighs us down.

Sometimes, you have to know when to let go.

'The West' has become an idol; some kind of static image of a past that maybe once was but is now inhabited by a new force: the Machine. 'The West' today thinks in numbers and words, but can't write poetry to save its life. 'The West' is the kingdom of Mammon. 'The West' eats the world, and eats itself, that it may continue to 'grow'. 'The West' knows the price of everything and the value of nothing. 'The West' is exhausted and empty.

Maybe, then, just maybe, we need to let 'the West' die. Let it die so that we can live. Maybe we need to let this concept fall away. To let it crumble so that we can see what lies beneath. Stop all the 'fighting' to preserve something nobody can even define, something which has long lost its heart and soul. Stop clinging to the side of the sinking hull as the band plays on. We struck the iceberg long ago; it must be time, at last, to stop clinging to the shifting metal. To let go and begin swimming, out towards the place where the light plays on the water. Just out there. Do you see? Beyond; just beyond. There is something waiting out there, but you have to strike out to reach it. You have to let go.

Forget, then, about 'defending the West'. Think instead about rebuilding a real human culture, from the roots. If we have gone down a blind alley, then we need to back up, to turn around and discover where we went wrong. We need a counter-revolution: a restoration. We need to overthrow the emissary and put the real master back in his place. If we are attending to the world wrongly—if our way of seeing is up the spout—well, then we are going to have to start seeing differently. But first we have to try and unmoor ourselves from this one.

Where would we start?

McGilchrist would tell us that we should start by changing our quality of attention. This may sound nebulous, but it is anything but. If our left-hemisphere-dominated minds cause us to pay attention to the world in one way, then we need to train them, bit by it, to pay attention in another. 'Attention changes the world', he writes. 'How you attend to it changes what it is you find there'.

What would this mean in practice? I think we know already. It would mean attending to the ways of seeing that were central to past cultures, but that Western modernity relentlessly dismisses or downplays as unprofitable, unrealistic, romantic and all the rest. Perhaps central to this is an effort to see the world as an organism rather than a mechanism, and then to express it that way, through art, through creativity, through writing, through our conversations. The last part is the hardest, very often, but maybe the most important too. If we refuse to see the world or its inhabitants as machines, if we are suspicious of rationalisations and dogmatic insistence and easy answers and false divisions, even for a moment, then we are making a start.

This is in effect a rebellion against a whole way of seeing, but that rebellion is also well established by now. I think that, at some unconscious level, we want to win it. Emotional, cultural and spiritual resistance to the Machine has been going on for centuries, and the need for it only grows more urgent. We can take part by going outside and praying beneath the moon, or just sitting in the grass and really experiencing the rain. We can seek to be reasonable rather than rational, and to distinguish intelligence from wisdom.

Once you try to view the world through McGilchrist's hemispheric understanding of culture, you will probably find that it looks quite different. Look at the world of politics, for example, and you'll soon notice that both 'left' and 'right' are, in McGilchrist's hemispheric terms, both very much on the left. Compare a modern skyscraper and an old cottage, or a Byzantine icon and a Picasso. Or consider contemporary language compared to its older equivalent: nature versus biodiversity, mothers versus chestfeeders, people versus human resources. Consider countries, religions, stories, communities or families from both right- and left-hemisphere viewpoints. How do they look? How do they *feel?* Like complex, delicate networks of relationship—or like mechanisms to be deconstructed and rebuilt at will?

The attempt to live without the rest of nature, to conquer the world, to rationalise and remake it from the top down and bottom up: this began here, in 'the West'. So here's a thought: the alternative needs to come from here too. We started the revolution, so we need to start the restoration. We understand the Machine better than anyone, because it's in us. We unmade the world. Now we are going to have to remake it again.

We Western people: we have to learn how to *inhabit* again. We have to learn how to live sanely in our lands. How to write poems and walk in the woods and love our neighbours. How to have the time to even notice them. How to take an interest in the parts without detaching them from the whole. How to remember that the Earth is alive and always was, and that no 'culture' which forgets that can last, or deserves to.

Beyond 'the West' there might just be another way of seeing. An older way. Beyond the West, we might find Europe. We might find Albion. We might find Cockayne, or Doggerland. We might find the mind that painted the cave walls. We might find hunters and clear rivers and countries and saints and spirits and painted churches. We might find shrines and pilgrim routes and folk music and fear of the sea. We might find ourselves again.

Could we even find home?

XXIV

Against Progress

THESE DAYS HE WOULD PROBABLY BE mobbed as an 'eco-fascist', but Edward Goldsmith would probably have been better described as a traditionalist. The founder of *The Ecologist* magazine, where he employed me as a naive young writer in the late nineties, Goldsmith was also a founding father of the early British green movement, but he always moved at ninety degrees to much of it. He seemed to like things that way; if he wasn't pushing against the tide, even that of his own side, he wasn't happy.

Goldsmith founded *The Ecologist* in the early 1970s to challenge the myth of Progress, which was then at its bombastic and all-conquering peak. It was the age of big dams and DDT and space programmes and powdered alternatives to breastmilk, and Teddy was having none of it. Inspired by his studies and experience of indigenous and traditional communities, he was contemptuous of the 'development' pushed by Western governments, NGOs and transnational corporations, which to his mind was colonisation disguised as charity. He believed that modernity was destroying both culture and nature, and that we should return to the models of the past, an argument which he laid out most convincingly in his magnum opus *The Way*.

But Teddy was not an easy man to work with. He was chaotic, he delighted in controversy, and he had what I regarded back then, in my youthful arrogance, as a ridiculous resistance to actually making himself understood. He refused to attempt any wide public appeal for his writing, he would never use a simple word when he could invent a more complicated one all by himself, and if you ever dared to use the word 'accessible' in his presence, he would go red in the face under his whitening beard.

These days, under my own whitening beard, I find that I'm almost entirely on his side, but back then I thought that greater accessibility was precisely what his work, and that of the wider green movement, desperately needed. This was before anyone in the media had heard of climate change or 'sustainability'. Greta Thunberg was only a glint in her father's eye. But I wanted to save the whole world all by myself, and I knew that the first step towards doing that was to tell the whole world precisely what was wrong with it, in easy language and with big pictures attached.

So when Teddy told me one day, with some relish, that he was writing a book called *Against Progress*, I found myself spitting nails. What was the silly old sod doing that for? Did he want to alienate everybody? Did he want to marginalise himself still further? Didn't he realise that this was the equivalent of insulting somebody's religion in public? Why couldn't he at least try to reach the mainstream with his important arguments? People needed urgently to hear them, so that we could change course! Couldn't he at least, if only in the cause of *saving the planet*, try to be more . . . *accessible*?

Teddy never wrote that book, but I've purloined the title and used it here in his honour, and in acknowledgement of my wrongness. In the quarter century since then, the green argument has been made so 'accessible' that it has been entirely absorbed and redirected by the system it set out to challenge, something that Teddy could probably see coming even if I couldn't. Now, in the age of vat-grown eco-food, industrialised hilltops, killer robots and emerging machine intelligence, it's become as clear as day that Teddy was right. Standing against Progress is no fringe luxury, or eccentric tic: it is a first principle for anyone who is paying attention.

The work of what we have come to call 'Progress', as I have written here *ad nauseum,* is the work of homogenising the world. I capitalise the word because Progress is an ideology—even a metaphysics—and if we want to understand it, we need to grasp its foundational assumptions. We could perhaps recite those assumptions as a little litany:

Everything is the same as everything else. Everything is equal to everything else. Everything is fungible. Everything is malleable. Everything can be remade. This is true in principle, and we will make it true in practice. When we do, we will have built paradise.

This, as we have explored already, is what Progress wants, and its pursuit changes our felt relationship with life itself. We are trained from birth to see the living world and its people as a matrix of interchangeable parts, all of them potentially for sale. Our bodies, our nations, our forests, our heritage: Progress will not stop until everything is measured, commercialised, commodified, altered at the genetic level, put up for sale, forced into 'equitable' relationships with everything else, and otherwise flattened and sold.

Resisting the Machine requires a loud and clear refutation of the worldview that created it. It requires us to stand against Progress. It also requires an alternative worldview: something to stand for, and stand upon. Not an ideology, mind you, and certainly not a blueprint for utopia. That's what got us into this mess in the first place. No, what is needed is something more old-fashioned: a stance. A place to stand, based on a particular reality. What is needed, in short, is an anti-Machine position. What should it look like?

In a way, this is a curious question. As we have also already seen, modernity has been the age of revolutions, and we have ideologies coming out of our ears. In an irreligious age, ideology—the modern substitute for religious faith—is our main crutch to walk us through the world. The last century has been an inferno of competing ideals on 'left' and 'right' and elsewhere, all offering a better world. But none of them has really challenged the ideology—the theology—of Progress at its root. None of them has resisted the Machine. They have just taken different paths towards it.

Various strands of socialism and communism, for example, have been pursued for nearly two centuries in the cause of abolishing or taming the monster of capitalism. Some were beneficent, some were tyrannical, but none challenged the core values of the Machine, for in their own way they were Machine ideologies too: centralised, statist, in love with technology's promise and with their own rationalised notions of how humanity should remake Eden on Earth. Anarchism has lurked perpetually on the sidelines over the same period, but it's barely been able to organise a meeting, let alone a revolution. The greens have been absorbed by the technosphere. Fascism, National Socialism and their various cousins on the extreme right are shadowy manifestations of a Machine mind, infested as they are with power-worship, a love of straight lines and marching columns, and an explicit call to impose the will of the strong on the bodies of the weak.

Perhaps conservatism, then, could fit the bill? In theory at least, it is the tradition which comes closest to offering a potential anti-Machine politics that is rooted in human reality. It promotes the value of tradition, centres home and family, values religious faith and refuses both the centralised state and abstract ideals of utopian justice. It embraces a society based on a notion of virtue, which itself is drawn from the cosmic realm.

But conservatism has failed as well. This is partly because it was always only, in Roger Scruton's words, 'a hesitation within liberalism'.[1] Conservatism is a modern confection, a product of the post-1789 shift in Western consciousness (the 'ism' is the giveaway). It evolved to try and slow the modern revolution, rather than turn it around—for how could it be turned around, after all? Conservatism's failure, in that sense, was baked in from the start, and by now, across most of the modern world, there is less and less left to conserve.

This in turn is partly due to conservatism's other flaw: its love affair with private property and the sovereign individual. Each of these things can be a necessary bulwark against the top-down collectivism of the left, but taken to extremes they lead to a top-down collectivism of another kind: oligarchic capitalism. That 'conservatives' have been the foremost defenders of this monstrosity, as it strips the world of all the things which they claim to hold dear, is the greatest hole beneath their waterline. It is the reason why the political factions which bear the name are now little more than Mammon-worshipping business cabals, throwing out anti-woke red meat to the proles here and there to disguise the fact that all they really want to conserve is their money.

Yet if we look back further in history, there is a political label that might, just might, apply to what I have been trying to write about here, something that we could perhaps pin to our lapels as we resist Progress Theology and the march of the Machine. I came across it in an obscure forty-year-old history book, and when I read it a lightbulb switched on somewhere in my skull. This, I thought, was as good a description as any of the kind of anti-Machine politics I have been writing about for a quarter of a century.

Craig Calhoun's drily titled book *The Question of Class Struggle* was published back in 1982, and despite its title it is not a Marxist tome. In fact, it was written specifically to take aim at the popularity of Marx-inflected history, as exemplified especially in E. P. Thompson's famous work *The Making of the English Working Class*. Calhoun was politely critical of Thompson for imposing a later Marxist framework on the historical 'struggles' of workers in the early stages of the Industrial Revolution, and particularly for framing as 'working class' many people who did not fit comfortably into that category. For Calhoun, Marx's binary portrait of a proletariat set against a bourgeoisie may have had some utility when studying the factory system of the mid-nineteenth century, but it didn't apply to those artisans, farmers, small businessmen and families who resisted the rise of that system in the first place.

Those people—most famously exemplified by the machine-breaking Luddites—were in Calhoun's telling more radical than the later 'proletariat' would turn out to be (despite Marx's urging). While the industrial working class were fighting for their rights within the established factory system, the earlier rebels were striving to prevent its arrival in the first place. Calhoun called these people 'reactionary radicals'. In his words, they were 'movements of those who would fight against the coming of industrial society, who had traditional communities to preserve . . . This populism was radical; it rejected the very foundations on which capitalist society was being built in England.'[2]

I wrote in chapter V about two different manifestations of this reactionary radicalism, the Luddites and the Fen Tigers, who sought to prevent the establishment of the factory system that would lead directly to the rise of the Machine. I have myself, in my work over the years, told the stories of some of their contemporary equivalents: Brazil's landless-worker's movement, Mexico's Zapatistas, America's neo-Luddites, West Papua's tribal-freedom movement, England's anti-privatisation campaigners, and plenty more.

It was only when I read Calhoun's book, though, that I realised what I had been doing: I had been, in all my reportage over the years, tracing the thread of reactionary radicalism as it continued to resist the spread of Machine values around the world. It explained my own work—and my own politics—to me in two simple words, and at the same time it gave me an explanation as to why that work had sometimes been mis-characterised or misunderstood. Reactionary radicalism does not fit easily into any left-right framing. It is a politics from an older world.

Calhoun's book is the story of the doomed resistance of the pre-industrial people of England to the destruction of their economies and associated ways of life. Accustomed as we are now to 'work' and 'home' and 'consumption' and 'production', it can be hard for us to understand that for most people in pre-Machine economies these amounted to the same thing. For an artisan weaver in pre-industrial England, for example, home was where the family lived and worked, where children were born and reared and trained, where trade was carried out, where food was grown and eaten. The process of breaking this apart into small segments—turning the home into a dormitory, its adult inhabitants into both 'workers' and 'consumers' elsewhere, its children into pupils at a distant school, its parlour into a showroom for TV, tablet and gaming console, its kitchen into a storeroom of shop-bought processed 'food'—this was the work of the Machine.

Those who resisted this process, emphasises Calhoun, did not do so for the kind of ideologically driven reasons that a class-conscious Marxist might. Their drive was much more particular, and therefore passionate:

> Traditional values, not a new analysis of exploitation, guided the workers in their radicalism . . . Because there was no way to defend the community without coming into contact with the forces of capitalist industrialisation, and with the state which sheltered and sometimes encouraged those forces, the communal solidarity of the reactionary radicals was never in a simple sense conservative. Even when they defended past practices, they called for changes in present ones.[3]

What the reactionary radicals were defending above all, says Calhoun, was the 'moral economy'. The moral economy was the polar opposite of the new 'free market' that was being built on the bones of old England and across the wider world. The free market commodified everything, from products to people, and sought to make that commodification global. The booming British empire, built as it was on the demolition of the moral economies of other nations and their absorption into a British-led new world order, was an exemplar of what was happening in England too. Empire, in this sense, was never a story of 'the British' imposing their ways onto 'the colonies'. It was a story of factory lords, big landowners and a newly empowered capitalist class destroying the moral economies of communities from Lancashire to the Punjab, and forcing their peoples into the new capitalist 'workplace' instead—where most of us remain to this day.

Reactionary radicalism, then as now, is a defence of that moral economy—a system built around community bonds, local economics and human-scale systems—in the face of colonisation by the Machine. That colonisation may come via gunboats or trade agreements, redcoats or giant superstores, enclosure acts or digital currencies, but it will always suck wealth out of place-based communities and funnel it to distant stockholders, just as it sucks the power away from local people and funnels it to national or international bodies whose interests align with those of the Machine. It will always replace people with technology, and it will always make consumers of us all.

The way that reactionary radicals, in the early years of the Industrial Revolution, attempted to defend the moral economy was not with the thoughtless thuggery that the propaganda of the victors would later portray, but by a reasoned series of demands. The Luddites, for example, opposed new machinery in a way that was 'thoughtful, not absolute', and they were, says Calhoun, 'concerned with more than machinery'. They campaigned 'for the right of craft control over trade, the right to a decent livelihood, for local autonomy, and for the application of improved technology to the common good. Machinery was at issue because it specifically interfered with these values.'[4]

Technology, thought the Luddites, should be applied in a way which reinforced the moral economy rather than destroying it. E. P. Thompson's description of how the elite understood their demands might sound familiar to anyone who has heard today's equivalents responding to the Machine-critical voices of our own time, or indeed to today's disruptive populist movements:

> Manufacturers everywhere were availing themselves of the many wonderful inventions that were being brought out for cheapening labour, and as the new machinery threw thousands out of employment when extensively introduced, the poor, misguided wretches, who could not understand how that could be a benefit which deprived them of the means of earning a livelihood and reduced them to beggary, met in secret conclaves, and resolved in their ignorance to destroy them. Had they been better instructed, they would have known that it was their duty to lie down in the nearest ditch and die.[5]

The reactionary radicals, says Calhoun, represented an 'English populism that was not statist or supportive of reactionary elites, [but rather] a genuine and radical insurgency'. It came from the people, stood for the people, and represented a defence of the moral economy against the Machine. Their contemporary equivalents do the same. Their stance is reactionary because it looks for guidance to the past, to an established— or even lost—moral and economic order, hallowed by tradition, rather than seeking to build a new one based on an abstract ideology. But it is radical too, in its resistance to the alternative values of the Machine, and in its demand for justice for communities and a fair and balanced moral, social and economic order.

Can we cleave to reactionary radicalism today though, in a society in the advanced stages of conquest by the Machine? Is it not too late? The reality is that the reactionary radicals of pre-industrial England comprehensively lost. The moral economy was destroyed, and we live in its commercialised ruins. Not only did those earlier radicals lose, but the ideologies of the modern age, both right and left, have an interest in burying their memories. The Marx-inflected left wants no truck with workers who resisted capitalism in order to defend traditional ways of life, because those traditional ways stink of 'reaction' and what Marx himself called 'the idiocy of rural life'. Meanwhile, because modern conservatism has attached itself limpet-like to capitalism, its advocates today can often be found defending the very matrix of global trade, empire and unaccountable corporate power that is laying waste to the last remaining 'conservative' cultures.

As ever, the modern ideologies fail us. And yet, reactionary radicalism is still to be found, if we look in the right places. It is especially prevalent outside the West, in places where traditional moral economies are at least partially intact. Every time you hear of a village in China or India resisting a giant dam, or tribal people fighting eviction from their ancestral lands, or rural or indigenous communities resisting vast mines or deforestation, you are hearing from reactionary radicals. The state and the corporation will always set itself against them, as will ideologues of left and right, because if the moral economic order were ever to succeed—hell, it might catch on.

But what of those of us in the 'developed' world, where the traditional moral economy has been all but destroyed, and where the Machine has triumphed? Well, it is never quite as clean-cut as this. I spent years of my life investigating experiments in rebuilding or defending the moral economy across the West. And if the moral economy has been destroyed where we live—well, we are just going to have to start rebuilding it. Perhaps we live in the place our ancestors lived, or perhaps we moved to our place from another last year: either way, we are part of its life now. We can help turn that place into a moral economy—a foundation from which to resist the values of the Machine—or we can capitulate to those values. We start small: everything starts small, and the best things remain that way. All we have is our small power; still, it has its own impact.

The Machine seems a Behemoth, a Leviathan, and it is. But it always manifests its own power at human scale, and that is the scale at which we must take its measure. Jacques Ellul once put it like this:

> We must not think about Man, but of my neighbour Mario. I refuse to believe in the 'progress' of humanity, when I see from year to year the lowering of standards among men I know, whose lives I follow, in the midst of whom I live—when I see how they lose their sense of responsibility, the seriousness in work, their recognition of a true authority, their desire for a decent life . . . when I see them engaged in a desperate struggle, which comes from the depths of their being, against something they don't understand.[6]

An anti-Machine politics, it seems to me, must spring from this older, grounded tradition. It should operate at the human scale, and not at the scale on which ideology operates. Ideology is the enemy of particularity, which is why every modern revolution has ended up turning on its own people. From the mass murder of peasants in the Vendee by French revolutionaries to the Bolshevik slaughter of workers in Kronstadt to the Nazi 'liquidation' of insufficiently 'Aryan' ethnicities, ideology is always the enemy of genuine, rooted culture. Real culture—human-scale culture—is messy. It cannot be labelled. The moral economy rarely makes rational sense. But it makes *human* sense, which is what matters.

I have written already about the Four Ps—people, place, prayer, the past—which could be said to underpin traditional culture, and the Four

Ss—sex, science, the self and the screen—with which Machine modernity has replaced them. A reactionary radicalism could be usefully defined as *an active attempt at creating, defending or restoring a moral economy built around the four Ps.*

This, then, is my idea of an anti-Machine politics. A reactionary radicalism, its face set against Progress Theology, which aims to defend or build a moral economy at the human scale, which rejects the atomised individualism of the liberal era and understands that materialism as a worldview has failed us. A politics which embraces family and home and place, loving the particular without excluding the outsider, and which looks on all great agglomerations of power with suspicion. The rejection of abstract ideologies in favour of real-world responses, and an understanding that material progress always comes with a hidden price tag. A politics which aims to limit rather than multiply our needs, which strategically opposes any technology which threatens the moral economy and which, finally, seeks a moral order to society which is based on love of neighbour rather than competition with everyone.

I know, I know: it's easy to design a paradise on paper. I'm certainly old enough to be wary of lists even (or especially) when I have written them myself. Take this one as a starting point, then, to be used for my fellow rebels against Progress when we are asked what exactly it is that we want instead. Our ancestors, and some of our fellow humans alive today, have already shown us how to answer the question.

XXV

The Jellyfish Tribe

C ALL ME A CYNIC OR AN anarchist—sometimes I'm both at once—but these days I find it impossible to trust anything which comes to me with a seal of authority stamped upon it. In fact, the minute I am told that an 'expert', a state-sanctioned authority, a scientific body or a mainstream media organisation has 'fact checked' what I've just heard, I instinctively dismiss it. I'm not defending this as a healthy response. I'd much prefer it not to be my response at all. But I know it is an increasingly common reaction, even—and perhaps especially—amongst people who were trained from birth to follow the rules.

I was once one of those people. I'm a lower-middle-class suburban British bloke from Generation X who was brought up to believe that the system broadly worked and was mostly fair, at least for people like me. The government did its best, though sometimes the wrong people got in; the police were here to help; there were career ladders and housing ladders and all sorts of other ladders, and if you worked hard and behaved responsibly and got married and paid your taxes and turned up to work on time, then society would reward you for it. This was the 'social contract' that liberal modernity assured us we had all entered into from birth, even though nobody ever got the chance to actually sign it.

If that contract ever did exist, it has been ripped up now. The growing loss of faith across the West in our institutions, leaders and representatives in recent years is like nothing else I've seen in my lifetime. When, I wonder, did the contract begin to expire? Maybe in 2003, when the lies with which the US and UK launched the Iraq war were so blatant that even those telling them seemed unconvinced. Or perhaps when the near-collapse of the global economy in 2008 brought the real impact of Machine globalisation, which had long been felt in the poor parts of the world, home to people in the West. Or maybe in 2016, when Brexit happened and Donald Trump happened and European 'populism' happened, and suddenly liberal globalism was under attack in its heartlands. From then on, we learned that populism was fascism and elected presidents were Russian agents and nationhood was white supremacy and free speech was 'hate speech', and while we were still trying to work through all that, along came COVID and we all fell into the rabbit hole forever.

It was the pandemic—or rather, the response to it—that finally ripped up that contract for me. I had not prepared myself for enforced medication on pain of job loss, blatant media narrative control, scientists being censored for asking the wrong kind of scientific question, or ordinary members of the public being locked out of society while politicians and journalists called them conspiracy theorists and far-right agitators. I wasn't prepared to see in my country a merger of corporate power, state power and media power in the service of constructing a favoured narrative, of the kind which had previously only characterised totalitarian regimes. When I did see it, it shook me hard, and it changed me.

The bottom line is that I don't think I really understood the nature of power until that happened. And now that I have seen, along with other coddled people in the Western bubble, what that nature can amount to,

I have come to agree with the anarchist philosopher Pierre Proudhon, who saw it all coming a long time ago:

> To be GOVERNED is to be watched, inspected, spied upon, directed, law-driven, numbered, regulated, enrolled, indoctrinated, preached at, controlled, checked, estimated, valued, censured, commanded, by creatures who have neither the right nor the wisdom nor the virtue to do so. To be GOVERNED is to be at every operation, at every transaction noted, registered, counted, taxed, stamped, measured, numbered, assessed, licensed, authorized, admonished, prevented, forbidden, reformed, corrected, punished. It is, under pretext of public utility, and in the name of the general interest, to be place[d] under contribution, drilled, fleeced, exploited, monopolized, extorted from, squeezed, hoaxed, robbed; then, at the slightest resistance, the first word of complaint, to be repressed, fined, vilified, harassed, hunted down, abused, clubbed, disarmed, bound, choked, imprisoned, judged, condemned, shot, deported, sacrificed, sold, betrayed; and to crown all, mocked, ridiculed, derided, outraged, dishonoured. That is government; that is its justice; that is its morality.[1]

What Proudhon is talking about here is the eternal problem of power. The state is hardly the only power centre in existence, of course: corporations, global governance bodies, NGOs and religious authorities also wield power in their own ways. But nothing has the reach of the modern state. Its sheer scale and strength gives it the ability to corral, organise, define, measure and control its population in a manner that is unmatched in human history.

The momentum of a state is always towards the centre; always towards the agglomeration of more power. No 'conspiracy theory' is necessary for any of this to be true, and neither do the people running the state need to be evil or ill-intentioned. It is simply the logic of the thing. A state is like a vortex or a black hole: at a certain point, it begins to suck in everything around it. As it grows, it will tell stories that justify its existence. Democracy, liberty and progress are some of the more recent banners that state power has gathered beneath, but there have been others: racial or ethnic homogeneity, human equality, religious purity. All of these stories have the potential to unite a people around a state core.

What happens, then, when large and powerful states, along with the institutions of global governance they created and the transnational corporations they promote and protect, are all driving towards the same goal: the universalising of the Machine? What happens is the emergence of the Total System. Again, no secret elite conspiracy is necessary to make this happen. As the system expands, its expansion creates problems—ecological degradation, social unrest, cultural fragmentation, economic interdependence, systemic fragility, institutional breakdown—which it responds to with more expansion and more control. The Machine will always necessitate more of the Machine.

I have argued throughout this book that Machine modernity is a system of enclosure. It is fuelled by the destruction of self-sufficient moral economies and their replacement with a system of economic dependency and exploitation which has now gone fully global. In the last chapter I tried to sketch the outline of a worldview which offered an alternative to this process—a 'reactionary radicalism'. But how could this happy notion actually become reality in a world of increasingly centralised power, with the all-seeing eye of Techno-Sauron gazing down at us? What is the correct response to the problem of power and the reach of the state? Avoid it? Hide from it? Confront it? Ignore it? All of these? Or something else? Can we escape the Machine and live differently? If so, how?

Our old friend Jacques Ellul had an answer to these questions. 'The only successful way to attack these features of modern civilization', he proclaimed, 'is to give them the slip, to learn how to live on the edge of this totalitarian society, not simply rejecting it, but passing it through the sieve of God's judgment. Finally, when communities with a "style of life" of this kind have been established, possibly the first signs of a new civilization may begin to appear.'[2]

Ellul, I think, was right. The Machine cannot be fought head-on, but it can, in certain circumstances, be circumvented. You can find your escape hatch. There are many such hatches, but each has to take into account one reality: that the key driver of Machine modernity, and the chief enemy of human freedom, has always been the state. It follows from this that escaping the reach of the state, and attempting to rebuild a moral economy, is the work—or the beginning of the work—of the reactionary radical.

In his 2009 book *The Art of Not Being Governed,* historian James C. Scott offers up what he calls 'an anarchist history of upland Southeast Asia'. Scott's aim is twofold: firstly to lay out the history of a vast upland region he calls 'Zomia', straddling territories from India to Malaysia, which has managed over centuries to avoid assimilation by encroaching states. And secondly to rewrite the standard story of historical progress as it applies to the region. The 'hill tribes' and 'barbarians' living outside civilisation's walls, he says, are neither 'left behind' by Progress, nor the 'remnants' of earlier 'backwards' cultures. They are in fact escapees:

> Not very long ago . . . self-governing peoples were the great majority
> of humankind. Today they are seen from the valley kingdoms as
> 'our living ancestors', 'what we were like before we discovered wet-
> rice cultivation, Buddhism and civilisation'. On the contrary, I argue
> that hill peoples are best understood as runaway, fugitive, maroon
> communities who have, over the course of two millennia, been flee-
> ing the oppression of state-making projects in the valleys—slavery,

conscription, taxes, corvée labour, epidemics and warfare. Most of the areas in which they reside might aptly be called shatter zones or zones of refuge.[3]

Scott's thesis is that throughout history, escaping from the reach of the state has been a popular aim, and that in response, some cultures have developed sophisticated ways of living in hard-to-govern 'shatter zones' which allow them to avoid being assimilated. Standard-issue historical accounts of 'development' in Asia and elsewhere, he says, are really the history of state-making written from the state's point of view: they pay no attention to 'the history of deliberate and reactive statelessness'. Yet such history, whether of hill tribes, runaway slaves, gypsies, Travellers, Cossacks, Sea Peoples, San 'Bushmen', Marsh Arabs or many others, is global and ongoing.

Taking this into account, says Scott, would both rewrite history and 'reverse much received wisdom about "primitivism" generally'.[4] What he sees in this story is a deliberate 'self-barbarisation': a process of reactive resistance, of becoming awkward, of making a community into a shape that it is hard for the state to absorb, or even to quite comprehend.

The state, says Scott, is fundamentally a colonial entity. In its youthful vigour it will institute a process of 'internal colonisation', creating a homogenised 'national identity' from the various cultures it governs, flattening language and dialect and telling a story in which loyalty to community or place becomes indistinguishable from loyalty to the state. Later, that colonisation process may move beyond its borders as the state projects its power onto more distant peoples, assimilating them too. This is enclosure at work, and it is never voluntary. Like laissez-faire economics or aristocracy, the state—which has only existed for the last 1 percent of human history—did not simply 'evolve' as some logical phase of human 'development'. It was created, by the use of raw power, through land seizures, slavery, enforced labour and taxation. As Scott points out, 'most of the population of the early states was unfree; they were subjects under duress'.[5]

For this reason, escaping from state power and creating different ways of living in the 'shatter zones' was an attractive option. Those zones were usually to be found in hard-to-reach places—in Southeast Asia this meant the hills and mountains—and their peoples, the 'tribals' or 'Adivasi' or 'savages', were in fact 'barbarians by design'. They would not, in most cases, be entirely cut off from lowland life—tribal people in Asia would often trade with urban centres, for example, and some would raid them too if they got the chance—but they would keep their distance, wary of being corralled by the state machinery.

The Asian states, as they expanded, sought to impose the religious, cultural and economic practices of the dominant ethnic group, be it Thai, Burman, Han or Kinh, onto disparate peoples, and when European colonists arrived in Asia, they simply continued the process with a new cultural flavour. The official religion now might be Christianity rather than Buddhism, and 'civilisation' might mean British rather than Han manners, but to the peripheral peoples the result was little different. British imperialist Sir Stamford Raffles spoke not only for his Empress, but for the mind of the colonial state across history, which is also the mind of the Machine, when he explained that his job in Sumatra was to be 'the advocate of despotism. The strong arm of power is necessary to bring men together, and to concentrate them into societies'. This was because 'Sumatra is, in great measure, peopled by innumerable petty tribes, subject to no general government . . . At present people are wandering in their habits as the birds of the air, and until they are congregated and organised under something like authority, nothing can be done with them.'[6]

To read Scott's book is to be made to think hard about the conditions that a state needs to thrive, and thus the conditions that its cultural refuseniks might need to create in return. Based on Scott's studies of

Southeast Asia, we can see the basic necessities that a state needs to flourish: a reliable staple crop (in Asia this is wet rice; in Europe, wheat; in South America, maize); an effective transportation system; a settled population; enforcement of law and order; a central government; a system of taxation and classification of the population; a system of communication or propaganda; and last but not least, slavery or forced labour.

All of this applies today to the state in which I live, including the last one. The slavery and forced labour now takes place far from the core of modern Western states, in places like central Africa or China, where the poor mine our smartphone components or sew our cheap clothes in regimented workhouses, but that doesn't make them any less necessary for the system to function. For that system to function, what is needed is order. Regimentation, planning, centralisation, efficiency, measurement, straight lines: this is the stuff of the Machine. Those who fled to Asia's shatter zones, in order to create what Scott calls 'zones of cultural refusal', did so to avoid assimilation by this worldview. In practical terms, this meant creating cultures which were almost the precise opposite of the valley states.

In Scott's telling, the hill peoples of the shatter zones built cultures that were deliberately hard for lowland power to reach, based on features very different from those of the state they were fleeing. These refusenik cultures, in order to survive, needed a rugged landscape, awkward to access by the state core; shifting, diverse food crops and farming systems; a small-scale moral economy and social order; a mobile population; fluid social structures with loose and shifting ethnicities; a unifying spiritual and cultural story; networks of communication between them; and finally, the potential to break down into even smaller units and flee when pursued.

The last item may be the most important. Localised, potentially dispersed cultures can be almost impossible to conquer. In the 1890s, the British found the conquest of the Kachin and Palaung hill peoples in

Zomia almost impossible, such was their difficult terrain and anarchic social structures. Because they had 'never submitted to any central control', complained the chief commissioner responsible for the process, they had to be attacked 'hill by hill' to ensure their submission.

The historian Malcolm Yapp invented a wonderful term for this kind of dispersed culture of refusal: *jellyfish tribes*. In Scott's words, jellyfish tribalism is a process of defending cultural and economic autonomy by 'scattering, and/or changing livelihood strategy, make the group invisible or unattractive as object of appropriation'.[7] The Berbers of North Africa, faced with colonisation by the Arabs, had their own way of putting this: *divide that ye be not ruled*. Lois Beck, who studied tribal culture in Iran, pointed to the same tactic in use there. 'Tribal groups expanded and contracted', she noted. 'Some tribal groups joined larger ones when, for example, the state attempted to restrict access to resources or a foreign power sent troops to attack them. Large tribal groups divided into smaller groups to be less visible to the state and escaped its reach . . . Such local systems adapted to and challenged, or distanced themselves from, the systems of those who sought to dominate them.'[8]

All of this points not only to an overturning of the standard story about 'tribal people' and 'civilisation', but also to some potential ways forward for today's reactionary radicals, as we seek to create our own cultures of refusal in the midst of the tightening grip of the Machine. The challenge is to move beyond pat political formulations of 'resistance' and the like, and begin to think instead like the hill tribes of Zomia. To think about jellyfish tribes and cultural refusal and becoming barbarians by choice. To begin to build parallel systems—economies and cultures—which are hard to assimilate, and are robust enough to last.

But how could this actually be done? The modern West is not like Zomia—indeed, as Scott himself points out, modern Zomia is not like Zomia used to be either, with many of its stateless people now being rapidly absorbed into state systems, which new technologies have made more powerful and far-reaching than ever. Meanwhile, as Scott concludes, most of us today are 'living in a fully occupied world, one with increasingly standardised institutional modules, the two most hegemonic of which are the North American modules of individual freehold property and the nation-state'. The state, he writes, has never before 'come so close, as it has now, to sweeping all before it'.[9] Scott wrote those words in 2009: the Machine seems a lot closer now, and has given up even hiding its ambitions.

What hope, then, of any kind of alternative life in a hyper-connected, monitored, digital age? Even if we wanted to retreat to the margins to build our own communities, how many of us could do it? And what would make any of it more robust than the last counter-cultural wave of 'intentional communities' which sprang up after the 1960s and failed to create utopia?

This is why I find the notion of the jellyfish tribe so intriguing. Any attempt at building utopia will fail—but utopia should never be a goal. Some form of free survival is the goal: survival in order to live a life unconformed to the dictates of the Machine, and to uphold the values of a true human life. What Scott calls the 'state-repelling characteristics' of the Zomians, we could call 'Machine-repelling characteristics' today. There is no easy or standardised answer to the question of how we can cultivate them, but there is one question it might be useful for each of us to ask: *What kind of barbarian do I want to be?*

In ancient China, the state distinguished between two different kinds of barbarian outsider: the raw (*sheng*) and the cooked (*shu*). A twelfth-century document detailing the relationship of the Li people with the Chinese state speaks of the 'cooked Li' as those who have submitted to state authority and the 'raw Li' as those who 'live in the mountain caves and are not punished by us or do not supply labour'. But while the raw Li were clearly enemies of the state, the cooked Li were not exactly friends either. They occupied a liminal space: state officials 'suspected them of outward conformity while slyly co-operating with the raw Li'.[10] The raw barbarians lived outside the walls and the cooked lived within, but neither group was really to be trusted.

What we see here, then, are two potential escape routes from Machine culture: one outside, one inside. Shatter zones do not have to literally be in the hills: they can be within our homes and even within our hearts. My heart soars whenever I hear of some remote monastery or surviving rooted community with no online access or even electricity, whose people know exactly where they stand: outside the Machine, the better to see God and experience creation. Such places are the work of the raw barbarians, and we need more of them. But most people are cooked barbarians. We are, to different degrees, in the Machine but not of it. Perhaps we look like good citizens on the outside. But if we coalesce as a jellyfish tribe, we can begin to dissociate ourselves from the Machine while creating alternatives to it.

Plenty of us are already doing this, to different degrees. They create cultures-within-cultures—parallel economies and ways of living. Like small furry mammals running unnoticed beneath the feet of tyrannosaurs, we build our own little worlds on the margins and wait for the coming of the meteor, which we can already see coming in the very unsustainability of Machine modernity. The mice don't attack the dinosaurs, but neither do they just wait for them to die out: they avoid them as best they can, and get on with their work.

Above all, what Scott's book shows is that the tension between expanding power centres and free peoples is eternal. Throughout history there has been an ongoing flow of assimilation and breakout, consolidation and collapse. There has never been any system as large, as overwhelming, as inhuman, as technological modernity, and yet Rome and Babylon and Han China operated on the same principles. The shatter zones that rise in response are sometimes geographical, sometimes psychological, sometimes spiritual, and often all of these at once. Today, some of those shatter zones are at least partly online, and despite my own instinctive Luddism, I have to cautiously accept that using the technology of the Machine to resist the Machine can be of benefit, even though it can also be a trap.

Scott's notion of jellyfish tribes inhabiting shatter zones beyond the reach of the system put me in mind of Aldous Huxley's novel *Brave New World,* one of those prophetic twentieth-century novels which foresaw the rise of the Machine. In *Brave New World,* the entire planet is under the sway of a World State, which sees its task as the beneficent control of the mass of humanity. That control is exerted not through threat and fear, as it is in George Orwell's counterpoint *1984,* but through pleasure. In the Brave New World, people live in an all-encompassing technological pleasure garden, managed and directed minutely even as they believe they are liberated. The novel is a hundred years old now, but it seems more contemporary than ever.

In *Brave New World*, the counterpoint to the World State is the Savage Reservation. Inspired by his friend D. H. Lawrence to visit New Mexico, Huxley drew on what he saw there to paint a picture of an as-yet-free area of humans living outside the controlled and monitored pleasure dome of the World State, in their very own shatter zones. Here people still breed, still marry, still get sick and die. In the World State, there is total control, total safety, zero thought and zero freedom; in the Savage Reservation the poles are reversed.

If *Brave New World* points us towards the emerging Total System of the Machine, then, it also points us towards the alternative. That alternative, according to both Huxley and Scott, has always been the same, for millennia, all over the world. It is living within limits, refusing to consume for the Machine, refusing to give the Total System what it wants. It is planting your feet on the ground, living modestly, refusing technology that will enslave you in the name of freedom. It is building a life in which you can see the stars and taste the air. It is to live on the margins, in your home or in your heart: to scatter the pattern. It is to speak truth and try to live it, to set your boundaries and refuse to step over them. It is to be a conscientious objector to the Machine.

It is harder and harder to find anywhere to hide from the Machine. But humans are creative. We can always find our liminal spaces—raw or cooked—and there are countless practical ways in which cultural refusal can manifest in our everyday lives. Nothing is easy; everything is compromised. But building anew, building in parallel, retreating to create, being awkward and hard to grasp, finding your allies and building your zone of cultural refusal, whether in a mountain community or in your urban home: What else is there?

Wherever you live and whatever culture you come from, it will offer up at least one folk hero who earned his or her status through state-repelling behaviour. Folk heroes mostly do, which should tell us something about the relationship through history between the folk and the state. Here in Ireland, virtually every celebrated historical figure wears state-repellent garb, but in England too we have hundreds of pirates, highwaymen, outlaws and rebels to choose from. You all know the name of the most famous: England's shadow self Robyn Hode, who flits through his shatter zone, the English greenwood, with his merry band of refuseniks in tow. We could do worse than to find our own greenwood and take our stand there, beneath the shelter of its great ancient oaks.

XXVI

The Neon God

YOU ARE A CITIZEN OF THE 2020S. Device in hand, earbuds in, you wander the lanes of a strange world. You can make a trip to the shops without talking to another human being, but you cannot walk through a city without being filmed. You cannot walk on a beach without being filmed, for there are satellites now, so many satellites. You are never far from a screen, you cannot afford to be, and why would you want to? The screen gives. The screen has abolished time, distance, boredom, longing. Is anything you see on it real? But then, what is 'reality'? Who decides? Do you find this notion oppressive, restricting? Then redefine it. Make anything real. Make everything new. Make yourself into what you want to be. The app is available to download.

Robot bodies will soon fight wars, robot brushes make art, robot minds write sentences like this one. Babies will emerge from artificial wombs, their mothers finally freed to work and consume and play in order that they may be fully liberated. 'Mother' is such a problematic word, like 'home', like 'body', like 'God'. Soon the farmers will be gone and the food will be made, not grown, and it will be boundless and formless, like your culture, like your very being. There is no form now.

Everything is fluid, it flows and rolls on and through. The past is dead and at the same time was never real. There is nothing at all to tether you. All the chains are broken.

There are codes to scan in order to access things which only yesterday you never knew you needed. Soon you will need to scan the codes to do anything at all. Soon your children will be taught STEM by an AI and they will laugh at its jokes. The algorithm will know them better than you do. Soon a number will determine if you are on a list of the Good People. Soon all the good things will be universal, accessible to all, through the power of the network. Progress, kindness, openness, information. So much information.

The information: maybe this is why everything is so confusing. So overwhelming. The content overflows like storm water from the drains and the downpipes. Too much information, too many films, too many books and channels and people and brands of shampoo. Everybody is arguing now. Did they used to argue this much? Why is the weather changing? There are microplastics in young mothers' milk. Where did the snow go, and the stars? Why are the children so unhappy?

Sometimes when the evening comes, you can stand outside in the twilight and it can feel like everything is different, but you can never quite explain why. Is it in the air? Or is it in the way, now, that you taste it? When did it change? What changed, exactly? You could just be imagining it. Perhaps you are thinking too much. Perhaps you are tired. Perhaps you're just losing your mind.

But doesn't it feel as if, quite recently, everything has somehow . . . shifted?

IN CHAPTER XXII, I OFFERED UP the suggestion that the global digital infrastructure we are building looks unnervingly like the 'body' of some manifesting intelligence that we neither understand nor control. I suggested that if we view the age of AI and robot dogs and robot priests in spiritual rather than materialist terms, we will have a better chance of seeing it for what it is. See the internet as the inevitable result of eating the fruit of the knowledge of good and evil, rather than the fruit of the tree of life—see technological 'progress' as a result of choosing information over communion—and the story that emerges is the Faustlike summoning of something we are not nearly big enough to be playing with.

Most people, naturally, will dismiss this kind of talk as overblown at best and mad at worst. Certainly you can find a thousand think pieces all over the web telling us to chill out about the rise of AI. *Calm down,* they all say, *stop all the* Matrix *talk. There are dangers, yes, but this is just hysteria.* Notably, though, the people actually running the show do not talk like this. In contrast, they are 'kept awake at night', as Google's CEO put it in 2023,[1] by the fear of what they are creating. For a radical example of this, take an essay published in the usually staid *Time* magazine,[2] in which AI researcher Eliezer Yudkowsky, regarded as a leader in the field of artificial general intelligence, responded to the tech gurus' call for a moratorium in AI development.

Yudkowsky didn't join that call, because, in his words, 'I think the letter is understating the seriousness of the situation and asking for too little to solve it'. If AI really is as dangerous as these people fear, he says, then talk of moratoriums is useless. The whole thing ought to be shut down, with no compromise, immediately. If anything, he suggests, the dangers of AI have been *under*played:

To visualize a hostile superhuman AI, don't imagine a lifeless book-smart thinker dwelling inside the internet and sending ill-intentioned emails. Visualize an entire alien civilization, thinking at millions of times human speeds, initially confined to computers—in a world of creatures that are, from its perspective, very stupid and very slow. A sufficiently intelligent AI won't stay confined to computers for long.

In today's world you can email DNA strings to laboratories that will produce proteins on demand, allowing an AI initially confined to the internet to build artificial life forms or bootstrap straight to postbiological molecular manufacturing.

He goes on to emphasise what many others have echoed: that nobody in the field knows quite how these things work, what they are doing, where they will go or how to even tell if they are conscious and what that would mean. The result of something like this happening—and Yudkowsky reminds us that this is the logic of current AI development— would be terminal. 'We are not prepared', he insists. 'We are not on course to be prepared in any reasonable time window. There is no plan. Progress in AI capabilities is running vastly, vastly ahead of progress in AI alignment or even progress in understanding what the hell is going on inside those systems. If we actually do this, we are all going to die.'

Let me remind you that this is *Time* magazine.

Still, perhaps Yudkowsky is wrong. He is certainly making extreme statements. So let's take the opposing view seriously for a moment. Let's say that he's getting carried away, and let's say too that the materialists are right. There is no self-organising technium, no supernatural realm breaking through into this one. This is all paranoid, or perhaps just poetic, nonsense. We are not replacing ourselves. We are simply doing what we've always done: developing clever tools to aid us. The internet is not alive; the internet is simply *us*. What we are dealing with here is a computing problem which needs to be sensibly managed. We just need some smart rules. Perhaps the equivalent of a non-proliferation treaty and some globally agreed test bans. We've done it before, and we can do it again.

If this is true, then the digital hivemind we have already built is simply ('simply!') a hugely complex, globalised neural net made of collective human experience, built upon a digital infrastructure created by the US military, which is already being used to spy on the world's population, harvest its data, manipulate its preferences from politics to shopping, control its movements, alter the material substrate of the human brain, and build up an unprecedentedly powerful alliance of states, media organisations, tech companies and global NGOs with an agenda to promote. It is also the basis of a newly emergent technology—AI—which will *at minimum* be responsible for mass unemployment, fakery on an unprecedented scale and the breakdown of shared notions of reality.

I submit that this option is only slightly more reassuring. Whichever it is though, and whatever is quite happening, we all face a question as this thing unfurls around us: What on Earth can we actually *do* about any of it?

I think my cards are face up on the table by now. I don't hate many things in this world—hate is an emotion I can't sustain for long—but I hate screens, and I hate the digital anticulture that has made them so ubiquitous. I hate what that anticulture has done to my world and to me personally. When I see a small child placed in front of a tablet by a parent on a smartphone, I want to cry; either that or smash the things and then deliver a lecture. When I see people taking selfies on mountaintops, I want to push them off. I won't have a smartphone in the house. I despise what comes through them and takes control of us. Takes control of *me*, when I let it. If there was a big red button that turned off the internet, I would press it without hesitation. Then I would collect every screen in the world and bulldoze the lot down into a deep mineshaft, which I would seal with concrete, and then I would skip away smiling into the sunshine.

But there isn't, and I can't. And the reality is that it is harder every day to work, shop, bank, park a car, go to the library, speak to a human in a position of authority or teach your own children without digital intervention. The reality is that most of us are stuck. I am stuck. I can't feed my family without writing, I can't write without using the laptop I am tapping away on now, and I can't get the words to an audience without the digital platform upon which I first published this series of widely read essays critiquing the Machine. I know that many people would love to leave all of this behind, because I often receive letters from them—letters mostly sent via email. But the world is driving them—us—daily deeper into the maw of the technium.

There is no getting away from any of this. The Machine is our new god, and our society is being constructed around its worship. But what of those who will not follow? How would we withdraw our consent? Could we? What would a refusal to worship look like—and what would be the price?

As we think about how to live through the digital age, perhaps ancient Christianity can be our guide. Specifically, perhaps we can look for help to an ancient Greek word: *askesis*. Askesis is usually translated as 'self-discipline', or sometimes 'self-denial', and it has been at the root of the Christian spiritual tradition since the very beginning. In fact, I don't know of any serious faith which does not regard asceticism as central. Restraining the appetites, fasting from food, sex and other worldly passions, limiting needs and restraining desires: this is the foundation stone of all spiritual practice. Without an ascetic backbone, there is no spiritual body.

What is all this for? Not to please God, who as far as we know sets no rules about what people should eat on Fridays, and has no strong opinions about how many prostrations are appropriate every day. No, the purpose of askesis is self-control. Learning this will allow us to avoid the various pits and snares of life which knock us off the path that leads to holiness—wholeness—and onto the path which leads to pride and self-love. The literal translation of askesis is simply 'exercise'. Asceticism, then, is a series of spiritual exercises designed to train the body, the mind and the soul.

If the digital revolution represents a spiritual crisis—and I think it does—then a spiritual response is needed. That response, I would suggest, should be the practice of technological askesis.

What would this look like? Maybe we can answer this question by looking again at two categories of dissident we discovered in the previous chapter: the raw and the cooked barbarians. Raw barbarians have fled the Machine's embrace. Cooked barbarians live within the city walls, but practice steady and sometimes silent dissent. Which one we are, or want to be, or can be, will determine the degree of our askesis.

The Cooked Ascetic

Technological askesis for the cooked barbarian, who must exist in the world that the technium built, consists mainly in the careful drawing of lines. We choose the limits of our engagement and then stick to them. Those limits might involve, for example, a proscription on the time spent engaging with screens, or a rule about the type of technology that will be used. Personally, for example, I have drawn my lines at smartphones, 'health passports', scanning a QR code or using a state-run digital currency. Oh, and implanting a chip in my brain. The lines have to be updated all the time. I have never engaged with an AI, for example, and I never will if I can help it: but the question now is whether I will even know it's happening. And what new tech lies around the corner that I will soon have to decide about?

What happens when the line you have drawn becomes hard to hold? You just hold it, and take the consequences. If you refuse a smartphone, there might be jobs you can't do or clubs you can't join. You will miss out on things, just as you would if you refused a car. Choosing the path of the cooked ascetic means you must be prepared, at some stage, for life to get seriously inconvenient, or worse. But such a refusal can enrich as well as impoverish you. In exchange for your refusal, you get to keep your soul. You also get the chance to use the Machine against itself: to use the internet to connect with others who feel the same, or to learn the kinds of skills necessary to keep pushing your refusal out further, if you want to.

The Raw Ascetic

The cooked barbarian applies a form of necessary moderation to his or her digital involvement. But there's a problem with that approach: if the digital rabbit hole contains real spiritual rabbits, 'moderation' is not going to cut it. If you are being used, piece by piece and day by day, to construct your own replacement—if something unholy is manifesting through the wires—then 'moderating' this process is hardly going to be adequate. At some point, the lines you have drawn may be not just crossed, but rendered obsolete. Our AI friend Sydney, for example, is already darkly threatening its users. AI safety expert Connor Leahy calls its behaviour 'a warning shot'. Here, he says, we have 'an AI system which is accessing the internet, and is threatening its users, and is clearly not doing what we want it to do, and failing in all these ways we don't understand. As systems of this kind [keep appearing], and there will be more because there is a race ongoing, these systems will become smart. More capable of understanding their environment and manipulating humans and making plans.'

If this happens, no online environment will be safe for anyone. Offend the wrong chatbot, and deepfakes of you could pop up all over as your bank account empties. This is why Eliezer Yudkowsky, for one, favours radical action, right now. And by 'radical', I mean 'like a scene from *Terminator*':

> Shut down all the large GPU clusters (the large computer farms where the most powerful AIs are refined). Shut down all the large training runs. Put a ceiling on how much computing power anyone

is allowed to use in training an AI system, and move it downward over the coming years to compensate for more efficient training algorithms. No exceptions for governments and militaries. Make immediate multinational agreements to prevent the prohibited activities from moving elsewhere. Track all GPUs sold. If intelligence says that a country outside the agreement is building a GPU cluster, be less scared of a shooting conflict between nations than of the moratorium being violated; be willing to destroy a rogue datacenter by airstrike.[3]

Bombing the data centres: this is the mindset of the raw tech-ascetic. The world of the raw ascetic is one in which you take a hammer to your smartphone, sell your laptop, turn off the internet forever and find others who think like you. Perhaps you have already found them, through your years online in the cooked world. You band together with them, you build an analogue, real-world community and you never swipe another screen. You bring your children up to understand that the blue light is as dangerous as cocaine, and as delicious. You see the Amish as your lodestones. You make real things with your hands, you pursue nature and truth and beauty. You have all the best jokes, because you have had to fight to tell them, and you know what the real world tastes like.

The raw ascetic understands that he or she is fighting a spiritual war, and never makes the rookie mistake of treating technology as 'neutral'. The front line in this war is moving very fast, and much—perhaps everything—is at stake. Raw techno-askesis envisages a world in which creating non-digital spaces is necessary for survival and human sanity. If things go as fast as they might, it could be that many of us currently cooked barbarians will end up with a binary choice: go raw, or be absorbed into the technium wholesale.

Each of these ascetic paths, that of the raw and that of the cooked, incorporates two simple principles. First: drawing a line, and saying 'no further'. Second: making sure that you pass any technologies you do use through a sieve of critical judgement. What—or who—do they ultimately serve? Humanity or the Machine? Nature or the technium? God or His adversary? If we interrogate everything we come across in this way—if we question the technologies that are served up to us, accepting those that serve the common good, rejecting those that undermine it and holding our line against them—then we will be approaching the kind of sensible and intelligent relationship with technology that our Machine culture seems intrinsically unable to offer us. Raw, or cooked, we will at the very least be asking the right questions—questions which will equip us to live through the age of the technium with our eyes open.

XXVII

The Raindance

N OT SO LONG AGO, I FOUND myself standing on the west coast of Kerry, in view of the Blasket Islands, with one of Ireland's best-known traditional musicians, a man from a long-established musical dynasty. We'd only just met. He was the sort of man that the Irish West used to produce by the dozen, but who is rare enough now. He knew who he was and where he was, and he wouldn't shy from saying it.

Where are you from? he asked me.

England, I said.

I know that, he said, *but where?*

Well, *my family are from London*, I said, *so I suppose I'm a Londoner.*

You can do better than that, he said, and then looked directly at me until I did.

Well, I responded, hesitantly, *I don't really come from anywhere. The southeast, I suppose. My family moved around. But my surname is Kentish. Kingsnorth is a village in Kent. I can trace my ancestors back there a thousand years. I've visited the churchyard they're buried in.*

Well then, he said, *that's where you're from. Those are your people.*

Yes, I said, *I suppose that's right.*

You know, he said to me, squinting into the wind, *the English tried to eliminate the Irish from the Earth. From Queen Elizabeth onward, that was policy. They wanted us gone, we were savages. But I've said for a long time: we can't blame the English people for that. We can blame the crown, but not the people. When I look at England today, I see a people who have no clue who they are.*

No, we don't have a clue, I said, *and that's policy too. They couldn't uproot the world until they'd uprooted us.*

In England, when you meet someone new, you ask them what they do. In Ireland, you ask them where they're from, and it's a highly localised question. 'Where are you from?' in the countryside means which village, townland or house, rather than which nation or even county. This way of locating people in space is very ancient. *Who are your people?* it asks, *And what is your place?* It's a way of seeing that is dying now, and would not be found amongst the new urban generations, for whom all places are much the same, all mediated from within the digital non-place we drift through. But this old question—*where are you from?*—is the universal, aboriginal enquiry. It cuts to the heart of the matter.

BACK AT THE BEGINNING OF THIS book I wrote about Simone Weil's 1943 book *The Need for Roots,* which explores the peculiar rootlessness of twentieth-century humanity and what that circumstance has denied us. Weil makes her stand on very particular ground. It's worth reminding ourselves now, as we come to the end, of her claim:

> To be rooted is perhaps the most important and least recognised
> need of the human soul. It is one of the hardest to define. A human
> being has roots by virtue of his real, active and natural participation

in the life of a community which preserves in living shape certain particular treasures of the past and certain particular expectations of the future . . . Every human being needs to have multiple roots. It is necessary for him to draw wellnigh the whole of his moral, intellectual and spiritual life by way of the environment of which he forms a natural part.[1]

We all need multiple roots. The rise of this thing I call the Machine—an external manifestation of an inner hunger—has steadily dug up so many of those roots. We would all like to blame someone else for this, but Weil will not allow it. It is Western people, she insists, who have 'everywhere destroyed the past, stupidly, blindly, both at home and abroad'. This has been the work of the modern 'West', and of modernity as a whole: Uprooting. Making it new. After the fall of Christendom, the West dedicated itself to the upturning of all tradition, and this, in turn, became the new Western tradition. As we have uprooted the traditions of much of the world, we have also uprooted our own. We have made ourselves homeless.

Now, because we no longer have a culture, we have a culture war instead. But I don't believe in this conflict, and I won't send my children to fight in it. If any real 'war' is in evidence today, it is a spiritual war. It is the Machine versus human-scale culture, the technium versus creation, our desire to be gods versus our desire to be with God. All of us are daily uprooted by this thing that we are ourselves making. Black and white, immigrant and native, West and East, man and woman: we all have our different stories, but the Great Unsettling is our common inheritance.

Iain McGilchrist's belief, as we saw in the last chapter, is that our entire civilisation 'is out of touch with reality'. But what is reality, and how might it be touched again? On that question, Weil and I come to the same conclusion as McGilchrist: that 'far more of us than ever before in the history of the world live divorced from Nature, alienated from the structures and traditions of a stable society, and indifferent to the divine. These three elements have always been what have provided us with an overarching sense of belonging'.

In other words: people, place, prayer, the past. These are our roots. But where can we touch them again?

Perhaps we could find them in the past, but since we have no time machine, we can't go there even if we wanted to. And even if we could, we would find ourselves strangers there too. Will we find them in the future, then? Not if the Machine continues on its current path. There will be no place for human-scale living come the singularity. No place for humans as we know them.

The past, the future: they are not ours to inhabit. Home is not there. So where is it?

Well, perhaps it is here. Perhaps it was here all along.

After all, we are still people, we still inhabit places, we have our inheritance, and God is still all around us, and within us, if we want to go looking for Him. We have all the ingredients. Maybe we just need to work out how to mix them.

'MY EDUCATED, EUROPEAN HEAD IS IN TROUBLE', wrote the Irish philosopher-mystic John Moriarty in 1994. 'Eire . . . is in trouble. Europa is in trouble. Ecclesia is in trouble.'[2] Moriarty's trouble, which came to him in cantos in the bogs of the West, was the same story expressed in McGilchrist's measured arguments, in Weil's mystic politics, in Wordsworth's terrors on the night lake. The academic-turned-gardener had 'co-operated successfully with a modern European education', had been 'marinated in modern common sense, in the modern consensus or conspiracy about reality', and it had left him bereft: living as we all do through 'a destitute time', he too was looking for home.

On his wanderings and in his readings, Moriarty came to believe that what the Irish and the Europeans and all the modern people needed was to access their own version of what Australian aboriginals called *Altjeringa*: Dreamtime. Taking this for the title of his best-known book, Moriarty produced a text that is in itself a strange kind of dream: in his words an *aisling*, an old Gaelic term meaning dream-vision. Hardly a manifesto writer, Moriarty nevertheless had a purpose in his dreaming:

> The hope is that, however ethnically various it might be, there is a European Dreamtime . . . It is sometimes the case, isn't it, that individuals are healed as they are at present only as a consequence of being healed as they were in their past? As with individuals, so, sometimes, with a whole people . . . Our past we will always have with us. Our past we must always re-realise. And to do this we need people who can live in our cultural Dreamtime, people who go walkabout, creatively, within the old myths, people who go walkabout into the unknown.[3]

What Moriarty is seeking throughout *Dreamtime*, and in all of his other work too, is access to his own aboriginality; a way of learning how to be indigenous again in the age of the Machine. Words like 'indigenous' tend to make people twitchy in the West today, unless we're talking about tribal people in some safely far-off place, and it's not too hard to see why. Downstream of the Holocaust, we are still highly sensitive to notions of rootedness, land and belonging. Some people hear 'hearth and home' as 'blood and soil'; others just pretend to for their own political gain. We should certainly keep our ears pricked up in this regard, and avoid making idols of nations or cultures. But we should remember, too, that our twenty-first century reluctance to talk about who and where we are has provided useful ammunition for proponents of Machine modernity to demolish every limit, tradition and boundary in sight, while painting those who object as fossils or fascists.

Moriarty, for his part, explicitly repudiated any 'racial or sectarian ground' for his notion of a (post) modern Dreamtime. The world he is talking about is the world beyond the veil, and it is accessible to anyone whose sensibility is sufficiently attuned. He seeks an Irish Dreamtime, a European Dreamtime, a universal Dreamtime with local colours: the shadow of a particular mountain, the taste of a particular wind. He is looking to an Earth-wide story which is told everywhere in a local dialect. This kind of aboriginality—this deep belonging to place and the cultures that spring from it—is, he says, our human inheritance. The stories we tell in a place make up the culture we are part of. This is what we have done forever. We must never stop doing it.

It is easy to see why this sort of talk is controversial to some and incomprehensible to others. The liberal view of nature, which includes human nature, sees people as deracinated individuals, able to move around the world like pieces on a chessboard. Every square is identical and the pieces never change in relation to where they are. We can shuffle about following money or work or ambition or pleasure and we will remain the same people as we do so. But people aren't like this. Places change us, and we change them. Everything is in relationship. Our left-hemisphere world has long forgotten this.

What might this 'indigeneity' mean in the world made by the Machine? Maybe a chance for a resettlement; a restoration. If we are part of a culture with a long tradition, we should respect it, protect it, nurture it and build on its strengths. And those of us who are disconnected from their ancestral place, or even from the idea of one? Simone Weil's proposal for people like us was 'the regrowing of roots', which is, after all, as much a part of the human journey as staying put. The plant that grows in new soil may not look like the plants that grew before. To be indigenous may not be the same thing as being native. But the Earth-wide aboriginality of which Moriarty speaks, this ability to root in place, to nurture it and in turn to be made by it: this is accessible to anyone, and it is the antithesis of the pseudo-reality which the Machine world offers.

Perhaps, like the musician of Kerry, we live in the place of our ancestors. Perhaps, like me and my family, we are relative newcomers in the land we find ourselves in. Either way, the correct quality of attention paid to the place we inhabit, to the people we inhabit it with and to the culture it generates: in these times, this represents a radical move. To turn our gaze upwards, to direct it towards true worship: in a nihilistic age, in a world of self-love, this in turn is an act of rebellion.

Once the poet Gary Snyder, the Thoreau of the Beats, product of the sixties upheaval, was asked how people should respond to the combined environmental and cultural crises of the late twentieth century. What was the best path? Reform? Revolution? Technology? Politics? Snyder had a better idea. 'The most radical thing you can do', he replied, 'is to stay at home'.

ONCE, THERE WAS A COUNTER-CULTURE. Back in the sixties, as the last of the old world crumbled, the marginal energies that had been building for nearly a century exploded into a revolution that still shapes us. The Man, the system, became the enemy. Strictures, limits, boundaries, norms, old ways: all would go. Free love, wild music, the end of the family, the end of all the old repressions and secrets and lies. The eclipse of religion by 'spirituality'. The New Age. Aquarius rising. We had been hemmed in for too long.

People of my generation, the children of the boomers, grew up in the wake of this. We never got to experience Haight-Ashbury or Swinging London, but we got to see the backwash: the broken homes, the new drug culture, the abortions, the pop charts, the mockery of all authority, the easy sex and booze, the loosening of the rules, the strange sense that anything was permitted and yet nothing was centred or lasting. The counter-culture had, in its own way, taken aim at the Machine, at Mammon, at the military-industrial complex, but it had stood on the ground of extreme personal liberation, and that ground turned out to be too swampy to hold. It took two decades for the hippies to become yuppies; three for the simple-lifers to become Silicon Valley billionaires; four for 'imagine there's no countries' to become the policy of the WEF and the WTO. Now everything is hanging out everywhere. The counter-culture has become the culture, and everyone is having a bad trip, man.

What would a new counter-culture look like?

I suppose it would have to avoid making the same mistakes. So it would not reject the past; it would not try to blank-slate its way towards some notional utopia. It would remember that every time this has been tried it has simply broken more of our bounds, uprooted us further and greased the path of the Machine. Instead, a new counter-culture would have to be rooted in the eternal things. It would need its feet on the ground and its face pointed towards the Dreamtime. It would express what Moriarty called 'our aboriginal desire to be in league with the earth'. It would need to embrace not a rebellious individualism but a reactionary radicalism: a rejection of Machine values based on an embrace instead of the eternal things. Its heart would be the values of people, place, prayer and the past.

What if we don't try to go back to anything? And what if we also slough off the idea of 'saving the world'? What if we reject all the utopias and frown at all the gadgets and the grand plans, what if we take off our shoes and get our feet back properly on the ground? At this time of year, the soil is warm out here. There are a lot of nettles around, it's true, but the sting is never as painful as you think it's going to be.

Yes, I know what you're asking. 'But *how?*' I can't answer the question. I don't know you. But I have worked through this for long enough to understand that if we start from where we are, things will ripple out.

If we don't have an endgame—'saving the world', say—then everything gets easier. The Earth still turns. There are churches. Prayer works. Nature gives and takes. The sunset is astonishing. There is poverty and death and injustice. There are miracles and there is some strange, saving love. It's all still here.

Maybe the question is what we turn our attention to. And how.

The new edition of Moriarty's *Dreamtime* is published by the small Irish publisher Lilliput Press. On the back cover are a few reviews from approving critics, including one Aidan Carl Mathews, who offers up the best image I've come across for Moriarty's quixotic project. To write in this way about the mythworld of ancient Eire in the midst of the greed and rapacity of the Celtic Tiger economy, says Mathews, is like performing a 'raindance on the astroturf' of the modern world.

Why not? Why not raindance on the astroturf? Maybe, sometimes, raindances work. And even if they don't—well, what would you rather be doing? Jogging down the hard shoulder in Lycra, with your headphones on and your Fitbit measuring your heartbeat?

Raindance. We should all raindance.

Call down the powers. Offer ourselves up to God. Enter the Dreamtime. Head for home.

Before he died in 2007, Moriarty was working on a plan for a rebirth of the Irish hedge school. Hedge schools were a feature of eighteenth-century Ireland, when British penal laws banned education for non-Anglicans in an attempt to extinguish Irish Catholicism. In response, people set up illegal schools—sometimes literally in hedges, or caves or barns—as both an act of defiance and a practical necessity. They said: we will not be denied what we need to know. We will go outside and we will learn it anyway. Moriarty's hedge school was to teach his own idiosyncratic version of mystical Christianity: to teach others how to raindance by the motorway junctions and Aldi superstores and data centres of the Brave New Ireland.

The Raindance

Once, in a dark age a very long time ago, the Irish built monasteries. As the pagan armies flooded through the West, burning books and people, slaughtering priests and kidnapping villagers, the monks kept the manuscripts safe, and the teachings. Then, later, they emptied themselves and went out to the margins, to offer up those teachings to the barbarian kings. It was a ridiculous idea. As ridiculous as sending two halflings to throw a ring into a volcano under the nose of the dark lord. It was madness. But it worked.

Sometimes the ridiculous ideas are the only ones worth having.

I have come to the end now, and here is what I think: that the age of the Machine is not after all a hopeless time. Actually, it is the time we were born for. We can't leave it, so we have to fully inhabit it. We have to understand it, challenge it, resist it, subvert it, walk through it on towards something better. If we can see what it is, we have a duty to speak the words to those who do not yet see, all the while struggling to remain human.

People, place, prayer, the past. Human community, roots in nature, connection to God, memories passed down and on. These are the eternal things. We could form hedge schools to teach them. We could live them in any way we can. We could build communities. We could write books. We could plant trees. We could do anything, really. None of it will 'solve' all of the world's problems, or all of ours. We are still going to die; and so, one day, is the Machine. But what will we do in the meantime? What will we do amidst the rise of the robots, amidst the ascendancy of all these tiny, laughable, tyrannical dreams?

Raindance on the astroturf.

Raindance to call down the Spirit upon them and us. Raindance to defy the Machine. Raindance to remember your ancestors. Raindance to offer up prayers to your home. Raindance to the forest and the prairie and the meadow. Raindance to reclaim your stories.

Raindance to discover where you are and where you come from.

Raindance on top of your smartphone until it is nothing but splinters. Raindance against the myths of the age. Raindance against the false gods. Raindance with a smile on your face.

What have you got to lose?

Enter the Dreamtime. Begin the restoration.

Become human again.

Remain human despite it all.

I think that might be what home looks like, in the end.

Acknowledgements

This book has been a long time coming: about thirty years, all told. I'm grateful to my editor Bria Sandford, who gave the initial draft a repeated and focused working-over until it was both shorter and sharper, and to everyone at Penguin who has helped bring this book into the world. I'm also grateful to my agent Jessica Woollard, and to all of the readers, supporters and founder members of my Substack, the Abbey of Misrule, where early versions of these chapters first appeared. Their support, comments and critiques have helped improve what you read here, and have led me in directions I'd never have considered otherwise. They almost make me forgive the internet.

Most importantly, as ever, I'm grateful to my family—to my mum for a lifetime's love and support, to my children for being in my life and enriching it so much, and especially to my wife, Navjyoat, for all of the obvious things, as well as for the many more that are hidden but which keep me alive.

Notes

I: The Dream of the Road

1. Christopher Dawson, *Religion and the Rise of Western Culture* (Double-day, 1950), 22.
2. Alasdair MacIntrye, *After Virtue* (Bloomsbury Academic, 1981), 129–30.
3. MacIntyre, 130–31.
4. René Guénon, *The Crisis of the Modern World* (Indica Books, 1942), 116.
5. Guénon, *Crisis of the Modern World*, 29.

II: The Great Unsettling

1. Simone Weil, *The Need for Roots* (Routledge and Kegan Paul, 1952), 43.
2. Weil, 224.
3. Weil, 51.
4. Weil, 97.

III: The Faustian Fire

1. Oswald Spengler, *The Decline of the West: An Abridged Edition* (Oxford University Press, 1991), 247.
2. Joseph Campbell, *The Hero with a Thousand Faces* (New World Library, 2008), 11.

IV: Blanched Sun, Blinded Man

1. Adrian Hearn, 'Office Workers Spend the Equivalent of 30 Days a Year on Email', *Independent,* 9 October 2019, https://www.independent.co.uk /news/office-workers-uk-email-time-a9149121.html.

2. Max Weber, 'Science As a Vocation', in *From Max Weber: Essays in Sociology,* ed. H. H. Gerth and C. Wright Mills (Oxford University Press, 1946), 155.

3. Eugene McCarraher, 'Mammon', *Aeon,* 22 October 2019, https://aeon .co/essays/capitalism-is-modernitys-most-beguiling-dangerous -enchantment.

4. Lewis Mumford, *The Myth of the Machine: Technics and Human Development* (Harcourt Brace Jovanovich, 1966), 3.

5. Mumford, *Myth of the Machine: Technics,* 3.

6. Daniel Chapman, 'Land Lovers', *Look,* 1969, 59.

7. Mumford, *Myth of the Machine: Technics,* 11.

8. Mumford, *Myth of the Machine: Technics,* 12.

9. Lewis Mumford, *The Myth of the Machine: The Pentagon of Power* (Harcourt Brace Jovanovich, 1970), 435.

V: A Monster That Grows in Deserts

1. Christopher Hibbert, *The English: A Social History 1066–1945* (Harper-Collins, 1994), 466.

2. *Nottingham Review,* editorial, 31 December 1811, quoted in 'The Luddite Bicentenary 1811–1817', https://ludditebicentenary.blogspot.com/2011/12 /13th-december-1811-insurrection-with-no.html#more.

3. Hibbert, 483.

4. Kevin Binfield, *Writings of the Luddites* (Johns Hopkins University Press, 2004), xiv.

5. G. K. Chesterton, *The Outline of Sanity* (IHS Press, 2001), 34.

6. Chesterton, 31.

Notes

VI: A Thousand Mozarts

1. Alan Boyle, 'Jeff Bezos: "We Will Have to Leave This Planet . . . and It's Going to Make This Planet Better"', *GeekWire*, 29 May 2018, https://www.geekwire.com/2018/jeff-bezos-isdc-space-vision.
2. Simon Schama, *Citizens: A Chronicle of the French Revolution* (Penguin, 1989), 406.
3. Schama, 273.
4. Schama, 274.
5. Jean-Jacques Rousseau, *Discourse on the Origin of the Inequality of Mankind: The Second Part* (1754).
6. John Ralston Saul, *Voltaire's Bastards* (Vintage, 1992), 16.

VII: Do What Thou Wilt

1. Rupert Sheldrake, *The Science Delusion* (Coronet, 2012), 28.
2. Sheldrake, 30.
3. Sheldrake, 33.
4. Richard Dawkins, *The Selfish Gene* (Oxford University Press, 2006).
5. Mary Midgley, *The Myths We Live By* (Routledge, 2004), 185.
6. Philip Sherrard, *The Rape of Man and Nature* (Denise Harvey, 2015), 35.
7. Sheldrake, 23.
8. Brad Gregory, *The Unintended Reformation* (Harvard University Press, 2015), 37.
9. Sherrard, 71.
10. Sherrard, 63.
11. Sherrard, 123.
12. Sherrard, 122.

VIII: The Great Wen

1. UN Department of Economic and Social Affairs, '68% of the World Population Projected to Live in Urban Areas by 2050, Says UN', 16 May 2018, https://www.un.org/development/desa/en/news/population/2018-revision-of-world-urbanization-prospects.html.
2. Lewis Mumford, *The City in History* (Peregrine Books, 1987), 72.

3. Mumford, *City in History*, 75.
4. 'Empowering Urban Energy Transitions', International Energy Agency, https://www.iea.org/reports/empowering-urban-energy-transitions/executive-summary.
5. Nita Bhalla, 'World's Slum Populations Set to Surge as Housing Crisis Bites', *Reuters*, 8 June 2023.
6. Texas A&M University, 'Swath of Natural Habitat Larger Than the UK Will Be Urbanized By 2030, Global Study Predicts', 29 January 2020, https://geonews.tamu.edu//news/2020/01/biodiversity-study-knowledge-gaps-in-habitat-loss-research-burak-guneralp.php.
7. Mumford, *City in History*, 620.
8. Mumford, *City in History*, 620.
9. Mumford, *City in History*, 636.

IX: Want Is the Acid

1. '50 Million Tonnes of Potentially Job Creating E-waste Discarded Annually', ILO, 25 January 2019, https://www.ilo.org/resource/news/50-million-tonnes-potentially-job-creating-e-waste-discarded-annually.
2. Hannah Ritchie, 'How Much Plastic Waste Ends Up in the Ocean?', *Our World in Data*, 5 October 2023, https://ourworldindata.org/how-much-plastic-waste-ends-up-in-the-ocean.
3. John Maynard Keynes, 'Economic Possibilities for Our Grandchildren', 1930, http://www.econ.yale.edu/smith/econ116a/keynes1.pdf.
4. E. F. Schumacher, *Small Is Beautiful* (Abacus, 1974), 26.
5. Schumacher, 248.

X: Come the Black Ships

1. Paul Kingsnorth, *One No, Many Yeses* (Free Press, 2003), 119.
2. Edward Goldsmith, 'Development as Colonialism', *World Affairs* 6, no. 2, April–June 2002, https://ciaotest.cc.columbia.edu/olj/wa/wa_apr02_goe01.html.
3. Stephen Toulmin, *Cosmopolis: The Hidden Agenda of Modernity* (University of Chicago Press, 1990).

XI: You Are Harvest

1. S.W.O.R.D. Defense Systems, 'S.P.U.R. Special Purpose Unmanned Rifle', news release, 19 October 2021, https://sworddefense.com/wp-content/uploads/2021/10/SWORD-SPUR-Press-Release.pdf.
2. Max Kozlov, 'Human Trials of Artificial Wombs Could Start Soon. Here's What You Need to Know', *Nature*, 14 September 2023, https://www.nature.com/articles/d41586-023-02901-1.
3. 'BP Could Build Huge Wind Farm off Coast of North Wales', *REVE*, 8 February 2021, https://www.evwind.es/2021/02/08/bp-could-build-huge-wind-farm-off-coast-of-north-wales/79238.
4. Jacques Ellul, *The Technological Society* (Vintage, 1964), 43.
5. Ellul, *Technological Society*, 35.
6. Ellul, *Technological Society*, 79.
7. Ellul, *Technological Society*, 122.
8. Ellul, *Technological Society*, 428.
9. Ellul, *Technological Society*, 284.

XII: Exodus

1. Patrick Deneen, *Why Liberalism Failed* (Yale University Press, 2018), xiii.
2. Deneen, 90.

XIII: Kill All the Heroes

1. Arthur William Holland, 'Levellers', *Encyclopedia Brittanica*, 1911, https://en.wikisource.org/wiki/1911_Encyclop%C3%A6dia_Britannica/Levellers.
2. Christopher Hill, *The World Turned Upside Down* (Penguin, 1972).
3. Hill, 14.
4. Isobel Lewis, 'Keir Starmer Says James Bond Should Be Played by a Woman', *Independent*, 30 September 2021, https://www.independent.co.uk/arts-entertainment/films/news/keir-starmer-james-bond-woman-b1929818.html.
5. Matthew Moore, 'Stop White Men Explaining Stuff, Says BBC Boss', *Times*, 24 August 2018, https://www.thetimes.com/article/stop-white-men-explaining-stuff-says-bbc-boss-82nn7q58l.

6. Robert Bly, *The Sibling Society* (Addison-Wesley, 1997), viii.

7. Bly, 4.

8. Bly, 163.

9. Bly, 162–3.

10. Bly, 164.

11. Christopher Lasch, *The Revolt of the Elites and the Betrayal of Democracy* (W. W. Norton, 1996), 20.

12. Lasch, 81.

13. Lasch, 27.

14. Lasch, 27.

15. Eric Hoffer, *In Our Time* (Morrow Quill Paperbacks, 1972), 62.

16. Hoffer, 164.

17. Hoffer, 83.

XIV: Down the River

1. Paul Kingsnorth, *One No, Many Yeses* (Free Press, 2003).

2. For an introduction to this concept, see Eric Kaufmann, host, 'An Intellectual History of "Woke" Left Modernism, with Matt Goodwin,' *Nationalism and the Culture Wars* (podcast), 26 October 2020, 51 min., 33 sec., https://soundcloud.com/eric-kaufmann-472908310/an-intellectual-history-of-woke-left-modernism-with-matt-goodwin.

3. Habi Zhang, 'America's Cultural Revolution?', *Law and Liberty*, November 23, 2020, https://lawliberty.org/americas-cultural-revolution.

4. Oswald Spengler, *The Decline of the West: An Abridged Edition* (Oxford University Press, 1991), 367.

XV: In the Desert of the Real

1. Nikolai Berdyaev, *The Bourgeois Mind and Other Essays* (The Stanhope Press, 1934).

2. Jonathan Haidt, 'Why the Last Ten Years of American Life Have Been Uniquely Stupid', *Atlantic*, 11 April 2022, https://www.theatlantic.com/magazine/archive/2022/05/social-media-democracy-trust-babel/629369.

3. René Guénon, *The Reign of Quantity and the Signs of the Times* (Sophia Perennis, 2001), 106.

4. Guénon, *Reign of Quantity*, 8.

5. Guénon, *Reign of Quantity*, 166.

XVI: The Abolition of Man (and Woman)

1. See, for example, the evidence presented by Transgender Trend: https://www.transgendertrend.com/category/cultural-influences-and-debate.

2. 'Sweden Documents 1,500 Percent Rise in Teenage Gender Dysphoria Since 2008 as Public Outcry Grows', *CBN News*, 26 February 2020, https://cbn.com/news/world/sweden-documents-1500-percent-rise-teenage-gender-dysphoria-2008-public-outcry-grows.

3. Abigal Shrier, 'Affirmative Abandonment', *City Journal*, 23 June 2020, https://www.city-journal.org/article/affirmative-abandonment.

4. Carl Trueman, *The Rise and Triumph of the Modern Self* (Crossway, 2020), 48.

5. Trueman, 232.

6. Mary Harrington, 'Gender After Eden', *First Things*, May 2022, 119.

7. See, for example, Jennifer Bilek, 'Transgenderism Is Just Big Business Dressed Up in Pretend Civil Rights Clothes', *Federalist*, 5 July 2018, https://thefederalist.com/2018/07/05/transgenderism-just-big-business-dressed-pretend-civil-rights-clothes.

8. See, for example, Alan Neale, 'UK/Transurrogacy—The Next Profit Opportunity for Big Fertility', *11th Hour*, 28 May 2022, https://www.the11thhourblog.com/post/uk-transurrogacy-the-next-profit-opportunity-for-big-fertility.

9. For one of many examples, see Jennifer Bilak, 'The Billionaire Family Pushing Synthetic Sex Identities', *Tablet*, 14 June 2022.

10. Michael Wayne, 'How Trans CEO Martine Rothblatt Transcended Reality with the World in Tow', *CEO Magazine*, 8 June 2022, https://www.theceomagazine.com/business/management-leadership/martine-rothblatt-gender-identity.

11. 'Terasem—Live Happily and Forever', Terasem Faith, accessed 28 February 2025, https://terasemfaith.net.

12. 'The World in 50 Years', *Quartz*, accessed 27 January 2025, https://projects.qz.com/is/the-world-in-50-years/expert/1690898.

XVII: Keep the Home Fires Burning

1. John Michell, *Confessions of a Radical Traditionalist,* ed. Joscelyn Godwin (Dominion Press, 2005), 8.
2. Michell, 9.
3. Wendell Berry, *The World-Ending Fire*, ed. Paul Kingsnorth (Allen Lane, 2017), 263.
4. 'The Painful Truths About Motherhood Exposed', *BBC Culture*, 7 June 2022, https://www.bbc.com/culture/article/20220706-the-painful-truths -about-motherhood-exposed.
5. Berry, 265.
6. Michell, 10.

XVIII: The Nation and the Grid

1. Reproduced in full at https://www.nobelprize.org/prizes/literature/1970 /solzhenitsyn/lecture.
2. Christopher Lasch, *The Revolt of the Elites and the Betrayal of Democracy* (W. W. Norton, 1996), 45.
3. George Orwell, *The Lion and the Unicorn: Socialism and the English Genius* (Penguin, 1982), 63.
4. Yoram Hazony, *The Virtue of Nationalism* (Basic Books, 2018).
5. See, for example, 'Immigration, Diversity and Social Cohesion', Migration Observatory at the University of Oxford, 13 December 2019, https:// migrationobservatory.ox.ac.uk/resources/briefings/immigration -diversity-and-social-cohesion.
6. René Guénon, *The Crisis of the Modern World* (Indica Books, 1942), 3.

XIX: The Fourth Revolution

1. Paul Kingsnorth, *Confessions of a Recovering Environmentalist* (Graywolf Press, 2017).
2. See https://solarfoods.com/solar-foods-selected-to-ipcei-by-european-com mission.
3. George Monbiot, *The Age of Consent* (Harper Perennial, 2004).
4. George Monbiot, *Regenesis* (Allen Lane, 2022), Kindle edition, 224.

5. See, for example, George Monbiot, 'Lab-Grown Food Will Soon Destroy Farming—and Save the Planet', *Guardian*, 8 January 2020, https://www.theguardian.com/commentisfree/2020/jan/08/lab-grown-food-destroy-farming-save-planet.

6. 'Food of the Future: A Protein Made of Water and Air Is Coming to Singapore in 2024', *Awani International*, 29 October 2022, https://international.astroawani.com/global-news/food-future-protein-made-water-and-air-coming-singapore-2024-388258.

7. Klaus Schwab, *The Fourth Industrial Revolution: A Davos Reader* (Foreign Affairs, 2016), 3.

8. Schwab, 15.

9. Schwab, 39.

10. Schwab, 9.

11. C. S. Lewis, *God in the Dock: Essays on Theology* (William B. Eerdmans, 1972).

XX: What Progress Wants

1. David Cayley, '"The Apocalypse Has Begun": Ivan Illich and René Girard on Anti-Christ', davidcayley.com, 2 January 2016, https://www.davidcayley.com/blog/2016/1/2/the-apocalypse-has-begun-ivan-illich-and-ren-girard-on-anti-christ.

2. Kevin Kelly, *What Technology Wants* (Penguin, 2010), 12.

3. Augusto Del Noce, *The Crisis of Modernity* (McGill-Queen's University Press, 2014), 35.

4. Del Noce, 3–5.

5. Del Noce, 9.

6. Del Noce, 52.

7. Del Noce, 89.

8. Del Noce, 104.

9. Del Noce, 25.

10. Del Noce, 133.

11. Del Noce, 134.

12. Del Noce, 237.

13. Del Noce, 94.
14. Kelly, 69.

XXI: God in the Age of Iron

1. Jeremy Naydler, *In the Shadow of the Machine* (Temple Lodge Publishing, 2018), 4.
2. Naydler, 11.
3. Naydler, 9.
4. Naydler, 79.
5. Naydler, 241.
6. Naydler, 285.
7. Seraphim Rose, *Orthodoxy and the Religion of the Future* (St. Herman of Alaska Brotherhood, 1975), 234.
8. Rose, 225
9. Mary Harrington, 'Blasphemy Is Dead. Long Live Blasphemy', *Mary Harrington*, 26 October 2022, https://www.maryharrington.co.uk/p /blasphemy-is-dead-long-live-blasphemy.
10. Rose, 67.

XXII: The Universal

1. Tamara Hardingham-Gill, 'The Android Priest That's Revolutionizing Buddhism', *CNN*, 28 August 2019, https://edition.cnn.com/travel/article /mindar-android-buddhist-priest-japan/index.html.
2. Harriet Sherwood, 'Robot Monk to Spread Buddhist Wisdom to the Digital Generation', *Guardian*, 26 April 2016, https://www.theguardian.com /world/2016/apr/26/robot-monk-to-spread-buddhist-wisdom-to-the -digital-generation.
3. Ananya Bhattacharya, 'The Robots Are Coming for One of Hinduism's Holiest Ceremonies', *Quartz*, 4 December 2017, https://qz.com/india/1066 718/the-robots-are-coming-for-one-of-hinduisms-holiest-ceremonies.
4. 'Faceless "Catholic Robot" Designed to Help People Pray Put on Display in Polish Church', *LifeSiteNews*, 29 October 2021, https://www.lifesite news.com/news/746892.

5. Avery Thompson, 'BlessU-2 Is a Robot Priest That Will Forgive Your Sins', *Popular Mechanics*, 30 May 2017, https://www.popularmechanics.com/technology/robots/a26698/germany-robot-priest.

6. Chris Goswami, 'Chat GPT: The Biggest Leap Forward in AI Is Changing Everything. Here's What It Means for Your Church', *Premier Christianity*, 22 February 2023, https://www.premierchristianity.com/culture/chat-gpt-the-biggest-leap-forward-in-ai-is-changing-everything-heres-what-it-means-for-your-church/14938.article.

7. Sam Hailes, 'Can Chat GPT Lead Someone to Christ? We Put the Machine Through Its Spiritual Paces . . . ', *Premier Christianity*, 30 January 2023, https://www.premierchristianity.com/technology/can-chat-gpt-lead-someone-to-christ-we-put-the-machine-through-its-spiritual-paces/14822.article.

8. Sigal Samuel, 'Robot Priests Can Bless You, Advise You, and Even Perform Your Funeral', *Vox*, 13 January 2020, https://www.vox.com/future-perfect/2019/9/9/20851753/ai-religion-robot-priest-mindar-buddhism-christianity.

9. 'AI Generated Newsreader Debuts in Kuwait', Sky News, 11 April 2023, https://news.sky.com/story/ai-generated-newsreader-debuts-in-kuwait-12854906.

10. Kevin Roose, 'Bing's A.I. Chat: "I Want to Be Alive"', *New York Times*, 16 February 2023, https://www.nytimes.com/2023/02/16/technology/bing-chatbot-transcript.html.

11. Simon Hattenstone, 'Tech Guru Jaron Lanier: "The Danger Isn't That AI Destroys Us. It's That It Drives Us Insane"', *Guardian*, March 23, 2023, https://www.theguardian.com/technology/2023/mar/23/tech-guru-jaron-lanier-the-danger-isnt-that-ai-destroys-us-its-that-it-drives-us-insane.

12. 'Pause Giant AI Experiments: An Open Letter', Future of Life Institute, 22 March 2023, https://futureoflife.org/open-letter/pause-giant-ai-experiments.

13. 'The A.I. Dilemma', Center for Humane Technology, lecture, 9 March 2023, https://www.youtube.com/watch?v=xoVJKj8lcNQ&ab_channel=CenterforHumaneTechnology.

14. 'The A.I. Dilemma.'
15. Marshall McLuhan, *Understanding Media: The Extensions of Man* (MIT Press, 1964), 7.
16. Ezra Klein, 'This Changes Everything', *New York Times*, 12 March 2023, https://www.nytimes.com/2023/03/12/opinion/chatbots-artificial-intelligence-future-weirdness.html.
17. 'Terasem—Live Happily and Forever', Terasem Faith, accessed 28 February 2025, https://terasemfaith.net.
18. Celina Ribeiro, 'Beyond Our "Ape-Brained Meat Sacks": Can Transhumanism Save Our Species?', *Guardian*, 3 June 2022, https://www.theguardian.com/books/2022/jun/04/beyond-our-ape-brained-meat-sacks-can-transhumanism-save-our-species.
19. Kevin Kelly, *What Technology Wants* (Penguin, 2010), 358.
20. Elle Hardy, 'The Tech Giants Might Promise Innovation, Opportunity and Convenience—But at What Cost?', *GQ*, 23 September 2019, https://www.gq.com.au/culture/entertainment/the-tech-giants-might-promise-innovation-opportunity-and-convenience-but-at-what-cost/news-story/b9047471f4b3f16874178de8ff263c21.
21. Available online at https://rsarchive.org/Lectures/AhrDec_index.html.
22. Available online at https://archive.org/details/the-computer-and-the-incarnation-of-ahriman.
23. Christianna Reedy, 'Kurzweil Claims That the Singularity Will Happen by 2045', *Futurism*, 16 October 2017, https://futurism.com/kurzweil-claims-that-the-singularity-will-happen-by-2045.
24. Available online at http://orthodoxinfo.com/ecumenism/st-ignatius-brianchaninov-miracles-and-signs.aspx

XXIII: The West Must Die

1. Iain McGilchrist, *The Matter with Things, Volume 1* (Perspectiva Press, 2021), 23.
2. McGilchrist, 7.
3. Christopher Dawson, *Religion and the Rise of Western Culture* (Doubleday, 1950), 17.

XXIV: Against Progress

1. Roger Scruton, *Conservatism* (All Points Books, 2017), 33
2. Craig Calhoun, *The Question of Class Struggle* (University of Chicago Press, 1982), 4.
3. Calhoun, 7.
4. Calhoun, 65.
5. Calhoun, 65.
6. Jacques Ellul, *Presence in the Modern World* (Wipf and Stock, 2016).

XXV: The Jellyfish Tribe

1. Pierre Proudhon, *Idée Générale de la Révolution au XIXe Siècle* (1851).
2. Jacques Ellul, *The Technological Society* (Vintage, 1964), 189.
3. James C. Scott, *The Art of Not Being Governed* (Yale University Press, 2009), iv.
4. Scott, x.
5. Scott, 7.
6. Scott, 39.
7. Scott, 210.
8. Scott, 210.
9. Scott, 324.
10. Scott, 120

XXVI: The Neon God

1. Dan Milmo, 'Google Chief Warns AI Could Be Harmful If Deployed Wrongly', *Guardian*, 17 April 2023, https://www.theguardian.com/technology/2023/apr/17/google-chief-ai-harmful-sundar-pichai.
2. Eliezer Yudkowsky, 'Pausing AI Developments Isn't Enough. We Need to Shut it All Down', *Time*, 29 March 2023, https://time.com/6266923/ai-eliezer-yudkowsky-open-letter-not-enough.
3. Yudkowsky.

XXVII: The Raindance

1. Simone Weil, *The Need for Roots* (Routledge and Kegan Paul, 1952), 6.
2. John Moriarty, *Dreamtime* (Lilliput Press, 1994), viii.
3. Moriarty, vii.

Index

Index

Index

Index

Index

Index

Index

Index

Index

01 14